MW01002018

THE
SCIENCE
OF RACISM

THE
SCIENCE
OF RACISM
**Everything You Need to Know
but Probably Don't–Yet**

KEON WEST

ABRAMS PRESS, NEW YORK

Library of Congress Control Number: 2024941008

ISBN: 978-1-4197-7437-9
eISBN: 979-8-88707-313-2

Printed and bound in the United States

10 9 8 7 6 5 4 3 2 1

ABRAMS The Art of Books
195 Broadway, New York, NY 10007
abramsbooks.com

For my wife, Zoe
And for my sons, Thelonious and Phoenix
The most important readership I'll ever have

Contents

Introduction

Here We Go Again
Toward a Better Conversation about Racism

On November 4, 2008, Barack Obama was elected as the first Black president of the United States of America. In November of 2016, Pamela Taylor, a former West Virginia official, called the First Lady, Michelle Obama, an "ape in heels." On May 19, 2018 in the UK, Meghan Markle married Prince Harry, making her the first person of color in memory to join the British royal family. On March 7, 2021, Meghan, now the Duchess of Sussex, revealed in an interview with Oprah Winfrey that a member of her new family had been concerned about the couple's son, born in 2019, being "too dark." On May 25, 2020 in Minneapolis, police officer Derek Chauvin murdered George Floyd by kneeling on his neck for almost ten minutes. As a result, the Black Lives Matter movement, which had existed since 2013, erupted into international prominence. On June 7, 2020, in Bristol, a statue of the slave trader Edward Colston was toppled from its plinth, defaced and thrown into the harbor. On January 5, 2022, those charged with illegally removing the statue were cleared of any criminal damages.

These events caused waves nationally and internationally. And yet, in each case, there were those who argued that it was all about race and racism, and those who argued that it had nothing to do with race or racism. Certain people argued that some of the events proved racism was over. Others argued that some of the events proved racism was alive and well.

Arguments like these have been going on for some time. As early as the 1990s, books such as Dinesh D'Souza's *The End of Racism* and, later, Larry Elder's *Stupid Black Men: How to Play the Race Card—and Lose* argued that racism was over. It was time to stop pretending to be victims. More recently, in 2020, books like Ijeoma Oluo's *Mediocre: The Dangerous Legacy of White Male America* and Layla Saad's *Me and White Supremacy* have argued that all White people are beneficiaries of, and perhaps complicit in, a continuing, active White supremacist system. New books are published each year on either side of this heated, polarized debate. We have arguments in abundance.

What we don't seem to have in abundance are facts.

This book will change that. It is not a political book, but a scientific one. As such, it will lay out empirical facts from the wealth of international scientific research on racism. While this research comes from countries as diverse as Australia, France, and Uganda, a disproportionate amount of it has been conducted in the US and in Western European countries like the United Kingdom. As a result, findings from those countries are overrepresented in this book and in the wider scientific literature. However, the central facts that emerge from this abundance of research are remarkably consistent.

This book is not about upending, or reaffirming, your cherished beliefs. Instead it will lay out the facts about racism, based rigorously and unerringly upon the best science we have at our disposal. There will be stories in it—some moving, some emotional, some eye-opening. But fundamentally, this book is about the scientific method, how we apply it to the study of racism, and what it reveals when we do. If you are a person who genuinely wants to know what the facts are and how we know them, this book is for you. Our values are the blueprint for the world we'd like to live in. Our politics are the roadmap directing us to that world. That much, I will leave up to the reader to sort out for themselves. But science is the best way we have of understanding the world as it is. Over the course of this book, I ask the reader to leave that to me.

The Science of Racism will start by highlighting how little agreement there is in society about contemporary racism, even at the most basic level. It will discuss how scientists build knowledge about contemporary racism, taking an in-depth look at one kind of experiment: the CV experiment. We will refer back to this type of experiment several times throughout the book, because it serves as a base upon which more complex and nuanced knowledge can be built. Having established *how* we know what we know through that narrow focus, the book will also take a broad look at *what* we know about the many areas of life (beyond employment) that may be affected by racism, from birth to death.

With the very basics of racism out of the way, we'll look at why we often know so little about racism and the psychological tools we use to hide the truth from ourselves. This will include topics like the unconscious bias narrative, deception, victim blaming, knowledge, meta-knowledge, and definitional boundaries of discrimination. Then we'll handle some of the most nuanced and delicate aspects of racism: racism between ethnic minorities, racism between members of the same ethnic group, and even "reverse racism" or racism against White people.

Finally, the book will turn to ways of responding to racism and what the science says about how well they really work. This section will include topics like color blindness, unconscious bias training, cross-group friendships, and collective action.

By the end of the book, you'll have a much clearer, more

scientifically accurate idea of what contemporary racism is, what it looks like, how to respond to it, and the complexities that surround it. Even better, perhaps, if you have doubts about any of it, you won't have to take my word for it. Instead you'll have hundreds of scientific references that you can check for yourself to make sure that what you've been told is the truth.

Racism is a difficult, complex topic, but we have much more scientific knowledge about it than most people realize. This book will share that knowledge with you.

PART I
HOW DO WE KNOW IF RACISM IS REAL?

Chapter 1

Do We Have a Problem?
Disagreements about Contemporary Racism

Few topics are as divisive as racism, so let's start with the disagreements.

Even the most basic question about racism is still, apparently, a source of great division and debate. Consider the simple question, "Does racism still exist?" By this, I don't mean, "Is it possible that one person's uncle somewhere in a small town still makes the occasional 'off-color' remark?" I mean something bigger than that, and I think most other people do too when they ask that question. If I had to translate "Does racism still exist?" into more rigorous terms, I think it'd be fair to phrase it something like this: "Is racism still enough of a feature in our society that it has detectable, significant effects on how people are treated and what their life outcomes are likely to be?" For example, does race affect how a crime is reported or interpreted? Does race affect how likely you are to be supported in your graduate studies, or hired for a job, or given the appropriate treatment by a doctor, or shot by a police officer? When we see certain people being followed around in stores, or treated like foreigners, or harassed by the authorities, is this because of racism or is it because of something else? Are people just using racism as a way to avoid taking responsibility for their own actions or failures? Or is there genuinely a system in society that works to the advantage of White people and the detriment of everyone else? Before you read any further, I'd like you to seriously consider what your answer to those questions would be.

Whatever you believe, about half the population agrees with you. I am being very literal about this: about half of the population in both the UK and the US believe in the existence of contemporary racism and about half (or, depending on the specific kind of racism, slightly more than half) do not. According to a representative 2018 *Guardian* poll of British adults, more than half of those polled thought minorities faced less or the same discrimination as White people in the news (53%), in TV or films (60%), in the workplace (54%), in access to finance (57%), access to jobs (52%), university (52%), or good schooling (54%). Results in the United States are somewhat similar. A 2021 Gallup poll revealed that slightly more than half of the White American population (59%) believe "racism against Blacks [is] widespread in the US," while slightly less than half do not (40%). In the meantime, according to the same poll, slightly less than half of the White American population (43%) believe "racism against Whites [is] widespread in the US," while slightly more than half do not (55%). These findings echo those of a 2011 study by Norton and Sommers which showed that a growing number of White Americans believed "reverse racism" or racism against White people was the more prevalent form of racial bias.

This kind of division in our society is a real problem, but it is understandable. People look to authorities to help them answer the big questions about life and society. But often, those in positions of authority offer no clear answers. Politicians frequently pretend to be experts on a host of scientific matters like racism—and vaccines, and climate change, and evolution—but they're not. If they don't have degrees or past careers in social psychology or climate science or evolutionary biology, then they are no more experts in the topic than you are. Nonetheless, they are our chosen representatives: a reflection of our collective beliefs and the kinds of societies we'd like to have. We have a reasonable expectation that we should take their views seriously.

Unfortunately, they are as sharply divided as the rest of us. In his inauguration speech in 2020, Joe Biden, the 46th president of the United States, said: "We face an attack on democracy and on truth. A raging virus. Growing inequity. The sting of systemic racism . . ." and "Our history has been a constant struggle between the American ideal that we are all created equal and the harsh, ugly reality that racism, nativism, fear, and demonization have long torn us apart." President Biden also overturned his predecessor Donald Trump's Executive Order 13950: the Executive Order on Combating Race and Sex Stereotyping, which aimed to put a halt to diversity training, anti-bias training, and many other interventions that were allegedly "teaching that men and members of certain races, as well as our most venerable institutions, are inherently sexist and racist." By doing this, Biden reopened the door to discussions of continued racism in American society and what to do about it. Democratic representative Alexandria Ocasio-Cortez makes frequent references to racism and White supremacy in her speeches and on her Twitter profile, where she has voiced opinions such as "Let this front page serve as a reminder of how white supremacy is aided by—and often relies upon—the cowardice of mainstream institutions," and "Your weakness will help build a monument to white supremacy."

On the other side of the American political aisle, Republicans are concerned that talk about racism and anti-racism has gone much too far. In 2022 a fierce debate began, and is ongoing, about "critical race theory"—specifically, whether it should be taught in schools. There is widespread disagreement, among its defenders and its detractors, about exactly what critical race theory is, but it seems to serve as a stand-in for all the aspects of racism that some people are tired of talking about. According to Senator Ted Cruz, critical race theory says that "every White person is racist" and that "certain children are inherently bad people because of the color of their skin." Christopher Rufo, a senior fellow at the Manhattan Institute (a libertarian think tank), wrote an article in *USA Today* called "What I Discovered about Critical Race Theory in Public Schools and Why It Shouldn't Be Taught." In the article, Rufo asserts that critical race theory is a form of "race-based Marxism." Similar to Senator Cruz, he claims that critical race theory ascribes "moral superiority" or inferiority to people based solely on their race: that White people are unfairly deemed inherently racist and ethnic minorities are unfairly deemed inherently virtuous. At the time of writing, at least five US states have passed critical race theory bills restricting what a teacher may talk about, or may be compelled to talk about. At least twelve other states are considering similar bills.

Not to be outdone by the Americans, the British government has weighed in in very similar ways. Kim Johnson and Dawn Butler are both Black women, both Labor MPs, and both of the opinion that the British police (and other institutions) are institutionally racist, as has been widely reported in the British media. This may have something to do with the fact that both women have been stopped and questioned by the police on what seemed to be very flimsy pretexts. In each case, once they identified themselves as members of parliament, the police very quickly lost interest or even apologized, but both women believe racism was part of the reason why they were stopped and questioned. Jeremy Corbyn, an MP and former Labor candidate for prime minister who is White and male, has also made his views on the matter clear. On April 22, 2021, he tweeted, "Today the struggle against institutional racism continues. From Stephen Lawrence to George Floyd, Black Lives Matter."

On the other side of the British political aisle is the (at the time) Conservative Women and Equalities minister—Kemi Badenoch MP, who, like Johnson and Butler, is Black and a woman, but not at all of the belief that institutional racism is a serious problem in the UK. She admits that there is some racism in the UK and that she has experienced some discrimination. But she strongly resists what she calls attempts to "politicize" her skin color. Like her counterparts in the US, Badenoch has claimed that critical race theory is an ideology that interprets mere Whiteness as oppression and mere Blackness as victimhood. She has further claimed that many people who support critical race theory aren't working toward any ideal future that we would recognize, but actually want reprehensible things like a segregated society. Further still, Badenoch has stated that British teachers would be breaking the law if they taught their pupils about a range of concepts, including critical race theory and White privilege, as if they were fact rather than merely one side's political opinion. This is more than just talk. In 2021, the British government, after assembling a Commission on Race and Ethnic Disparities and conducting its own research, went on to publish the Sewell report, which found "no evidence of systemic or institutional racism" in the UK.

It's hard to know what to believe. It's hard to say which has more credibility: a peer-reviewed publication, a government report, a book, or any other kind of media. It's hard to know which sources are reporting facts and which are just spouting opinions. And it's often not clear who has the authority, expertise, or methodology to back up their claims. Lots of very clever people with impressive-sounding degrees have published lots of books that wildly disagree with each other.

As an example, whether you agree with her or not, you may

have heard of Dr. Robin DiAngelo. She is White, a woman, and the holder of two bachelor's degrees (in Sociology and History) as well as a PhD in Multicultural Education from the University of Washington. She has published several books about the persistence of racism in today's society and has gone as far as to say that "all White people are racist." She has clarified that statement by adding that she didn't mean that all White individuals were consciously, intentionally doing hurtful anti-Black things, but that they have all absorbed a certain amount of racist ideology—and that this ideology shapes the way they see themselves, the way they see the world around them, and the practices and policies that they set up in that world. If you are a fan of Dr. DiAngelo's work, you likely believe in widespread racism on both an interpersonal and institutional level.

However, there are books that disagree. Dinesh D'Souza is another author you may have heard of, whether or not you agree with his work. Mr. D'Souza is an Indian American and the holder of a bachelor's degree in English from Dartmouth College. He has consistently published books saying that racism isn't a problem in society anymore, and that the issues we face today are largely cultural faults within ethnic minority groups themselves. We can look at specific examples, such as some of D'Souza's claims that came out in an interview with Ben Wattenberg for the television show *Think Tank*. Here, D'Souza said that it was wrong to believe, as liberals apparently do, that racial discrimination wholly or even largely explains the failures of Black people in America. Rather, D'Souza blames these failures—crime, babies born out of wedlock, and so on—on problems with Black culture, including heavy, "virtually parasitic" reliance on the government. If you are a fan of Mr. D'Souza, you probably believe that people should stop trying to blame racism for their problems and just take responsibility for their own lives.

There is no shortage of people willing to write books on whether racism still exists or is still a problem, and there is no shortage of disagreements between these authors. And now you are reading a new book, by a new author, saying that this time it's going to be different. So what makes this book more useful or more accurate than the flood of literature you've already encountered so far?

One word: *science.*

Science is a rigorous, self-correcting system of making hypotheses—that is, predictions about how the world works—and testing those hypotheses against objective, reliable, external data. If the data don't match the predictions in your hypotheses, your hypotheses have failed and you have to change them or abandon them. If your hypotheses make more accurate or precise predictions than others, then your hypotheses win, and should be accepted over the others. If your hypotheses can't make any predictions at all, then you're not even doing science and you should just leave. Evidence is the coin of the realm in science. Not eloquence, not popularity, not even formal philosophical syllogisms, but evidence: the ability to make predictions about the real world that are more specific and more likely to come true than anyone else's predictions.

And this means that in science, you can't have wildly differing opinions on whether racism exists in society. Politicians can disagree on these things. Philosophers can disagree on these things. Pundits, activists, demagogues, and professional debaters make their living out of disagreement. But in science, if there is a disagreement, sooner or later somebody is going to make a prediction and test it, or they'll have to admit that they were wrong. By its nature, science tends toward consensus.

This is not to say that there are no disagreements in science at all. Even from my own research, it's easy enough to point to examples of me disagreeing with other scientists about a number of higher-level ideas. Science always has frontiers, and it always takes time to sort out the answers to new questions. But disagreements cannot last for very long, and the question of racism is not a new one. It is a very old one. We have had a consensus on it for a long time—and by the time you've finished this book, you'll know what that consensus is and how we got to it.

Chapter 2

Show Me What You Got
The Scientific Consensus on Racism

I've said that I am going to give you the scientific consensus on the existence of racism—I should clarify what I mean by that. I don't mean that I'm going to give you my opinion as a scientist or an expert in the field. I could do that. With a doctorate in Social Psychology from Oxford University, over fifteen years of research experience in the field, more than seventy-five empirical, peer-reviewed papers which have been cited over 2,000 times, and a professorship at the University of London, I could just tell you my opinion as an expert. But, as I said before, opinion isn't the coin of the realm in science—not even expert opinion. Other people, with different opinions, could also claim to be experts. Indeed, some of them might genuinely be experts, perhaps with even more publications and citations than I have. But you don't achieve consensus in science by comparing degrees. What matters in science is not the years of experience, books written, or the number of people you can get to agree with you. In science, what matters is evidence: specifically testable, verifiable, quantitative evidence published in peer-reviewed scientific journals.

My opinions, expert or no, would be of no use to you, and I would not expect you to accept anything on my say-so. Quite the contrary: every time I tell you about a scientific finding, I will give you the names of the authors of the paper, the year in which they published it and (in the reference section) the journal in which they published it. This is to make sure that you don't have to take my word for anything. I want you to be skeptical. I want you to check for yourself. Please go so far as to read the papers and see if the researchers found what I say they found. I would honestly welcome that. There are far too many examples of advertisements or blogs or snake-oil salesmen claiming that "science has discovered this" or "science has confirmed that." But without identifiable, traceable, scientific sources, those claims are worthless and should be treated with the utmost suspicion. I'm going to tell you what the science has actually found, and I'm also going to give you the tools to verify that for yourself.

Science, as stated, is about the ability to make predictions. Philosophers can have the same debate for thousands of years without arriving at a consensus. Indeed, they have repeatedly done just that. A 2014 survey of 931 philosophy faculty members by Bourget and Chalmers found very low levels of agreement on a host of basic millennia-old questions such as whether free will exists, how truth should be defined, what personal identity means and whether there are such things as abstract objects. But in science, any meaningful belief must be translatable into a prediction about something in the real world. It's very "put up or shut up" in the scientific arena. A belief that can't be used to make any predictions at all isn't scientific, and any predictions that aren't supported by empirical data can be discarded as wrong. So if there is a disagreement, all you have to do is clarify what your divergent predictions are, then test them to see which ones are more accurate.

Let's start with one very simple prediction, and let's base that prediction on the opposing perspectives on racism outlined in the last chapter. Recall Dr. DiAngelo's views about the ubiquity and importance of contemporary racism, and compare them to

Mr. D'Souza's views that racism isn't a good or important explanation for the "failures" of Black people in today's society. These two contrasting positions must imply some different expectations about observable behavior in the real world. If not, science wouldn't consider them meaningful positions at all.

If I had to distill the words of DiAngelo and D'Souza down to a simple scientific prediction, it would sound something like this: *in a given situation in which a Black and a White person were otherwise identical, the White person would/would not receive detectably favorable treatment.* I know the language in that prediction might sound clunky and robotic. That's because the style aims to maximize clarity, even at the expense of feeling easy or natural. There can be no room for excuses. Science can't abide vague predictions that would allow anyone to claim victory. We all need to be in total agreement about what the conditions are (that is, a Black and a White person have to be otherwise identical—not similar, or related in some way, but identical) and what the outcomes are that would prove one person correct and the other incorrect (that is, the White person either would or would not receive treatment that is preferential, and this preference must be objectively detectable to both parties and to independent external observers).

Given what she's said, I would expect Dr. DiAngelo to agree with the "would" version of that prediction—that Black people are (at least sometimes) treated worse than White people for no other reason than their race. Similarly, I would expect Mr. D'Souza to agree with the "would not" version of that prediction, in which we should not find different outcomes for Black and White people who are otherwise the same as each other. Indeed, D'Souza's outlook strongly implies that the different outcomes for Black and White people should be due to some difference in the things they do. Once Black people and White people do the same things, they should be treated in much the same way, and get much the same results. This seems like a very clear-cut case of a difference in predictions. You may interpret those stances differently, or think that they point toward a different set of predictions, and that's fine. What matters is that your interpretation, whatever it is, permits some testable prediction about real-world events.

Now that we have a general prediction (which says that "in a given situation in which a Black and White person were otherwise identical, the White person would/would not receive favorable treatment"), all we have to do is pick a specific instance and test it. However, we should be careful here. This can be tricky to do properly, and it's where a lot of people who think they're relying on the data start to make mistakes.

For example, some people point out that the unemployment rate for Black people in the United States is much higher than the unemployment rate for White people in the United States (15.4% vs. 10.1%, according to data from the US Labor Department). In the UK, though the overall unemployment rate is lower, the gap is much worse, with unemployment rates among Black British people being twice as high as those among White British people (8% vs. 4%, according to the Office for National Statistics). Some people use this as evidence of racial discrimination against Black people in the workplace. However, by itself, it isn't. Let's think about it. Would these rates allow us to differentiate between Dr. DiAngelo's and Mr. D'Souza's beliefs about racial discrimination? The answer is clearly no. DiAngelo could say that the different unemployment rates are a clear sign of anti-Black discrimination. D'Souza could say that the discrimination is small, if it's there at all, and that the real issue is Black culture, or a lack of workplace ambition, or something else. Merely observing a relationship between race and some outcome doesn't tell us why that relationship is there. That is why scientists often say "correlation does not equal causation."

We also have to avoid relying on anecdotes. For every story about a Black person who says they faced discrimination at the hands of some employer, we could find a story about a White person who says they were passed over for a job due to affirmative action or some other form of reverse discrimination. Even if we were bizarrely naive and simply took all these stories at face value—accepted that the people in question accurately understood their situations, and accepted that they each relayed that understanding perfectly to us—we still wouldn't be able to filter out the effects of a thousand other potential factors, of which the people in the situations might not even be aware. In each case, we still wouldn't know how much the person's own performance, workplace behavior, age, location, or even their appearance might have contributed to the situation. We can't go back in time and magically change the race of a person, and *only* their race, to see how the situation would have been different. Hence, we still can't draw definitive conclusions from these stories, no matter how many we collect. That is why scientists often say that "the plural of anecdote is not data."

It should also go without saying that it's not a viable option to simply ask a large number of people whether they do or do not discriminate against ethnic minorities. Some research works this way, and it can be useful in particular circumstances. In 2020 I conducted a study like that myself, which I will come to later. But for this particular question, it would be an obvious mistake, because people might lie. Indeed, many people have strong reasons to fudge the truth, at least a little. Research by Crandall and colleagues in 2002 and by McConahay and colleagues in 1981 has shown that there are very, very strong anti-discrimination norms in Western societies, and even people who knowingly respond more negatively to some groups than to others can be careful to hide their feelings in order to avoid the social or legal consequences. Whether you agree with these social norms or not, there is no escaping the fact that they sometimes make us hide our true feelings and beliefs. Or, as D'Souza himself was cited saying in a 2000 paper by Van Boven, "the topics of race and to a lesser extent gender have been taboo in our society, particularly in the universities. What people say in public is not the same as what they believe in private." Scientists don't have a catchy phrase to sum up this lesson, but it's still a good lesson: you can't just ask people about stuff like discrimination.

So is all hope lost? Is there any way to truly, scientifically test whether discrimination is happening or not? Of course there is; otherwise, this would be a very short book. All it takes is a little bit of knowledge about the scientific method and experimental design.

Experimental design

Actually, it takes more than "a little bit" of knowledge. Over the decades, psychological science has leaped forward several times. We now have much more rigorous standards around experimental design, statistics, transparency and replicability than we used to. Doing it right—conducting good scientific research—can be quite complex, and even the people with PhDs can still make mistakes. Gone are the carefree days when you could just lock a pigeon in a box, or trap a handful of male university students in your basement, or frighten the living bejesus out of a baby with a pair of cymbals and then jot down whatever observations seemed important to you. (Yes, these are all real experiments that actually happened; check out the work of Haney, Banks and Zimbardo in

1973; Skinner in 1948; and Watson and Rayner in 1920.) Nowadays, things are much more rigorous, and it would be wrong to give you the impression that it's all very simple.

That said, you don't really need to understand all the statistics and the advances in design and reporting. The basic principles are easy enough to grasp and they still form the bedrock of psychological science (and science in many other fields) today. In essence, here is how the scientific approach would solve our problem. If you want to test whether one thing causes another thing, then what you need is a genuine experiment. And it can't just be any experiment. The best kind is what we call a randomized controlled trial.

What does that mean? Let's start with the "randomized" part. In this kind of experiment participants are randomly assigned to be in one group or another, or to receive one treatment or another. This is very important because we want to be sure that any differences we find after the experiment are due to the things we did during the experiment, and not due to some systematic differences that already existed before the experiment. If the participants in different groups aren't based on random assignment but are instead consistently different in some other way (for example, if they were chosen from two different workplaces or classrooms), then you can't tell whether or not this preexisting difference is the real explanation for your results. That's what we call a "confound:" some difference, other than the one you're interested in, that systematically varies between the groups you're testing. A confound is disastrous for any experiment as it destroys the ability to confidently say where the effects came from.

"Controlled" means a lot of things, but essentially it means that the experimenters whittle away any potential explanation for the results other than the specific thing they are trying to investigate. This is why genuine experiments need a "control group"—a group that gets every single thing that the experimental groups get, *except* the one thing that you're interested in. So if you want to know whether a drug improves academic performance, you need to compare a (randomly assigned) group of people who took the drug to a (also randomly assigned) group of people who experienced exactly the same thing as the people who took the drug, except the drug itself. If one group went to see a doctor or psychologist, the other group should also go to see the doctor or psychologist. If one group took a pill from a big shiny bottle, the other group should also take a pill from a big shiny bottle. Even very subtle, discreet nonverbal behaviors of the experimenters can skew the results; so, for instance, if experimenters in one condition (i.e., one group of randomly assigned participants) expect the participants to do better on a maths test, the experimenters in the other condition should also expect the participants to do better on the maths test. Indeed, we now recommend that neither the experimenter nor the participant should have any idea which group they happen to be in. Preferably the participants should have no idea what the experiment is even about, or how many groups there are. This is what's called a double-blind experiment, and it's the best way to stop our expectations from making us produce flawed data.

What's crucial here is the following basic principle: if you want to know whether someone's race affects anything, then you need to design an experiment (a double-blind, randomized, controlled trial) where the only thing that varies is the race of the stimulus or target. Everything else should be the same. If you successfully do that, and you still find differences in the responses that reliably vary by race, then you can confidently say that these differences in responses are due to race and race alone. That is how you scientifically test for discrimination.

The CV study

Applying that knowledge to a specific situation, we can make our general prediction more precise. Instead of, "In a given situation in which a Black and White person were otherwise identical, the White person would/would not receive favorable treatment," we could say, "In a situation in which a Black and White person had otherwise identical CVs, the White person would/would not be treated more favorably when they apply for a job."

With that formulation, it's easy to see how the test could be done. All you need is a CV. You can then make hundreds or thousands of copies of that CV. The number you make depends on your budget and how confident you want to be that your results are both real and generalizable, rather than a statistical artifact or only applicable to a small section of the population. There are all kinds of fancy, science-y considerations to help you determine the exact number you'd need, depending on your experiment's design and the hypothesized size of the effect. But for now, a good rule of thumb is that this kind of experiment should contain about 100 people if you're keeping things simple, and about 1,000 people if you want to make things very complex or ensure you have a more representative population.

Now, you take your hundreds (or thousands) of CVs and keep them all exactly the same except for one thing: the identity of the person who ostensibly sent the CV. Again, this identity could be changed in a number of ways. However, for this example, let's keep things simple and say that half the names on the CVs are edited to make it look as though they're being sent by a Black person and the other half are edited to look as though they're being sent by a White person. Now we've accomplished that coveted controlled status that weeds out any effects except those of the thing we care about: race.

We're almost done. All we have to do is send these hundreds (or thousands) of CVs to potential employers. At this stage it's important that we do nothing to tip the employers off as to what's going on. They should have no idea which condition they're in (Black CV vs. White CV), they shouldn't even know how many conditions there are, and preferably (though you can't always do this because of the ethics boards) they shouldn't even know that they're in an experiment, or that there are any conditions in the first place. All they should know is that, one day, a CV landed on their desk and they had to make a decision about whether to call that person in for an interview or toss the CV in the bin.

And then we wait.

We give it a while, however long we think it should take for the potential employers to make up their minds. Then we just have to count the number of callbacks each version of the CV got and we'll have our answer about whether or not racism is still a factor in contemporary hiring decisions.

Remember, science is about making predictions and proving that those predictions are accurate. If you're unwilling to put your cards on the table and make a prediction, then this isn't the game for you. Those of you who agree with DiAngelo should predict that the CVs will get very different callback rates; specifically, the White CVs should get a higher rate of callbacks than the Black CVs. Those of you who side with D'Souza should predict that the CVs will get very similar callback rates. There may be a tiny difference in one direction or the other, but this difference shouldn't be consistent or different from the results of random chance. It should not be, as the scientists would say, statistically significant.

So, now that we've explained what the design of our CV

experiment should be, here is the big question: if you conducted an experiment like this, what would you find? Would the responses to the CVs be based on their merits? Or would the race of the person sending the CV make a difference?

This is a question I would really like you to answer. As I've said, science is about making accurate predictions. So make one! Making a prediction about the outcome of an experiment is the best way to see how scientific your views are. This is no time to chicken out, and the rest of the chapter will be a lot more fun if you put your prediction out there. Feel free to use the format below to specify what your prediction is:

Who would receive more callbacks?
☐ White CVs   ☐ Black CVs   ☐ Neither
How many more callbacks would they receive?
☐ 10%   ☐ 50%   ☐ 90%

These are very broad, ballpark figures, but they're still good enough to see whether our predictions roughly match the data. And now that we have a specific prediction, let's find out if we were right.

The consensus: Is racism a factor in hiring decisions?

Rather than give you a simple yes or no, we'll go through examples of research that has used the design I've described, and we'll see what they found.

In 2003, Devah Pager hired four twenty-three-year-old university students, two of whom were Black and two of whom were White. These students were Pager's confederates: people recruited by experimenters to play important roles in their studies. This could mean pretending to be a bystander, another participant in the experiment or, as in this case, an applicant for a job. According to Pager, the students were "matched on the basis of physical appearance and general style of self-presentation." For the purpose of this experiment, all the relevant details on their CVs were also matched, including their educational attainment and work experience. They then looked for jobs that were advertised in the Sunday classified advertisement section of the *Milwaukee Journal Sentinel*, plus some extras that they found on Jobsnet—a job-seeking website. They applied for 350 jobs at the rate of about fifteen every week. In each case, they visited the potential employers, filled out the application process, and proceeded as far as they could go during the course of the visit.

Pager used the employers' measurable responses to the applicants as the outcome data. If they were invited back for an interview (that is, if they received a callback) or if they were hired on the spot, these were counted as positive responses.

You've probably noticed that there's some information I didn't give you. Who was Devah Pager? Where did she grow up? What was her skin color? What university did she work for? Which department was she in? How many papers had she published? What were her political leanings? I left all of that information out, and I left it out deliberately, because in science none of that matters.

Politicians, pseudo-scientists and propaganda artists love to focus on that kind of information. It is one of their most frequently used rhetorical tricks to offer a list of fancy people, with fancy degrees from fancy universities, and claim that those people agree with them. That tactic is perfectly understandable because it works. Many of us would naturally find Pager's conclusions more convincing if we were told that she worked at Harvard University (which she did), or that she was a renowned sociologist (which she was) who had published about seventy academic works that have been cited over 16,000 times (which she had).

The unscientific approach would be to use Pager's credentials to argue that her conclusions on racism in employment were sound. But the scientific approach ignores all of that. The only things that matter in science are the methods she used and the observations that resulted from those methods. In other words, what did she do, and what did she find? Any other information is a distraction. Or worse, it is an attempt to use authority, real or fabricated, as a substitute for empirical data. The only reason I gave you Pager's name and the year in which she published was so that you could look up her paper yourself in the reference section and check that I am representing her findings accurately. This will also be my approach with all other research cited in this book. We will ignore the fluff and focus on the data.

So, 350 job applications later, what did Pager find? Overall, the Black applicants had a 9.5% callback rate. And the perfectly equally qualified White applicants? They had a 25.5% callback rate. That is over two times higher. In other words, despite having completely identical CVs and being matched on all the conceivably relevant characteristics, for every 100 jobs the Black people applied for, they heard back from about 10 of the employers, and for every 100 jobs the White people applied for, they heard back from about 26 of the employers.

The response matrix we used earlier doesn't have the numbers to represent such an extreme result. This is a 160% difference, and the highest number we anticipated was a 90% difference. Still, it's useful to compare our predictions to what we found. That's how we do science, after all. So, if we had to plug Pager's findings into our response matrix, it would look something like this:

Who received more callbacks?

■ White CVs   ☐ Black CVs   ☐ Neither

How many more callbacks did they receive?

☐ 10%   ☐ 50%   ■ (>)90%

That, however, is only one result. And we'd be pretty poor scientists if we based all our beliefs on a single experiment from Milwaukee. Have any other experiments tested this phenomenon in similar ways? Yes. In 2004, Marianne Bertrand and Sendhil Mullainathan sent in CVs in response to job ads in Chicago and Boston newspapers and measured the number of callbacks for interviews each résumé received. In total, they sent over 5,000 CVs in response to over 1,300 employment ads. The number of CVs was so high because the experiment was rather complex; the scientists wanted to have enough versions of the CVs to see how the response rates were affected by more than one thing. While all their results were eye-opening, the one that we're interested in right now is how race affected the callback rates the CVs received. Again, it's important to remember that for each set of CVs, the Black and White CVs were identical in every way. In fact, Bertrand and Mullainathan only indicated the race of the applicant by varying their name to be stereotypically White or stereotypically Black (e.g., Emily vs. Lakisha). All the other details were the same, and at no point did the experimenters or any confederates interact with the potential employers, so there was no chance for expectations, nonverbal behaviors, or any other extraneous factors to affect the results.

So, what did they find? In the researchers' own words: "Applicants with White names need to send about ten résumés to get one callback whereas applicants with African American names need to send around fifteen résumés to get one callback. This 50 percent gap in callback rates is statistically very significant. Based on our estimates, a White name yields as many more callbacks as an additional eight years of experience."

That finding is not as extreme as Pager's 2003 result, but is still large, and very much in the same direction. If we put Bertrand and Mullainathan's 2004 findings into our response matrix, it would look like this:

Who received more callbacks?
■ White CVs   ☐ Black CVs   ☐ Neither
How many more callbacks did they receive?
☐ 10%   ■ 50%   ☐ 90%

There are many possible explanations for the difference in the size of the effect. For example, it is possible that Pager's hired university students let some of their expectations show, despite having been trained to keep them in check. It's also possible that Bertrand and Mullainathan's manipulation was weaker than Pager's because a name is only an indication of whether a person is Black or White, but you can't be 100% sure. It's definitely conceivable that a person named Emily West, Emily Morgan, Emily Bernard, or Emeli Sandé is a Black woman. In contrast, Pager's manipulation of the race of the applicant was rock solid. The employers could see a real human being filling out the application, and it was clearly either a Black person or a White one.

No experiment is perfect. There are pros and cons to every conceivable experimental design. Even with an infinite well of resources, there may still be questions about the findings. This is why we build a consensus in science. We use a variety of different tweaks to the design, in a variety of different places, over a considerable amount of time, to increase our confidence in the findings. So let's look at another.

In 2006, in New York, Eden B. King, Saaid A. Mendoza, Juan

M. Madera, Mikki R. Hebl, and Jennifer L. Knight asked 155 White men to rate an applicant based only on his CV. Of course, you know what's coming next. The CVs were all identical except for one thing—the race of the person who was applying. King, Mendoza, Madera, Hebl, and Knight actually used four racial categories, which they manipulated by changing the name on the CV: Asian American ("Lee Chang"), Black ("Jamal Jenkins"), Hispanic ("Jose Gonzales"), or White ("James Sullivan"). The results for the Asian and Hispanic names are interesting and we will get to them in a later chapter. But, for now, for consistency, let's keep looking at the Black and White examples. Given that the CVs were identical, did they receive identical ratings? No, they did not. This experiment didn't use callbacks as the outcome data. Instead, it used the participants' ratings of the applicants. Nonetheless, we can compare these findings and try to squeeze them into our response matrix. Overall, the White applicants were rated as reasonably suitable for the potential jobs (with a mean score of 3.42 out of 6), while the identically qualified Black candidates were perceived as significantly less so (3.19 out of 6). This is about a 10% difference in their perceived suitability, so we can enter the findings in our results matrix as follows:

Who received more callbacks?
■ White CVs   □ Black CVs   □ Neither
How many more callbacks did they receive?
■ 10%   □ 50%   □ 90%

Again, we see that the size of the effect varies. The smaller effect here could be due to geography (King's experiment took place in New York, while Pager's took place in Milwaukee), or the kind of job, or to the fact that perceived suitability may not be the main driver of racial discrimination in the job market.

It is possible that employers still discriminate against Black people even when they perceive them to be capable or suitable for the post. Nonetheless, the direction is remarkably consistent. Across a range of areas, a range of jobs and a span of time, White applicants are perceived and treated more favorably than Black ones.

Let's quickly go through a few more. In an experiment published in 2009, Pager, Western, and Bonokowski hired testers (Black, White and Latino) to apply for 340 real entry-level jobs over the course of nine months in New York City. According to the researchers, "They were matched on the basis of their verbal skills, interactional styles (level of eye-contact, demeanor, and verbosity), and physical attractiveness." As always, the CVs they used were also matched indicating "identical educational attainment, and comparable quality of high school, work experience (quantity and kind), and neighborhood of residence." Still, despite identical CVs and matching in all other conceivable ways, Black applicants had a 15.2% callback rate, and White applicants had a 31% callback rate—over twice as high. Plugged into our matrix, that would be:

Who received more callbacks?
■ White CVs   ☐ Black CVs   ☐ Neither
How many more callbacks did they receive?
☐ 10%   ☐ 50%   ■ 90%

In an experiment published in 2012, Booth, Leigh and Varganova applied for over 4,000 jobs in Australia between April and October. They used a set of CVs that were identical except for, you guessed it, the ethnicity of the name of the person supposedly applying for the post (Anglo-Saxon, Indigenous, Chinese, Italian, and Middle Eastern). Despite otherwise identical CVs, the Black (i.e., Indigenous) applicants had a 26% callback rate and the White applicants had a 35% callback rate—1.35 times higher. Plugged into our matrix, that would be:

Who received more callbacks?
■ White CVs ☐ Black CVs ☐ Neither
How many more callbacks did they receive?
☐ 10% ■ 50% ☐ 90%

In 2016, Kang and Decelles responded to 1,600 job postings across a variety of metropolitan areas in the United States. As always, the CVs they used were identical except for the apparent ethnicities of the people who were applying for the posts. They looked at the effects of both identifiably Black and identifiably East Asian names, but, again, for now we'll only look at the Black ones. Identifiably Black CVs had a 10% response rate, while CVs that were whitened to remove any traces of Blackness had a 25.5% response rate—over 2.5 times as many (or a difference of 150%). Plugged into our matrix, that would be:

Who received more callbacks?
■ White CVs ☐ Black CVs ☐ Neither
How many more callbacks did they receive?
☐ 10% ☐ 50% ■ (>)90%

In 2019, Di Stasio and Heath applied for approximately 3,200 jobs in the United Kingdom using identical CVs that (I'm sure you know the drill by now) were identical except for the name of the person who was ostensibly applying for the post. They found that applicants with Black-sounding names (whether Nigerian, Ethiopian, Somalian or Ugandan) had a 12.3% callback rate. Despite their completely identical CVs, applicants with White,

British-sounding names had a much more successful 24.1% call-back rate: almost twice as high. Plugged into our matrix, that would be:

Who received more callbacks?
■ White CVs   ☐ Black CVs   ☐ Neither
How many more callbacks did they receive?
☐ 10%   ☐ 50%   ■ (>)90%

There are many, many more studies like these on workplace discrimination conducted across a variety of locations, looking at many different types of jobs, going back several decades. But I think we can stop here. If this list of studies has not convinced you, it is unlikely that a longer list of similar studies would do the trick. Furthermore, there is one more type of study we must consider before we can really work out what the scientific consensus on a topic is: the meta-analysis.

The meta-analysis

The data from all these studies point in a similar direction, but it's noteworthy that the magnitude of the results varies from one study to another. A scrupulous, scientific thinker might then point out that we haven't really solved the problem of anecdotes, we've simply elevated it to a slightly higher level. After all, depending on politics, one scientist could select a handful of studies that find a huge difference in responses to CVs based on race, and another scientist could select a different handful of studies that find very small differences, if any at all. The discussion can descend into a "citation war," with each side choosing only the studies that best support their argument.

Is there a way to get a clear, objective, bird's-eye view of what all the studies say?

Yes, there is. Enter the meta-analysis. A meta-analysis is what it sounds like: a level of investigation one step higher than individual studies. In fact, it treats each individual study like a single data point and can thus combine all the insights from a large number of studies to produce a single, clear, compelling answer. There are rules around meta-analyses which exist to ensure that you can't just pick the studies you like and ignore the ones you don't like. Researchers doing meta-analyses have to declare their inclusion criteria in advance and meticulously stick to them, no matter what the findings end up showing. They have to scour all the peer-reviewed journals, even the ones they're not a fan of or that are less popular. They even have to run statistical analyses to detect "missing studies"—that is, studies that were conducted, but never ended up in a peer-reviewed journal. How they do that involves complex statistical techniques such as looking for an unusual skew or missing data points in what should be a more normal distribution. The effect is that a meta-analysis gives us an objective view of a large field of study, distilling the findings of many disparate studies into one simple result.

Indeed, they do more than that. A meta-analysis can look at studies over a number of decades to tell us whether an effect has changed over time. It can look at a variety of studies to tell us if an effect varies by region. It can take hundreds of studies on employment discrimination and tell us whether and how an effect varies by type of job, or level of seniority, or some other important factor. Armed with meta-analyses, we can finally get a hold of that all-important scientific consensus.

At this point, what the meta-analyses show may not surprise you. In 2017 Quillian, Pager, Hexel, and Midtbøen published a meta-analysis of the available field experiments on hiring discrimination against Black people and Latinos in America. This included 28 studies published over multiple decades, in which almost 56,000 applications were submitted for about 26,000 positions. Looking at this wealth of field experiments, the researchers found that White people receive, on average, 36% more callbacks than African Americans, and 24% more callbacks than Latinos who apply for the same jobs with exactly the same qualifications. Applying that to our answer matrix, the results would look like this:

Who received more callbacks?	White CVs
How many more callbacks did they receive?	About 36%

More frightening, perhaps, was what the researchers found when they examined how the data changed (or didn't change) over time. Though there is a widespread assumption that racism is steadily declining, the authors found no support for this claim. Instead, though they found "modest evidence of a decline in discrimination against Latinos," they found "no change in the level of hiring discrimination against African Americans over the past twenty-five years." There is discrimination in the system, and things are not getting better.

However, in 2019, Heath and Di Stasio published a meta-analysis of the available field experiments on hiring discrimination against ethnic minorities in the UK, and their results were entirely different!

I'm joking, of course. Their results were very much the same. Many of the studies they looked at were slightly more complex and included numerous points of comparison. They were also interested in a larger set of comparisons between ethnic groups, so their final analysis included 43 comparisons between White, Black, South Asian and East Asian targets; the results of their analysis are therefore a bit complicated. However, if we focus on the different results for White and Black people, the authors say this: "The summary discrimination ratio is a substantial and highly significant 1.56 . . . In this series of studies, black Caribbean applicants had to make about 50 percent more applications than their white British counterparts in order to receive a positive response." We can summarize that like this:

Who received more callbacks?	White CVs
How many more callbacks did they receive?	About 50%

And this is what is meant by the scientific consensus. It doesn't mean that all scientists agree. Indeed, different social psychologists or sociologists may have very different opinions on the matter. It certainly doesn't mean that every random biologist or chemist understands these studies or is even aware of their existence. If you really searched, you could almost certainly find someone with some kind of scientific degree, or even someone with "Professor" in front of their name, who would be willing to give their opinion that racism is not a factor in hiring decisions. If you're very politically savvy, you could make sure that this person was an ethnic minority, making their opinion seem all the more credible.

However, you would not be able to find empirical experiments or meta-analyses that consistently show Black people and White people getting identical treatment for identical CVs. You would definitely not find studies consistently showing Black people getting favorable treatment over White people. Instead, you would consistently find experiments that show White people getting a distinct, significant advantage, even when all other explanations for that advantage are whittled away. That is what is meant by the scientific consensus. That is how we know, scientifically, that racism is still a factor in hiring decisions, and that it has been a factor for a very long time.

Chapter 3

Everything, Everywhere, All at Once
The Pervasive Ubiquity of Racism

On May 6, 2019, Archie Harrison Mountbatten-Windsor was born. He is the son of Meghan, Duchess of Sussex, the son of Prince Harry, Duke of Sussex, the great-grandson of the then-reigning monarch, Queen Elizabeth II, and the grandson of the current reigning monarch, King Charles III. Archie was born into a family of unimaginable wealth, power, and significance—the very definition of the upper class (whether you like the notion of an upper class or not). At 6.09 p.m., within hours of Archie's birth, BBC Radio host Danny Baker tweeted a picture of a monkey in a suit, with the caption "Royal baby leaves hospital."

On December 17, 2022, a mother took her three-week-old baby to the beach at Scarborough Park in Sumner, New Zealand. While they were there, an eighteen-year-old man jumped on the baby while saying "Go back to your country," and "You don't even speak English." The man was with a group of friends, one of whom was carrying a metal bar. They fled the scene after the local imam, Gamal Fouda, intervened. The baby was taken to hospital.

On May 16, 2010, Aiyana Mo'Nay Stanley-Jones was seven years old, and that was as old as she was ever going to be. That night, she was asleep on her grandmother's sofa in Detroit, Michigan, when a flash grenade exploded in the room. After this, accounts vary. The grandmother, Mertilla Jones, says that the flash grenade set the child on fire. She ran to her burning granddaughter, but got there too late. Officer Joseph Weekley had already fired his submachine gun, possibly before he had even entered the room. The bullet had already pierced Aiyana's neck. Aiyana was already dead. Officer Weekley claimed that the grandmother had grabbed his gun, causing it to fire and kill Aiyana, although none of the grandmother's fingerprints were ever found on the gun. After a series of trials, mistrials and retrials, all charges against Officer Weekley were dropped. He returned to duty soon afterward.

On April 29, 2022, Amrita Varshini Lanka was eight years old. She told her parents that her stomach hurt. She was vomiting. She had a fever. Her parents did what most sensible parents would do and took her to their local children's hospital in Melbourne, Australia. They waited two hours to be triaged. At about nine p.m. Amrita was given an intravenous drip, but her condition continued to worsen. She told her mother she was experiencing "hard breathing." Her mother immediately pressed the staff assistance button, but after twenty or twenty-five minutes she was still waiting for someone to respond. That night, Amrita's mother alerted the hospital five times about her daughter's breathing difficulties. Each time, her concerns were brushed aside. At six a.m. on April 30, a member of the hospital staff realized that Amrita was in a critical condition, but they were too late. At 10.17 a.m., within twenty-one hours of arriving at the hospital, Amrita Lanka was dead.

Chikayzea Flanders was twelve years old in September 2017, on his first day at the Fulham Boys School in London. He was told that his hair, which he wore in dreadlocks, did not comply with the school's uniform and appearance policy. He would have to cut it off or be suspended.

Tamir Rice was twelve years old on November 22, 2014. He was playing with a toy gun at a park in Cleveland, Ohio. Someone called the police about "a male" with "a pistol." The 911 responder asked a specific question three times before dispatching officers to the scene:

"Is he Black or White?"

"Is he Black or White?"

"Is he Black or White?"

Officers Timothy Loehmann and Frank Garmback arrived first. Both later reported that they were continuously shouting "Show me your hands" through the open patrol car window, and that it looked like Tamir was about to pull the gun on them. However, the video footage of the incident shows that Loehmann shot Tamir almost immediately upon arrival. The car hadn't even stopped. Tamir Rice died the following day.

Oprah Winfrey is one of the wealthiest and most recognizable people in the world. In 2013, while she was shopping in Zurich, a sales assistant refused to show her a black handbag on the grounds that it was "too expensive" and that "she couldn't afford it." On August 9, 2013, the Swiss tourism office apologized to Oprah for the "misunderstanding." However, the incident led one journalist to wonder whether a Black person "can . . . ever be rich enough or famous enough or beautiful enough to not be racially profiled while shopping?"

In June 2020, sixty-two-year-old Millard Scott was shielding from the Covid pandemic at his home in London, spending most of his time caring for his son, who had cerebral palsy. Millard was upstairs when the police pushed their way into his home, past his fifty-two-year-old partner, who was screaming "Don't touch me." The police were looking for someone who did not live at the Scotts' home. When Millard came out onto the landing to investigate the noise, a police officer shot him with a taser. He lost consciousness and collapsed, falling down the stairs. Months later, Millard Scott's family reported that he was still limping, still in pain.

At first, May 14, 2022 was just another Saturday. Aaron Salter Jr., a fifty-nine-year-old ex-police officer, was working security at a Tops Supermarket in Buffalo, New York. One of the patrons that day was Ruth Whitfield, an eighty-six-year-old grandmother who, the newspapers would say, had devoted her life to her family. While Ruth was shopping, Payton Gendron—a White man, self-described ethno-nationalist, and supporter of White supremacy—shot her dead. Gendron had come to the Tops armed with a Bushmaster AR-15 style rifle and concerns about White people being "replaced" through violence, immigration, and interracial marriage. Gendron killed nine Black people in the store that day, including Ruth. Nine people with families and friends and lives were snuffed out in about five minutes. Even though he was woefully outgunned, Aaron Salter Jr. heroically tried to stop Gendron. Gendron killed him too, making the number of Black people he killed that day ten.

More than just hiring discrimination

Racism neither starts nor ends at hiring discrimination. Could you imagine a world in which we were able to give birth to our children, go to the beach with our babies, or let our seven-year-olds sleep on their grandmother's sofas, or take our eight-year-olds to the hospital when their tummies hurt, or let our twelve-year-old children play at the park, or let them go to school with their natural hair, or shop in a high-end store—or any store, really—or even stay home and take care of family members, and have nothing racist happen in any of those situations? Can you imagine how it would be to live our lives from birth to death with no racist incidents, except for some occurrences of hiring discrimination? That would be a dream come true for many people of color around the world, including myself. Unfortunately, racism is not so obliging as to restrict itself to a single domain. As the examples above suggest, racism is in everything, everywhere, all at once.

I say "suggest" because, as I outlined in Chapter 2, the plural of anecdote is not data. These true stories, though they may be moving, revealing, exhausting, or even tragic, are not the same thing as rigorously collected, objectively analyzed, quantitative, empirical data. It will probably not surprise you to hear that each of those events has been interpreted in very different ways by many different people. Some people think they reveal racism in contemporary society, while others claim that they have little or nothing to do with racism at all. Even in the case of Payton Gendron, who murdered Ruth Whitfield, Aaron Salter Jr., and eight other Black people on a normal Saturday afternoon in Buffalo—and who explicitly said that he was doing so for racist reasons—some have argued that the focal explanation should be Gendron's mental health problems, not his racism.

And, speaking purely as a social scientist, I must admit that there is some justification for skepticism about the causes of these events based on anecdotes alone. No anecdote, or collection of anecdotes, no matter how shocking, or captivating, or terrible, can scientifically prove that people of color are treated worse than White people in schools, in hospitals, in public spaces, at stores, or by the police. Data is what we'd need to make statements about the prevalence of racism in all these areas of life: rigorous, empirical data.

Fortunately, data is precisely what we have.

I could write a version of Chapter 2 for each of those areas of life. I could do a deep dive into the research around racial discrimination in, for example, healthcare, that is similar to the deep dive I have done for hiring discrimination. I could cite a long list of studies about racism in healthcare from different settings at different times, all generally pointing in the same direction, and then top it off with meta-analyses that clarify the size, reliability, and generalizability of the effects, as well as the scientific consensus around those effects. I could then repeat the entire process for each of the other topics: racism in education, racism in finance, racism in service industries, racism in policing, racism in dating, and so on.

You will be relieved to know that I am not going to do that.

Or, at the very least, not in such detail for each topic. The point of Chapter 2 was not just to deliver a simple message about racism in hiring practices. Rather, it was to give you a glimpse into the scientific methodology, the decades of work, the hundreds of thousands (if not millions) of data points, the rigorous experimental designs, and the exacting statistical standards behind the simple statement: "It is a scientific fact that there is widespread, significant racism in hiring practices." With the basics of scientific methodology and how we arrive at those conclusions understood, there is no need to repeat the process for each new topic.

However, while you now have a reasonably good grasp of the depth of the scientific evidence, you may not yet have a grasp of its breadth. This chapter will rectify that. It will touch on more of the areas, from birth to death, in which racism plays a role. It will not include all the available published research. That would be impossible. There's simply too much of it, and new research is being published every year. Nonetheless, it will highlight some of the interesting scientific findings about racism, even about things that you didn't realize could be studied scientifically. I will, of course, include the names of the authors and the dates when they published their papers. But I also encourage you to get hold of the papers and read them for yourselves. Take nothing I say on faith. Science never asks for faith, only for a rigorous and honest examination of the evidence.

I will also begin to highlight more research beyond randomized controlled trials. Indeed, this is probably a useful time for me to be explicit about my own research focus and areas of expertise. I am an experimental psychologist by training; this is the field I know best and the type of research that I find most convincing. Consequently, most of the research you read about in this book will focus on experimental designs. It will involve quantitative results—that is, results that can be interpreted numerically—and it will look at racism from a contemporary perspective and from the perspective of the individual. However, there is also a wealth of excellent research out there that is qualitative (non-numerical) or that focuses on the historical or the systemic. I will touch on some of those methodologies and perspectives throughout the book (see, for example, Chapter 4), but if you'd like to know more about them, I would strongly recommend the work of people like Phia Salter, David Olusoga, Joe Feagin, or one of my personal favorites, fellow Jamaican Rhodes Scholar Stuart Hall.

However, even when staying doggedly within the realm of quantitative research, and even despite acknowledging randomized controlled trials as the gold standard in science, we must also acknowledge that even they have their limitations. While randomized controlled trials are very good at clarifying causal relationships between specific, predetermined variables, they are less good at other aspects of the scientific process. They usually aren't designed to capture bidirectional or cyclical relationships between variables. They often involve manipulations that deviate, however slightly, from the way things happen outside the lab. They sometimes can't be used at all on very large epidemiological questions. This isn't to say that randomized controlled trials are flawed. It's just that scientific knowledge is built on a lot more than just that one specific kind of experiment. Now that the randomized controlled trials have (hopefully) convinced you that racism is at least part of the explanation for the effects we're investigating, we are free to include evidence from other types of research.

For example, we can include large-scale data analyses that are excellent for gathering representative samples and precisely estimating the sizes of effects across a population. We can also include longitudinal studies, in which the same data are collected multiple times from each participant across several time-points. These are excellent for investigating effects that take a long time to occur, for identifying changes over time and for specifying the order in which variables change relative to each other. We can also include observational studies, in which there is little or no manipulation from the researcher. These are excellent for discovering what participants do when we don't interfere with them at all. They are the researchers' closest approximations to real life. Or, as the scientists say, they have very high levels of "external validity." All these types of studies, and many more, are tools that scientists use to understand racism and its effects. And, as you will see, there is an awful lot to discover.

Mountains o' Things: Racism in many areas of life

Education

In 2016, Gilliam and colleagues recruited 135 teachers and other classroom staff who were attending a large, annual American conference of early care and education professionals. Gilliam and colleagues asked them to participate in an experiment that was ostensibly about trying to understand "how teachers detect challenging behavior in the classroom." Each participant was shown six minutes of clips of preschoolers in a classroom and asked to press the enter key on a computer every time they spotted a preschooler engaging in "challenging behavior."

What the participants didn't realize, however, was that there were no challenging behaviors in any of the videos. The real purpose of the study was to understand which children teachers look at when they are expecting challenging behavior. To accomplish that, Professor Gilliam used eye-tracking devices on the participants to accurately measure how much time they spent looking at each child. The researchers found that teachers who were expecting bad behavior in the classroom spent most of their time looking at Black children, particularly Black boys, and significantly less time looking at White children.

In a similar study, in 2011, Shepherd recruited 57 experienced school teachers from the Los Angeles area and asked them to evaluate the spoken responses of different children in the second and third grade. All the children responded to the same set of relatively mundane questions, like "Why do we celebrate Thanksgiving?" and "What does the American flag stand for?" All the children also gave exactly the same responses. This is because Shepherd provided them with pre-written answers. All the children also delivered the responses with the same cadence, fluidity, and quality of sound. To accomplish this, Shepherd took hundreds of recordings and then selected the ones that were matched in all relevant qualities for all the children. The only detectable difference between the children was that some of them were (and sounded like) White children, while the others were (and sounded like) ethnic minority children. Still, despite all the responses being identically worded and delivered in the same way, the teachers evaluated the responses from ethnic minority children (and boys in general) more negatively than the responses from White children.

In 2015, Milkman and colleagues, pretending to be prospective doctoral students, sent over 6,500 emails to professors at top universities across the US. The messages were identical, except that the names of the students were changed to sound like either White or ethnic minority names. Despite the fact that all the names sent identical messages, the researchers found that students with ethnic minority names received significantly fewer responses from the professors than students with White names.

Also, as we saw when we looked at employment discrimination, these effects were not limited to any one place—they could be reliably found across multiple countries. For example, those prior studies were conducted in the US, but in 2009 Burgess and Greaves compared the external and internal assessments of over two million (exactly 2,255,383) eleven-year-old British students across 16,557 schools. The external assessments were graded by people who never met the students and consequently had limited information about their demographic categories. The internal assessments were determined by the teachers' personal evaluations of each child, based on their performance in school and on the teachers' interaction with them over the course of the year. The teachers were thus very aware of the children's demographic categories.

Burgess and Greaves hypothesized that, if the teachers were letting racial stereotypes affect their assessment of students, they should find a pattern of consistent underestimation of the ethnic minority children. In other words, ethnic minority children should (more often than White children) have internal assessments that were lower than their external assessments. And that is exactly what Burgess and Greaves found. Just looking at the children's English scores, for example, while only 12.4% of White students received lower internal assessments than external assessments, this number increased to 17.2% for Black Caribbean children, 18.3% for Black African children, and 20.2% for

Pakistani children. Similar patterns of underestimation were found for other subjects.

The research is clear. Even when ethnic minority and White students behave exactly the same way, educators expect lower levels of achievement and higher levels of negative behavior from the ethnic minority students. They rate their work less favorably, offer them less support and give them fewer opportunities than they give White students. This bias starts very early, when the children are still in preschool, and follows them through to the highest level of education.

Work and business

But it works both ways. In 2010, Bavishi and colleagues recruited 375 students preparing to go to university and showed them the CVs of some of their potential future professors. The CVs were, of course, all equivalent except for the apparent gender and ethnicity of the professors presented. The results showed that the students judged the supposedly Black professors as less competent, less legitimate and lower in interpersonal skills than the identically qualified White professors. Similarly, in 2019, Chisadza and colleagues asked 1,599 first-year undergraduate students to rate university lecturers based on a particular presentation. Even though all the presentations used identical narrated slides, the students gave the Black lecturers lower ratings than the White lecturers.

In 2009, Schreer and colleagues sent Black and White "shoppers" (actually they were confederates) to a number of high-end stores. Each shopper approached an employee to make the same request: they asked whether a salesperson would remove the security tag on a pair of expensive sunglasses so that they could try them on. While the salesperson did remove the security tag in all cases, they also showed significantly higher levels of suspicion when dealing with the Black customers. They were much more likely to stare at them, and much more likely to follow them around the store while they had the sunglasses in their possession.

In 2011, Ayres and Banaji posted baseball cards for sale on eBay. Though they always posted exactly the same cards for sale, the accompanying picture either showed the cards being held by a light-skinned (apparently White) hand or a dark-skinned (apparently Black) hand. They found that the cards sold for approximately 20% less if they were being sold by Black people instead of White people.

Across several studies on workplace treatment, businesses and customer experiences, results have shown that ethnic minorities are perceived as less competent, less legitimate and less likeable. They are treated with less respect and more suspicion; they are offered less money for doing the same job, even when they are equally qualified and when they are providing identical goods or services.

Friendships and relationships

Of course, there is more to life than work. In 2019, Perszyk and colleagues recruited 30 young children in America (the average age was four and a half years old), and asked them to do a series of tasks in which they sorted images of other children by a number of positive and negative traits (for example, "nice" vs. "not nice"). By varying the race of the children in the images, the researchers were able to get a measure of the children's explicit biases: these are the biases that people are consciously aware of and fine admitting in public.

In a second task, the researchers asked the children to sort a set of unfamiliar Chinese characters. However, unknown to the children, using a technique called backmasking, each Chinese character was subtly paired with an image of a child. Backmasking takes advantage of human visual processing speeds to show two images in quick succession while leaving the participant conscious of only the second image, but totally unaware of the first image. By varying the race of the children in the hidden images, the researchers were able to get a good measure of the children's implicit biases: these are the biases that people are less aware of and less likely to admit to others (or sometimes even themselves). In the end, however, the distinction between the explicit and implicit biases hardly mattered. The researchers found that, whether assessed through explicit or implicit means, "[the] children revealed a strong and consistent pro-White bias."

In 2005, Rutland and colleagues had used similar techniques to measure the attitudes of 136 three-to-five-year-olds in the UK. Much like Perszyk and colleagues years later, Rutland not only found evidence of racial bias in children, but also found that it followed a consistent and predictable pattern: the most favorable attitudes were shown toward White children, Asian children were in the middle, and the least favorable attitudes were shown toward Black children. The results are clear. By the time a child is three to four years old, they likely already have significant, detectable biases against ethnic minorities.

In 2020, I asked 3,453 White British participants how likely they would be to casually have sex with, or to marry, someone from four different ethnic groups: White, Black, East Asian, and South Asian. Interestingly, no deception at all was used in this study. The participants understood what I was asking and why I was asking it. Nonetheless, the participants showed a strong and significant preference for White partners over any other ethnicity. Furthermore, they showed a relative preference for marriage (over casual sex) when considering White partners, but a relative preference for casual sex (over marriage) when considering ethnic minority partners.

From friendships to romantic relationships, from earliest childhood to adulthood, ethnic minorities are considered less desirable partners, and this preference is often explicit as well as implicit.

Police and the justice system

In 2007, across a number of studies, Correll and colleagues put police officers and members of the community into a video-game-like simulator. The participants were told that some people were going to pop up in the simulation. They had to shoot the people with guns and not shoot the people without guns. That seems simple enough. However, to keep things interesting, Correll and colleagues not only varied whether the simulated people had guns, they also randomly varied whether the simulated people were Black or White. The researchers were interested in whether and when the participants got things wrong. Did they shoot people who weren't holding guns? Did they fail to shoot people who were holding guns? And did the targets' race affect the likelihood of making those mistakes?

It will not surprise you to learn that the participants overall were significantly more likely to fail to shoot a White person who had a gun than a Black person who had a gun, showing the potential protective power of being White. Conversely, the participants were more likely to erroneously shoot a Black person who didn't have a gun than a White person who didn't have a gun. Black people holding wallets or can openers were often fired on by the participants.

What a powerful argument for rigorously controlled gun ownership. I am a Black person. I own a wallet. For some reason, I own multiple can openers. Life and death should not hinge on so little.

Correll and colleagues found other interesting results as well. While both police and community members were quicker to shoot Black people overall, the police officers were much more controlled than the community members (whom the researchers described using the official psychological term "trigger happy"). In a 2014 review of multiple studies, Correll and colleagues concluded that police officers do have similar biases to members of the community, but that they generally learn to keep their responses in check through training and exercising cognitive control.

However, other researchers' findings are less optimistic. Much research from the US—such as work by Edwards, Lee, and Esposito in 2019, and by Schwartz and Jahn in 2020—has found that the per capita rate of fatal shootings by the police is about 2.5 to 3 times higher for Black Americans than for White Americans. These differences can't be explained by other relevant factors, such as civilian behavior or socioeconomic status. Quite the contrary: research by Nix, Campbell, Byers, and Alpert in 2017 shows that Black victims of police shootings are twice as likely to be unarmed as White victims. These issues also don't start and end at the point of getting shot. Large-scale analyses of police stops in the United States by Pierson and colleagues in 2020 show that Black drivers are more than twice as likely to be stopped than White drivers. Furthermore, as Kramer and Remster found in 2018, when they do encounter the police, "Black and White civilians experience fundamentally different interactions," particularly, as Khan, Goff, Lee, and Motamed found in 2016, "concerning the use of force."

And before the British readers point out that those results come from American studies, the British police show similar patterns to the American ones. There are fewer guns in the UK, and even the police are much less likely to carry them or use them. However, the powers that the police do wield are often used in racially disproportionate ways. Research by Bowling and Phillips in 2007, and also Joseph-Salisbury, Connelly, and Wangari-Jones in 2020, has found that depending on the region and the year, Black people in the UK are between 6 and 27 times more likely to be stopped and searched by the police than White people. Recent statistics from Mellor in 2021 also show that the British police are nine times more likely to use their tasers on Black people than on White people—a pattern that is yet to be explained by any other characteristic of the interactions.

Across two studies in 2018, together with a psychologist friend of mine, Jo Lloyd, I showed 120 participants identical newspaper stories about real crimes committed by real criminals. As you can probably guess at this point, the stories were identical within each study except that the names of the alleged criminals were randomly changed to make them appear to be either White Christians or Arabic Muslims. Even though the behaviors were exactly the same, we found that participants rated the criminals' behavior as both worse and more terrorist-y when they thought the criminal was Muslim.

In 2019, Howard asked 121 participants to read two versions of a newspaper article about an individual who had been wrongfully convicted of a crime following a false confession, but was later exonerated. Despite the stories being otherwise identical, the participants in the study perceived the Black exoneree to be more aggressive, less deserving of government assistance, and more likely to commit a crime upon release than the White exoneree.

In 2003, Pager conducted a CV study very similar to the CV studies seen in Chapter 2 of this book. A set of nearly identical CVs were distributed that differed only in the apparent race of the person sending the CV: Black or White. However, Pager added an interesting new twist to the study. As well as varying whether the ostensible applicant was Black or White, Pager also varied whether or not they had a criminal record. That created four possible versions of the otherwise identical CVs: Black with a criminal record; White with a criminal record; Black with no criminal record; and White with no criminal record. At this point, nobody was surprised to learn that White people received more callbacks than identically qualified Black people. Nor was anyone surprised that people without criminal records received more callbacks than people with criminal records. The shocking thing was the outcome of the two effects when they were added together. Pager found that even White people with criminal records had a higher proportion of callbacks (17%) than identically qualified Black people who did not have criminal records (14%).

In every respect, the justice system is harder on ethnic minorities than on White people. They are more likely to be stopped by the police in the first place, and police officers are more likely to use force (sometimes deadly force) against them. They are perceived more negatively than White people who commit the same crimes. They are perceived as guiltier and more dangerous than otherwise identical White people even if they are exonerated of their crimes, and they are still perceived as less desirable employees than White ex-convicts even if they—the ethnic minorities—have committed no crimes at all.

Healthcare

In 2020, Wisniewski and Walker called 804 randomly selected US doctors' offices while pretending to be White, Black, or Hispanic. Despite presenting the same information (other than race), they found that the supposedly Black and Hispanic callers were more frequently asked about their insurance status. Furthermore, despite having the same insurance status, the Black and Hispanic callers were offered appointments further in the future, making them wait longer than otherwise equivalent White callers.

In 2007, Green and colleagues tested 287 medical professionals on their levels of explicit anti-Black bias, implicit anti-Black bias, and their recommended treatment for myocardial infarction for particular patients. You may not know what myocardial infarction is. I didn't. It's more commonly known as a heart attack, a serious medical issue that can kill you. According to Green's paper, the best way to deal with myocardial infarction is something called thrombolytic therapy. If you aren't sure what that is either, just know that it can save your life.

What matters most here is the pattern of results that Green and colleagues found. Even though the physicians reported no explicit bias against Black people, the researchers found significant levels of implicit bias against Black people, who were perceived as less cooperative with medical procedures than White people. Furthermore, doctors with higher levels of implicit anti-Black bias were also less likely to offer Black patients—but not White patients—thrombolytic therapy (that is, the life-saving treatment) for their myocardial infarctions (that is, the deadly condition). In a similar study conducted in 2004, Gilligan and colleagues found that prostate-specific antigen tests were less likely to be used on Black men than White men. This pattern leads to a higher incidence of potentially deadly advanced prostate cancer among Black men.

Put together, all this research paints a devastating picture of what life is like for ethnic minorities in predominantly White countries. In the earliest years of their lives, as soon as scientists are able to test for it, we find significant racial bias among their teachers and their friends. This bias stalks them throughout their lives, affecting their friendships, their romantic relationships, their educational and employment opportunities, their interactions with the police, the justice system and the healthcare system. In a multitude of ways, this racism can literally kill them. Given how aggressively the deck is stacked against them, it is a marvel that any person of color manages to succeed in contemporary society.

That said, some people of color clearly do manage to succeed. They become wealthy, powerful, highly educated, highly respected individuals within our societies. Two of the most obvious examples are President Barack Obama and Prime Minister Rishi Sunak: both ethnic minorities, both highly educated, both wealthy (the latter being very, very wealthy) and both heads of state of predominantly White countries. This brings me to an argument that I sometimes see used against the weight of all this empirical evidence for the existence of racism. A person will sometimes point to a successful, rich, or highly educated ethnic minority individual and attempt to use that individual as evidence that the bias found in these many, many empirical studies does not exist. Sometimes they will go a step further and point to a person of color who claims never to have personally experienced any racism.

In response to these people, I will once again reiterate that central lesson from Chapter 2: the plural of anecdote is not data. It doesn't matter if you don't personally think you've ever experienced racism, or even if you can find 100 Black people all willing to say that they've never experienced racism, or 1,000 Hispanic or Asian people who are all doing fantastically well in some field or other. It doesn't matter if you find an endless list of people who say that they have personally always been treated fairly by their teachers, their co-workers, and the police. Scientifically, none of that matters at all. Nobody cares.

What matters, as always, is the result of rigorous, carefully controlled, expertly analyzed, empirical data. And that data reliably points in the same direction: racism is, essentially, in everything. There is no aspect of life that is unaffected by it, and there are very few people (if any) who can pass through society without being touched by it in some way. Scientists don't decide whether racial discrimination exists because one Black person says it happened to them, or because another Black person says it didn't. We *know* that racial discrimination occurs because the empirical research clearly shows that it does, in almost everything, almost everywhere, almost all the time. That is why, as Yale professor Beverly Daniel Tatum pointed out in 1999, "Every measurable social indicator, from salary to life expectancy to health to housing accessibility, reveals the advantages of being White."

Chapter 4

Power
Understanding Systemic Racism

Maurice Harold Macmillan, 1st Earl of Stockton, had a problem. It was 1962, and he was the prime minister of the United Kingdom. That was not the problem. The Second World War had been over for some time, and the UK was furiously rebuilding its services and infrastructure. That was certainly not the problem. However, to carry out this rebuilding, the British required some help, and that was where the problems began.

A lot of the people who came to offer their help were from the colonies—places like Jamaica, Trinidad and Tobago, South Asian countries, and the like. Hundreds of them. Thousands of them. One ship alone, HMT *Empire Windrush*, brought over nearly 500 of them in 1948. Later, in the 1950s and 60s, over 191,000 people traveled from Jamaica alone to settle in the UK, plus goodness knows how many from the other colonies. Hundreds of thousands of them!

To be fair, they made themselves useful. Many of the earliest arrivals were veterans of the war; they had been loyal subjects of the King in 1948 and were now, in 1962, loyal subjects of the Queen. This loyalty to the Crown was in their favor. Also, many were trained nurses, teachers or professionals of other kinds whose expertise the UK badly needed. Furthermore, multiple surveys had been done to check whether people were coming over to the UK just to be lazy freeloaders, and the government had found no evidence to suggest that was the case. They had come to work, these dark-skinned immigrants—and apparently, they were indeed working. So that wasn't the problem either.

The problem was that they weren't leaving.

Quite the opposite, in fact. They were sending for their families, increasing their numbers every day. They were buying houses. Some of them were even marrying British people and firmly planting their proverbial flags in the soil of London, and in other British cities too. Whole neighborhoods were becoming saturated with them and they clearly planned to still be here several generations down the line. This was definitely a problem.

As noted by Rudlin in 2021, Macmillan was neither the only nor even the first British prime minister to be concerned about this supposed problem. Three prime ministers earlier, back in the 1940s, Clement Attlee had received a letter from twelve of his MPs reminding him that the British were "blessed in the absence of a color racial problem" and warning him that the "influx of colored people domiciled here is likely to impair harmony." Two prime ministers before Macmillan—this time in 1955—Winston Churchill had toyed with the slogan "Keep Britain White" in response to the steady influx of these people to British shores. The Churchill government never used that slogan in the end, and the "colored" immigrants just kept coming.

And now it was 1962. Somebody finally had to do something about the problem, and it looked as though that somebody was going to be Harold Macmillan.

But fixing the problem wouldn't be so simple. You see, there was a second problem. The UK was a bright, forward-thinking, shining beacon of civilization and fair-mindedness. British people certainly weren't nasty racists like those Nazis had been. So, even if there was some popular support for keeping Britain

White, the government couldn't just pass a law saying, "No coloreds." That simply wouldn't do. It would make them look bad. What they needed was a clever way of getting rid of all those colored immigrants, or at the very least, stopping any more from coming over, without ever openly admitting that this was what they were trying to do.

Fortunately, Macmillan's government found a solution. It came via the introduction of a skills-based system of immigration. Here's how it worked. White immigrants generally came from countries in which their educational and training institutions provided documentation that the British government considered acceptable. The ones that weren't White? Not so much. Their institutions generally didn't provide the right sort of documentation. So, as the chairman of the committee assigned to the problem put it (again, as noted by Rudlin in 2021), a skills-based system was "the only workable method of controlling immigration without ostensibly discriminating on the basis of color."

As historian David Olusoga notes in his documentary on the Windrush generation, *ostensibly* was the important word here. Of course, the law would be discriminating on the basis of color. But, when scrutinized, one would find within it no mention of race at all—only mentions of skills and documentation. The government had found a way to keep the coloreds out while preserving its shining, non-biased image. The Right Honorable Richard Austen Butler, Baron Butler of Saffron Walden, and the Home Secretary in 1962, put it best: "The great merit of this scheme is that it can be presented as making no distinction on grounds of race or color . . . although the scheme purports to relate solely to employment and to be non-discriminatory, its aim is primarily social and its restrictive effect is intended to and would, in fact, operate on colored people almost exclusively."

Richard Austen Butler was Britain's First Secretary of State between 1962 and 1963. He died in 1982. Harold Macmillan was prime minister between 1957 and 1963. He died in 1986. But the skills-based immigration system is alive and well, and still operating in the UK today.

Defining systemic racism

This is probably a good place to define some terms. To quote the British government's controversial (and, I'll be honest, entirely unscientific and erroneous) 2021 "Report of the Commission on Race and Ethnic Disparities," "The linguistic inflation on racism is confusing, with prefixes like institutional, structural and systemic adding to the problem." On this point, I am forced to agree with the government's report. Many people use terms like "systemic racism" or "institutional racism" without first defining what they mean, and this can lead to a lot of unnecessary confusion. People sometimes use these words interchangeably, or in a way that differs from the understanding of their listeners, all of which makes matters worse. I am not the kind of pedant who strongly believes that words have a "correct" definition; language is an evolving and collaborative process, after all. But good communication is impossible without clarity on both sides. I am therefore going to set out some working definitions, just so we can all be on the same page.

With that in mind, I would like to describe all the racism we've discussed up to this point as "individual racism." By that, I mean that each of the examples of racism referenced in the last few chapters—selecting friends and romantic partners, offering people educational or employment opportunities, the treatment of people in the healthcare and justice system, and so on—required some individual person, or a large number of individual persons, to be racist in order for the racism to happen. These persons might be hard to identify; they might behave in subtle ways; they might even be unaware of what they're doing. Still, for each of those situations, racist individuals exist somewhere to drive the racist effects.

However, there is another kind of racism—a kind I will refer to here as "systemic racism." The *Cambridge Dictionary* offers definitions of both systemic racism and institutional racism; these definitions are extremely similar, and their slight differences are not central to this chapter. For this reason, I will focus only on systemic racism and allow it to stand in (for now) for both terms. The British government will have to forgive me.

With that in mind, the *Cambridge Dictionary* defines systemic racism as "policies and practices that exist throughout a whole society or organization, and that result in and support a continued unfair advantage to some people and unfair or harmful treatment of others based on race." This definition seems fine, but in my view, it does not sufficiently clarify the distinction between individual racism (as discussed in Chapters 1, 2, and 3) and systemic racism, which I'm trying to highlight now.

Many people, for example, would characterize the employment discrimination I outlined in Chapter 2 as systemic, because it's widespread and reliable, and has far-reaching effects. In this instance, "systemic racism" appears to be barely distinguishable, if distinguishable at all, from "a lot of racism." While I do recognize this use of the word "systemic" (that is, sufficiently widespread that it affects an entire *system*), it unfortunately hides an incredibly important distinction between racism that is individual but widespread, and racism that is truly systemic. I see these two types of racism as qualitatively different. To explain why, I'd like to offer a different definition of systemic racism, and it goes like this: *Systemic racism is the kind of racism that's built into the rules*

*of a society or organization, so that it still produces racist effects
even if there are no individual racists at all in the system.*

Using that definition, the employment discrimination discussed in Chapter 2 could be ubiquitous, and it could be devastating, but it would not be "systemic"—because the second you
removed all the racist people from the hiring committees, the
evaluating boards and the human resources departments, that
specific kind of racism would entirely disappear. Employment
would immediately cease to be a domain in which racism affected
outcomes.

The UK's immigration system, however, would not. The system was designed to be racist, and to continue to be racist long
after all the people who had created the racist policies were dead.
Even if every single individual person working in the British immigration system from 1963 (the end of Harold Macmillan's term as
prime minister) to the present day was perfectly egalitarian, the
immigration system would still have produced racist effects, as it
was intended to do, through the application of carefully chosen
rules that favored White immigrants and made things more difficult for non-White immigrants.

There are, of course, other examples of systemic racism. Some
of them, like the British immigration system, have a convenient
smoking gun: the dutifully recorded words of a politician or busi-
nessperson explaining how their new rule would be "ostensibly"
egalitarian, but "would, in fact, operate on colored people almost
exclusively." More often, however, when doing racist things, people
in power aren't so obligingly honest, or they don't keep such
immaculate records, so uncovering the systemic racism requires
a bit more work. Fortunately, it is still possible to uncover, because
systemic racism tends to leave a statistical trail and often follows
a familiar two-step pattern.

Step 1: Identify something that differs between White and

non-White people but is not necessarily important or relevant to your central issue—for example, different rates of access to specific documentation that proves their skills or education. *Step 2*: use the unimportant difference you identified in Step 1 as a prerequisite for accomplishing the thing you *really* care about. For example, make specific skills-based documentation a requirement for immigration to the UK. And you're done!

Step 2 contains no reference to race or ethnicity but, because of its relationship to Step 1, your outcomes will nonetheless be racially biased. Furthermore, they will continue to be racially biased long after all the racist people are removed from the system, so long as nobody changes the rules you initially set up.

With that in mind, we are ready to talk about voter identification laws.

Voter identification

Let's go through the same two-step process with voter identification. Imagine that you are a lawmaker who wants to prevent ethnic minorities from voting. How would you do it? You can't just hang signs on the voting booths that say "No coloreds." First of all, it hasn't been 1960s England for a long time, and younger voters might not even understand what you mean if you use that language. Second, and more importantly, it would make you look bad, particularly if you happened to live in the land of freedom, the land of liberty and justice for all, the land where "all men are created equal and endowed by their creator with certain inalienable rights." In this context, any move that so brazenly tried to stop ethnic minorities from voting would be perceived rather poorly.

However, you could find something irrelevant or unimportant

that differentiates between White people and ethnic minorities, and then tie the right to vote to that difference. What about some kind of identification document? Not all countries require identification to vote. The UK didn't require any kind of voter ID until 2023 and nonetheless saw astonishingly low levels of voter fraud. According to the British Electoral Commission, only thirteen cases of alleged personation fraud were recorded by police forces in 2022, and only seven of those cases involved allegations in polling stations (the only place identification would make a difference). Furthermore, none of those cases actually required the police to take further action, "because there was no evidence or insufficient evidence." The UK is a country of 68 million people. Within a rounding error, seven cases of voter fraud (the kind that could be addressed with voter ID) is essentially no voter fraud at all. Other European countries do require IDs to vote, but often every person who is eligible to vote is also given a form of identification that is easily or automatically provided, as well as either very cheap or completely free. This means that, barring very unusual circumstances, everyone who is entitled to vote can vote.

In the US, things are different. According to a 2021 report by the American Civil Liberties Union (ACLU), millions of Americans (about 7%) do not have a form of government-issued identification that would be acceptable for voting. These forms of identification also usually cost a significant amount of money to obtain, especially when one factors in the cost of prerequisite documentation, travel, and time taken off work to acquire them. This can run into the hundreds of dollars, which is prohibitive for anyone on a tight budget. Speaking of travel, sometimes identification offices are so remotely located as to be inaccessible for people without access to a car. The ACLU cite the example of rural Texas, where a person may have to travel about 170 miles to get to the nearest ID office.

With all of that in place, it is unsurprising that ethnic minorities—who already tend to be disadvantaged by the racism we discussed in Chapters 2 and 3—are less likely to have forms of identification that would allow them to vote. According to a 2015 report by Project Vote, Black Americans were almost three times as likely (13%) to lack government-approved voter ID compared to White Americans (5%). So, if you want to discourage ethnic minorities from voting, you don't have to do anything so crass as hanging a sign that says "No coloreds." Even if every individual at every polling station is perfectly egalitarian, you just have to strictly enforce voter ID laws, and the rules of the system will ensure that the racism occurs anyway.

Indeed, this is precisely what has happened (except, perhaps, the part about every individual being perfectly egalitarian). In 2017, Hajnal, Lajevardi, and Nielson examined data from the Cooperative Congressional Election Study (CCES). This dataset contained over 50,000 votes, each from a different person, which were validated by checking them against actual state voter files. The researchers used the data, plus data on the strictness of voter identification laws in each state (derived from the National Conference of State Legislatures) to assess whether the strictness of voting laws predicted voter turnout, and whether it did so differentially for White voters versus ethnic minority voters.

And, of course, it did! As the researchers put it, "these laws serve not only to diminish minority participation but also to increase the gap in the participation rate between whites and nonwhites." These gaps would vary depending on the ethnic minorities in question and the kind of election in question, but the effects of voter ID laws were sometimes very large indeed. In primary elections, the Asian–White participation gap more than tripled from 5.8 points to 18.8 points in states with strict voter ID laws. The Latino–White participation gap almost quadrupled in primary elections from 3.4 points to 13.2 points in states with strict voter ID laws. And in general elections, the Black–White participation gap more than quadrupled from 2.5 points to 11.6 points in states with strict voter ID laws.

Hajnal and colleagues performed a number of follow-up statistical analyses to weed out other potential explanations for their findings. They looked at political conditions in the states that implement these laws, the voting intentions of the different ethnic groups, and other state-level and campaign-specific factors. They found that none of these factors substantially altered the main findings related to the impact of voter ID on minority participation in voting. Their conclusions were inescapable: "[Voter ID laws] do, in fact, have real consequences for the makeup of the voting population. Where they are enacted, racial and ethnic minorities are less apt to vote . . . and the relative influence of White America grows."

Interestingly, the researchers also found that the strict voting laws had no effect on White people's voting. If anything, White turnout increased slightly in states with strict identification laws. In other words, American voter ID laws are another example of "rules that would be ostensibly egalitarian, but would, in fact, operate on colored people almost exclusively."

This is systemic racism.

Bringing the individual and the systemic together

You might be uncomfortable with calling voter ID laws an example of systemic racism. Perhaps you, like author and journalist Douglas Murray, see voter ID laws as something that can "unite the American Left and Right . . . an attempt to uphold the integrity of the vote." Maybe, like the British government, you believe that voter ID laws will "prevent voter fraud and protect democracy," especially from those seven people who may or may not have tried something dodgy in the voting booth in 2022. Maybe you see support for voter ID laws as motivated by concerns that are noble or, at the very least, racially neutral. If you do, the scientific evidence on this point might surprise you.

In 2013, Wilson and Brewer analyzed survey data from a representative sample of 906 American participants. The survey included a number of variables such as political ideology and party affiliation, media use, perceptions of voter fraud, and various demographic identifiers. However, the two variables we're most interested in are the participants' support for voter ID laws, and something Wilson and Brewer referred to as "racial resentment." This second variable was measured by getting participants to indicate their level of agreement with statements such as: "African Americans bring up race only when they need to make an excuse for their failure," and "I disapprove of any special considerations that African Americans receive, such as in college admissions or in the workplace, because it's unfair to other Americans." As you can tell, this was a pretty explicit measure of anti-Black racism.

If support for voter ID laws was purely driven by concerns about "preventing voter fraud and protecting democracy," the researchers should have found that perceptions of voter fraud were predictive of support for voter ID laws, and that very little else should have mattered once perceptions of fraud were accounted for. Explicit racism (or racial resentment) shouldn't have been relevant, and therefore shouldn't have predicted support for voter ID laws.

Of course, this is not what Wilson and Brewer found. Unsurprisingly, even when all the relevant predictors were taken into account—even after adjusting for the effects of politics, and media, and even knowledge about voter ID laws—racial resentment remained a significant predictor of support for these ID laws. In the researchers' own words: "the effect found for racial resentment suggests that ostensibly race-neutral voter ID laws carry racial symbolism."

There's that word again: *ostensibly.*

In 2016, Banks and Hicks recruited 723 White American participants for an experiment that took place over two waves. In the first wave, participants completed measures indicating how they felt about Black people. It's worth noting that these were measures of both explicit racism and implicit racism. Then, a few days later (to give the participants enough time to shake off any effects from completing Wave 1), the researchers asked the participants to return and complete the second wave of the experiment.

This second wave was more interesting. As you've probably guessed, it involved measuring the participants' support for voter ID laws. However, before participants indicated their support for voter ID laws, they were randomly assigned to one of three conditions, each of which (via a well-established technique that uses a combination of pictures and writing tasks) induced a different emotional state: relaxation (the control condition), anger (condition 2), or fear (condition 3).

Just like Wilson and Brewer before them, Banks and Hicks also found that higher levels of racism predicted greater support for voter ID laws. That much was unsurprising. The more interesting finding concerned the effects of the emotional manipulations. Explicit racism predicted more support for voter ID laws no matter what emotional state the participants were in. However, implicit racism was a particularly strong predictor of support for voter ID laws when the participants were afraid. That's right: if you scare White people, the ones with high levels of implicit racism respond to this fear by strengthening their support for voter ID laws.

This is how systemic and individual racism work together. Voter ID laws would have racist effects even if nobody in the entire world was racist at all. But, of course, we're not so lucky. Some individual people do have racist views and take part in racist behaviors. One manifestation of their individual racism is to increase their support for pillars of structural racism, at least under certain circumstances. Though they might not acknowledge it explicitly, on some level people do recognize the systemic racism of voter ID laws. And, when they're feeling afraid, they are willing and able to weaponize that knowledge.

So far, in this chapter, I've focused on two manifestations of systemic racism: immigration laws and voter ID laws. This focus has allowed me to outline some of the history and the research supporting our understanding of systemic racism. However, there's a lot that I haven't discussed—I haven't discussed poll taxes, literacy tests, or residency requirements as prerequisites for voting. I haven't discussed recent bans on providing water and food to those lining up to vote. I haven't discussed the geographical distribution of polling stations or transportation to them.

Beyond the domain of voting, I haven't discussed the links between property taxes and funding for children's education in America. I haven't discussed the UK's stop and search laws, or the American practice of "redlining," which means designating certain areas (surprise! These just happen to be mostly ethnic minority areas) as "hazardous to investment" and therefore not lending money or providing mortgages to people who live in those areas. I haven't discussed the banning of hoodies in shopping areas in the London borough of Romford, or in the Wolfchase Galleria mall in Memphis, Tennessee. I haven't discussed the fact that many places in the UK still explicitly ban a range of hairstyles from schools and places of work, many of which just happen to be natural Black hairstyles. I haven't mentioned that, as of 2022, only eighteen of the fifty American states have passed laws prohibiting discrimination based on hair texture. I wear dreadlocks myself, and so, even today, I can legally be prevented from accessing certain employment or services in many British establishments and almost two-thirds of US states.

Nonetheless, I hope the point has been made. The purpose of Chapters 2 and 3 was to show that a lot of people, in a lot of circumstances, do a lot of racist things. The purpose of this chapter has been to show that even the severe, ubiquitous, sometimes dangerous racism that those earlier chapters outlined is far from the whole picture. Even if you rubbed a magic lamp, or snapped your fingers, or wriggled your nose, and somehow removed all the racism from the hearts and minds of all people alive today, quite a lot of racism would simply grind forward unabated. It's built into the system itself. No individual support required.

PART II
ON CONSCIOUS AND UNCONSCIOUS BIAS

Chapter 5

They Know Not What They Do
The Unconscious Bias Narrative

A perpetually vexing aspect of the study of racism is the apparent lack of any actual racists. As Chapters 2 and 3 have shown, racism is real, significant, empirically detectable and almost everywhere. But if that's true, then why can't we tell where it's coming from? Who are the people doing all these racist things, and why can't we identify them?

This is no small problem, and for a time it was a matter of genuine scientific concern. If you enter any company or speak to any search committee and ask them if they discriminate against ethnic minorities in their hiring practices, they will all (or nearly all) tell you that they don't. And yet, if you then send them a few hundred (or thousand) identically qualified CVs, they will predictably and reliably select the White CVs more often than the Black ones. Similarly, if you ask any teacher or educator if they discriminate against ethnic minority students, they'll say that they don't. And yet, when you hand them a hundred or a thousand pieces of equivalent work, they will rate the work by Black students as worse than the work by White students. If you ask any medical professional if she or he discriminates against ethnic minorities, you're likely to get a stern dressing down and a request to leave the premises immediately. However, when you run the numbers, you'll see that the ethnic minority appointments are scheduled to occur later than the ones for White people and that the ethnic minorities are less likely to be offered crucial life-saving treatments. And if you ask any three-year-old or four-year-old if they prefer White people to Black people . . . well, a lot of them will just say yes, because kids are like that and most of them haven't learned about the finer points of social norms (remember, for example, the 2019 findings of Perszyk and colleagues mentioned in Chapter 3). But I think we can all accept that the three- and four-year-olds aren't the ones responsible for all this racism in hiring, policing, customer service, healthcare and essentially everything else. So what's going on?

Frustratingly, the problem goes even deeper. Even if you ask people anonymously, even if you ensure that they know there will be no negative consequences for revealing their true thoughts or feelings, you'll still find that almost nobody thinks of themselves as a racist person. This is not a claim I make idly. In 2019, West (that's me) and Eaton published interesting findings on just this topic. For our study, we asked 148 people to judge how racially egalitarian they were compared to both people in the wider society and to other people in the room with them at the time. We gave them a rating scale of 0 to 99, such that "0 would indicate that you are at the very bottom . . . or more racist than almost everyone else, 50 would indicate that you were 'exactly average,' and 99 would indicate that you were at the very top, or less racist than almost everyone else." If the participants were rating themselves accurately, we should have found that about half of them gave themselves scores that were lower than 50 (indicating that they were more racist than average) and half of them should have given themselves scores that were higher than 50 (indicating that they were less racist than average).

This, however, was not at all what we found. Instead, we found that everyone gave themselves scores that were higher than 50, regardless of the context in which they were comparing themselves. That means that even when they were just considering how they ranked compared to the other people in the room with them on that day, every single person thought that they were less racist than the average. You don't have to be much of a mathematician to understand that this is not how averages work.

How can we possibly square these two findings—a world in which there is widespread, significant, detectable racism in almost everything, but simultaneously a world in which hardly anyone, anywhere admits, even to themselves, that they think, feel, or do racist things?

This is the problem that research on implicit bias was perfectly poised to solve.

Implicit bias research to the rescue

Few things are more boring than a pedant who is a stickler for the terminology of their field of expertise. Sadly, I must take that role now. Forgive me.

I want you to note that I did not use the term "unconscious bias," although I know that it is now a very widely used term. For example, in the 2022 documentary series *Harry & Meghan*, Prince Harry, Duke of Sussex (whom I consider both well intentioned and reasonably well informed about racism for a very rich, very privileged, very White man), used it to explain both his earlier racist behavior and some of the attitudes of other members of his family. There are many, many books about unconscious bias: *The Leader's Guide to Unconscious Bias* by Pamela Fuller; *Sway: Unraveling Unconscious Bias* by Pragya Agarwal; *Unconscious Bias: Everything You Need to Know about Our Hidden Prejudices* by Annie Burdick; *UNBIAS: Addressing Unconscious*

Bias at Work by Stacey A. Gordon—and the list goes on. Even in books that I really like and that have been reviewed as excellent guides to contemporary bias, books such as *The Authority Gap* by Mary Ann Sieghart (I recommend that you read this book), the term "unconscious bias" is used very liberally, and quite a lot of bias is attributed to unconscious beliefs and motives.

However, "unconscious bias" was not the term used by Greenwald, McGhee and Schwartz, the team of scientists who, in 1998, invented and popularized these now widely used measures of hidden prejudice. In fact, they only mention the word "unconscious" once in their original 1998 scientific paper. The term they use most often, the term that shows up ninety-one times in the original paper, is "implicit." This seemingly subtle difference in terminology is a matter of some importance, because, as you'll see, "implicit bias" and "unconscious bias" mean quite different things.

Let's return to the problem that scientists were trying to solve. Scientists knew that there was a lot of bias out there, but they were having a hard time identifying the people most likely to behave in biased ways. Some mechanism was needed that could detect bias in individuals whether or not they admitted to it—a mechanism that could then be used to predict an individual's likelihood of behaving in certain specific biased ways.

These were the implicit measures of bias. I'll briefly describe how they work here. However, I would strongly recommend that you visit the Project Implicit website and do an Implicit Associations Test yourself. This will only take a few minutes and will give you a much more visceral understanding of their mechanisms than anything I can say now. Nonetheless, to explain briefly: the Implicit Association Test (IAT) and many other implicit measures of bias work by seeing how quickly and accurately you can respond to stimuli in particular combinations. For example, the test might quickly display a set of words on a screen one at a time and ask you to categorize them under the headings "good" (for example, love, happiness) and "bad" (for example, sadness, death). The test might also display a set of faces on the screen one at a time and ask you to categorize them under the headings White and Black. The scientists can then see how easily you can combine certain categorization tasks. For example, most people find it very easy to use the same computer key to categorize "good" things and "White" people, but very difficult to use the same computer key to categorize "good" things and "Black" people. When they try to do that second task they take longer, and they make more mistakes. By comparing their performance across different combinations, the scientists can generate a single score (their implicit bias test score) that indicates the person's level of bias. The Project Implicit website makes it even easier for you by offering you an interpretation of your test result (for example, "strong automatic preference" or "slight automatic preference" for one group or another), instead of just your numerical score.

The Implicit Association Test, which was invented in 1998, is now old enough to drink, drive and get married. Many follow-up experiments have dismissed potential criticisms of the test, such as suggestions that the results were merely due to the order of the tasks, or to irrelevant associations with other concepts (for example, White and Black as colors). If you are really interested in such discussions, I recommend that you read Nosek and colleagues' (Nosek, Greenwald, et al. 2007) paper, "The Implicit Association Test at Age 7: A Methodological and Conceptual Review." For now, however, all you really need to know is that the Implicit Associations Test (and other tests like it) can produce a score for an individual's level of implicit racial bias.

Best of all, these individual implicit bias scores don't rely on the person's awareness of their own bias or their willingness to honestly tell you. Or, in the words of Professor Anthony

G. Greenwald and colleagues in 2002: "There are well-known problems with self-report measures, because they depend crucially on (a) subjects' willingness to report private knowledge and (b) subjects' ability to report such knowledge accurately. Consequently, self-report measures can go astray when respondents are either unwilling or unable to report accurately." In other words, you can't just ask people how racist they are and expect to get a useful answer, because you're depending on them to both accurately know how racist they are and to be willing to tell you honestly. Neither of those two conditions can reasonably be assumed to be true. At least, not all the time.

Implicit measures of racism (and of other biases) are therefore any measures of bias that get around these two problems; they are measures that can detect bias in objective, quantifiable ways, even when an individual is "unwilling or unable" to report their levels of bias to you.

As the original researchers in 1998 hoped it would, further research has shown that this score usefully predicts actual behavior toward ethnic minorities. Recall, for example, the 2007 study by Green and colleagues on whether or not doctors would offer Black people with a deadly condition (myocardial infarction) the life-saving treatment (thrombolytic therapy). If the researchers had had access only to the doctors' explicit declarations of how they felt about Black and White patients, then they would have reported that the doctors showed no preference for White over Black people, and it would have been a total mystery as to why some of these doctors failed to offer Black patients the correct treatment. However, Green and colleagues didn't just have the doctors' explicit statements; they also had access to their Implicit Association Test scores. And with these scores, they were able to see that some of the doctors *did* have biases against Black patients and in favor of White patients. They were able to tell which doctors had the strongest biases, and were able to use that information to successfully predict which doctors were least likely to offer Black patients the correct treatment. In this case, implicit racism scores were useful predictors of doctors' behavior toward Black people.

Similarly, in 2010, Rooth tested whether scores on the Implicit Association Test could be used to predict hiring discrimination. To do this, he first did the usual CV experiment, with which you should all be very familiar at this point. Across two experiments, he recruited 351 employers: 193 in the first experiment and 158 in the second. He then sent these employers the CVs of some potential employees. As ever, these employees were identically qualified, but half of them had White-sounding names (in this case, they were White Swedish names, because the experiment was conducted in Sweden), while the other half had ethnic minority names (in this case, Arab-Muslim sounding names). Unsurprisingly, as in so many other experiments of this kind, Rooth found that applicants with White-sounding names had a higher callback rate than otherwise equivalent applicants with Arab-Muslim sounding names: 9% higher in the first experiment, and 17% higher in the second.

Rooth then went one step further. He contacted the employers again and convinced them to complete Implicit Association Tests to get a score of their bias in favor of White people and against Arab-Muslims. He then tested whether this implicit score could predict which employers would be most likely to pick the White-sounding applicant over the identically qualified Muslim-sounding applicant. And it worked! Higher levels of implicit anti-Muslim bias predicted a greater likelihood of rejecting the Muslim job applicants and over-selecting the White job applicants.

There are other examples. In 2016, Jacoby-Senghor, Sinclair

and Shelton recruited 210 White people and asked them to take on the role of an instructor who would deliver a lesson to another participant in the experiment. The second participant (let's call them the learner) was randomly varied to be either White or Black. The instructors also completed a seemingly unrelated task, which was actually a test of their implicit anti-Black biases (not an Implicit Association Test this time, but still an implicit bias test). The instructors were then given time to prepare and allowed to deliver their lessons to the learner. All the lessons were video-taped to see how well the instructors were performing, and all the learners took a test at the end of the lesson to see how effective the instructors had been.

At the end of the experiment, Jacoby-Senghor and colleagues found that the White instructors who were teaching Black learners were more anxious and delivered lower-quality lessons. The Black learners also performed worse overall than the White learners. Before you're tempted to say that this last result might have occurred because the Black learners were simply less able than the White learners, I'll point out that the researchers also found a clear relationship between the instructors' implicit bias scores and the learners' performance.

Implicit bias had no effect on how the instructors interacted with the White learners, so we'll ignore that for now. Also, if the instructors had low levels of implicit bias, the White and Black learners performed the same on the test. However, if the instructors had high levels of implicit bias, and if they were teaching Black learners, their anxiety went up, their lesson quality went down, and the learners' performance on the tests declined. The ethnicity-based achievement gap only appeared when the instructors had high levels of implicit bias. It's hard to imagine a clearer indication of the power of implicit bias in educational settings. The results of Jacoby-Senghor's experiment clearly showed that instructors with high levels of implicit bias lead to worse outcomes for ethnic minority learners—learners who would have performed just as well as their White counterparts if the instructors' levels of implicit bias had been lower.

In 2019, three years after Jacoby-Senghor's research was published, Richard Adams, the education editor of the *Guardian*, published an article on the "degree gap" between White and ethnic minority students. The article mentioned that Black and Asian students obtained upper seconds or firsts (these are the highest-rated university degrees in the British system) for their undergraduate degrees at significantly lower rates than their White counterparts. The article covered many recommendations on how to reduce this ethnicity-based achievement gap: "BAME students [Black, Asian and Minority Ethnic students] would benefit from a racially diverse campus environment," "university leadership teams are not representative of the student body," "curriculums do not reflect minority groups' experiences," "a poor sense of belonging might be contributing to low levels of engagement," and so on. But nowhere, absolutely nowhere in the article did Adams mention even the merest possibility that the racial bias of the instructors might be a factor. This is why knowledge of implicit bias research, like Jacoby-Senghor's, matters. Otherwise, we end up with articles on racial achievement gaps with no mention of racial bias in instructors. Racism without racists.

There are still more examples of the utility of implicit bias measures. In 2007, Rudman and Ashmore found that Implicit Association Test scores predicted participants' self-reported use of racial slurs, their social exclusion of ethnic minorities, their likelihood of causing ethnic minorities physical harm, and their desire to cut the budgets of ethnic minority organizations. In each case, the implicit scores predicted these behaviors even *after* statistically controlling for the participants' explicit racial attitudes. In 2008, other researchers (Greenwald, Smith, Sriram, Bar-Anan, and Nosek) found that the Implicit Association Test could predict which Americans would vote for John McCain or Barack Obama in the US presidential election, even after their explicit attitudes were taken into account. In 2021, Bell, Farr, Ofosu, Hehman, and DeWall found that the Implicit Association Test predicted which hopeful parents were less willing to adopt a Black child. Indeed, their implicit bias scores were better predictors than their explicit bias scores. I could go on, but hopefully the point has been made. As Greenwald and colleagues hoped back in 1998, implicit bias scores have proven their usefulness in the scientific community. They allow us to detect bias and to predict who is most likely to behave in a biased way, even if the person is "unwilling or unable" to admit it.

Dangers of the unconscious bias narrative

So far, this all sounds really good. From what I've said, the scientific research has clearly demonstrated the existence of implicit bias, and has clearly shown that implicit bias scores can be useful for predicting actual discriminatory behavior: medical discrimination, hiring discrimination, educational discrimination, political discrimination, familial discrimination, and so on. So, if that's all true, why do I keep hinting darkly at a problem with the unconscious bias narrative? Wasn't Prince Harry, Duke of Sussex, correct to attribute his past behavior and the current behavior of some of his family members to unconscious bias?

To explain my concerns, I'd like to return to the interesting phrasing that Greenwald and colleagues used when describing implicit bias: bias that a person might be "unwilling or unable" to tell you about. Why, exactly, might a person be "unwilling or unable" to accurately report their own levels of racism? There are many, many possible reasons, which I've condensed under three general headings. The first and most obvious of these is that a person may be perfectly aware of their levels of bias, but deliberately misrepresenting these levels to you in an attempt to deceive you. In layman's terms, I believe this is often referred to as "lying." The second reason could be that a person is partially or imperfectly aware of their levels of bias, but employing a set of psychological mechanisms to protect themselves from recognizing or admitting their biases. This second reason, which I'll put under the general heading of "psychological trickery," is, to me, the most interesting one, and it will get a much fuller treatment in Chapter 7.

For now, however, the third and final reason why someone might be unwilling or unable to tell you how biased they are could be that the person is completely unaware of their own level of bias, only discovering this after taking some kind of implicit bias test. This last reason is the only one that matches the "unconscious bias" narrative that has become so popular in recent years.

This is why I am so pedantic about the distinction between "implicit bias" (which the scientists like to talk about) and "unconscious bias" (which the newspapers like to talk about). Research on implicit bias covers a multitude of different types of bias that individuals are "unwilling or unable" to report explicitly and accurately. From the very beginning, its goal has been to take types of bias that are difficult to detect and make them easier to detect. It is a set of tools that allows us to better predict who will pick the White CVs over the Black CVs, who will rate the White student's work as better than the Black student's work, or who will schedule the White patient's appointment sooner than the Black patient's appointment—even if the person in question is "unwilling or unable" to admit to doing those things.

In contrast, the unconscious bias narrative sweeps away two of the important reasons why someone might be unwilling or unable to report their levels of bias. It ignores both simple deception and complex psychological trickery, leaving us with a narrative in which most or all people are entirely, and innocently, unaware of their own biases. As such, the problem with the unconscious bias narrative is not that it is inaccurate. Unconscious bias does exist. It can be objectively detected and it can be used to predict certain kinds of biased behavior. Rather, the problem with the unconscious bias narrative is that it ignores and downplays other real, damaging manifestations of bias. The unconscious bias narrative is restrictive and myopic.

And this myopia is dangerous.

As an example, in 2019 Daumeyer and colleagues conducted four studies on how people interpret and respond to bias. In one of these studies (Study 1B), they recruited 299 participants and got them to read stories about doctors who were treating their patients differently depending on their group membership—in other words, doctors who were behaving with detectable bias toward some of their patients. All the participants read the same scenarios with only one crucial difference. Half of the participants also read that the "doctors were somewhat aware they were treating patients differently," while the other half of the participants read that "the doctors had no conscious knowledge that they were treating patients any differently." In other words, in one condition Daumeyer and colleagues got the participants to assume that the bias was conscious, while in the other condition they got the participants to assume that the bias was unconscious.*

---

* It is noteworthy that Daumeyer and colleagues used the words "explicit" and "implicit," but they did define implicit bias rather narrowly to the participants as "attitudes or stereotypes that affect our understanding, actions, and decisions in ways that we are typically not aware of." In that light, it seems fair to treat this as a manipulation of beliefs about unconscious bias, rather than the broader category

After the participants had finished reading the stories and the crucial conscious/unconscious bias manipulation, the researchers asked each participant to indicate their level of agreement with a new series of statements. These statements assessed several points. First, how accountable the participants thought the doctors should be for their biases (for example, "Doctors should be held responsible for any biases they have that may impact how they interact with patients"); second, how much they agreed that there should be some form of punishment for biased behavior ("Doctors who repeatedly demonstrate biases toward patients should have their license to practice medicine suspended"); and third, how much concern the participants felt about doctors' biases ("The bias I read about in the article is concerning"). By comparing these responses, the researchers could discern the effects of framing bias as either conscious or unconscious.

And what did the researchers find? In this study, and in the other studies in the paper (all of which were variations on the one already described), Daumeyer and colleagues found that framing bias as "unconscious" made the participants care less about the bias. Specifically, even though the doctors' behaviors were the same and the effects on their patients were the same, Daumeyer's participants were less concerned about the bias, thought that the doctors should be less accountable for it, and were less convinced that anyone should be punished for it, if they thought of the bias as unconscious rather than conscious. In the researchers' own words: "Scholars of stereotyping and prejudice have long expressed concern that emphasizing the role of unconscious, automatic beliefs in engendering discrimination might reduce the perceived culpability of its perpetrators . . . The present

---

of implicit bias, which covers both lack of awareness and lack of willingness to disclose.

findings suggest this concern was well founded." The danger of the unconscious bias narrative is that it preserves the apparent innocence of the person committing the biased behavior, and reduces the likelihood that we will do anything about it.

As a social psychologist, these findings put me in a tough position. A huge number of people still don't even believe that contemporary racism exists. Despite the mountains of empirical evidence confirming that racism is a part of almost everything, almost everywhere, almost all the time, people are still stuck in a conversation about whether or not it is even happening. In that light, one would think that the proliferation of the unconscious bias narrative is the answer to a social psychologist's prayers. Finally, people are acknowledging that bias is real and pervasive. Finally, everyone is talking about contemporary bias and even referencing some scientific papers when they do it. From this perspective, one might assume that the unconscious bias narrative is a blessing.

But it is not.

I have appeared on radio and television many times to discuss bias. I've written in many newspapers about bias. I've been invited to explain my publications about bias. Increasingly, after I have presented the research, at least one well-meaning person frames the conversation in such a way as to imply that all contemporary bias (or at the very least, most of it) is now unconscious—a perspective that the scientific research has never suggested and would not support. I find myself repeatedly explaining that some bias is definitely still conscious and that there are many other, more interesting and accurate perspectives on bias than the black-and-white (pardon the pun), all-or-nothing, totally explicit or totally unconscious model. Yet, despite my protestations, the dominance of the unconscious bias narrative continues unfettered. People invite me to talk about unconscious bias even when my research is about very conscious kinds of bias. People thank me for explaining unconscious bias even when I have explained something else entirely.

And I'm sure it feels like we're doing something good with all this discussion of unconscious bias. It is, after all, important to finally acknowledge our biases. However, the research shows that if all we're acknowledging is unconscious bias, then what we're really doing is protecting our own perceptions of innocence, reducing our concerns about the bias we claim to be addressing, and ensuring that nobody is ever held accountable for it. This is not what doing something good looks like. This is doing something bad.

Chapter 6

Deception
Doing Racist Things and Lying About It

In an experiment published in 2009, Pager, Western, and Bono-kowski hired testers (Black, White and Latino) to apply for 340 real entry-level jobs over the course of nine months in New York City. I know what you're thinking. You're thinking: "Haven't we already done this one in Chapter 2? Isn't this the one where the applicants were matched on qualifications, neighborhood of residence, verbal skills, interaction style and physical attractiveness? Isn't this the one where, despite being matched in every conceivable way, the White applicant had a callback rate that was over twice as high as the Black applicants?"

You are correct, of course. I did tell you about this study in Chapter 2. However, there are some very important things that I left out. You see, when Pager and colleagues conducted this study, it was already scientific knowledge that White candidates were treated significantly better than otherwise identical ethnic minority candidates (particularly Black candidates) when they applied for the same jobs. But even when we know that an effect happens, it doesn't mean that we should stop replicating the research. We need to keep conducting experiments to see how this effect varies by location, by types of job, by levels of seniority, across time, and in many other ways. Furthermore, Pager and colleagues wanted to go beyond showing that White people are treated better than otherwise identical ethnic minorities. The team of scientists wanted to take a look under the proverbial hood, to open the proverbial black box, and see how this discrimination occurred.

So far, a lot of experiments had sent identical or equivalent CVs (or actual people) to apply for the same jobs and observed that the White applications received better treatment than the ethnic minorities. But what exactly happened between the applications and the callbacks? That part of things was a bit of a mystery. What were the employers actually doing with these applications? Were they reading them all carefully and then coming to the conclusion that the White people were (for some reason) better suited or qualified than their otherwise identical ethnic minority counterparts? Were the employers misreading or misremembering aspects of the CVs in ways that made the White applicants look more hireable? Were some of them just tossing the ethnic minority CVs straight into the bin without even looking beyond the name? Most fundamentally, Pager and colleagues wanted to know the answer to one very important question: were the employers aware of what they were doing?

This is where Pager's 2009 study really shines, even in the context of other excellent scientific research. In the authors' own words: "By observing the interactions that characterize each of these behavior types, we gain a rare glimpse into the processes by which discrimination takes place." As Pager and colleagues had sent real people (not just CVs) to apply for the same job at, or very near to, the same time, the applicants themselves could observe these potential employers and see the mechanisms that led to their racially biased behaviors.

The results were most revealing. Pager and colleagues noted that very few employers revealed any overt hostility toward racial minority applicants. At this point, you might be tempted to believe that the employers' biases were thus "unconscious:" that they were not aware of their discriminatory decisions. However, this was not the case. As discussed in Chapter 4, it is hopelessly naive to split all bias into the cartoonishly overt or the entirely unconscious. It omits the possibility of deception.

And deception is exactly what Pager found.

In one example, all three applicants (White, Black, and Latino) showed up at the same time to apply for a job. A woman herded them in and had them all fill out an application on the spot. However, when they had finished filling out the paperwork, she told them all that they could leave because "there's no interview today, guys!"

Since there were apparently no interviews, all three applicants left to catch the bus. However, when they had made it across the street to the bus stop, the woman came out and motioned for them all to return. She said that she "needed to speak" to the White and Latino applicant. Apparently, the White and Latino applicant had forgotten to sign something. The Black applicant could go. Of course, this was a lie. Once they were back in the office, the woman asked the White and Latino applicants if they could come back at 5 p.m. that day to start work. She hired them on the spot. At this point, the equally qualified Black candidate was already catching a bus back home, unemployed.

The paper is clear about what happened. The woman didn't suddenly have a sequence of implausible memory lapses or misconceptions that resulted in her accidentally or unconsciously hiring the White and Latino applicants but not the Black one. In fact, she was very open with the White and Latino candidates about what she was doing, explaining the lie to them in very straightforward terms. She even expected them to be co-conspirators in her racial discrimination. As the White candidate reported in the paper: "she seemed pretty concerned with not letting anyone else know." Let's be absolutely explicit here. There was nothing unconscious about this woman's racism. It was pure deception.

In another example, one of the Black applicants tried to apply for a position at a retail clothing store, only to be told that the position had already been filled. The Latino applicant tried for the same job shortly afterward and got a very similar response: the position had already been filled. But then the White applicant, who applied last, had a very different experience. When he asked if they were taking applications for the position, the person in charge took his application and asked, "You can start immediately? Can you start tomorrow?"

In another incident, all three applied for a job at an electronics store. The Black applicant was allowed to complete an application, but was also told that the store would have to check his references, so it would be a while before he could be called in for an interview. The White and Latino applicants, in contrast, were interviewed on the spot. Furthermore, the store manager never called to check the Black applicant's references. Two days later, the White applicant received a call offering him the job.

It is important to note that if the applicants had not all had access to each others' experiences it would have been very difficult, if not impossible, to know that racial discrimination had occurred, or that deception had been a key element of that racial discrimination. Had this been a real job application, the Black candidate would have had no way of knowing that he was exactly as qualified as the White and Latino candidates. He would have had no way of knowing that the managers lied when they said that the other applicants forgot to sign something, or that the positions had already been filled, or that the store needed to check his references. He would have simply returned home and continued looking for employment, with no way of knowing that racism had just cost him a job, or two, or three. The only people who would have known that racism was a factor in these hiring decisions were the managers themselves and the few others they drew in as co-conspirators to their racism. And, as you can see from the effort the managers put into disguising their true behaviors, the Black applicant would never find anything out from them. Sometimes the reason that someone is "unwilling or unable" to accurately communicate their racism has nothing to do with unconscious bias. Sometimes it's just deception.

Sometimes I catch myself thinking about this 2009 study by Pager, about the kind of racism revealed by those Black, White, and Latino job applicants. I thought about it when I was on holiday in Greece a few years ago. I was looking for a place to stay and was told that several hotels were full, sometimes by hostile, rude people, sometimes by apologetic, smiling people. Later, some White people I was traveling with, who knew that I was looking for a place to stay, would direct me to those very same hotels: "We just asked," they would say, "and they said they had loads of rooms available."

I thought about this study when I was invited to be the keynote speaker for a counseling and psychotherapy conference in Stratford-upon-Avon, in the UK. A keynote is an address of some prestige and importance at a conference. The speaker can reasonably expect to be treated with respect, if not deference. Not so, apparently, in Stratford-upon-Avon. At the conference hotel, I watched as all the White conference attendees strolled in unchallenged. I was asked to show proof that I was staying at the hotel.

I think about this study when I remember the many, many times that I've been followed around a store for the simple crime of earning money and trying to spend it. I think about it when I go to a restaurant or a store with a White person and the servers ignore me entirely.

I think about it when people argue that I can't possibly know that these are examples of racism, as if that wasn't the whole point. As Pager's 2009 study revealed, people go to incredible lengths to do racist things, but to do them in such a way that proving the racism is next to impossible. In real life, we don't have access to a set of White and Latino doppelgangers who can try to stay at the same hotels, or give the same keynote speeches, or shop at the same stores, or eat at the same restaurants. If the people in all those places want to be racist and sneaky about that racism, they have many available strategies for accomplishing just that.

I also think about Pager's experiment when I read yet another newspaper article or blog post calling evidence of discrimination a sign of "unconscious bias." I think about it when even people I like and respect attribute their past behavior, or someone else's current behavior, to unconscious bias alone. This, as the young people would say, is gaslighting in the extreme. Yes, unconscious bias does exist. Yes, *some* behaviors are unconscious. But many behaviors—lying about people having to sign imaginary forgotten forms, lying about positions being filled, lying about having to check references, lying about hotel rooms being unavailable, "randomly" checking the status of the Black person and only the Black person at a conference—are not. These behaviors are very conscious indeed.

The aggressive dominance of the unconscious bias narrative obscures the fact that some people are very much aware of their racism and not even trying to be less racist. Matt Rowan, a former youth pastor and sports announcer in Oklahoma, wasn't trying not to be racist in 2021 when he called a group of high-school girls "fucking niggers." He just thought that his microphone was off. When he later discovered that his microphone had been on during his outburst, he blamed his diabetes for somehow making him say racist things. In 2018, Jo Marney (then the girlfriend of the leader of the UK Independence Party), wasn't trying not to be racist when she texted a friend to say that she would never have sex with a "negro" because they are "ugly." She wasn't trying not to be racist when she said that Prince Harry's new fiancée would "taint" the royal family's blood. Indeed, when her friend responded that she was racist, she replied "LOL, so what?" Marney didn't mind being racist. She just didn't expect the texts to be leaked, or the reaction to them to be so negative.

In 2002, employees at Target weren't trying not to be racist when they admitted (in the course of a lawsuit) to "routinely destroying the job applications of Black individuals who attended job fairs held at several Milwaukee universities." In 2002, the then Mayor of London and eventual prime minister Boris Johnson wasn't trying not to be racist when he referred to the people of the Commonwealth as "flag-waving piccaninnies" with "watermelon smiles." In 2017, Conservative candidate Derek Bullock wasn't trying not to be racist when he commented, "shoot the Pakis on the spot" under a post about the Manchester Arena bombing. In 2018, Buford (Georgia) City Schools superintendent Geye Hamby wasn't trying not to be racist when he said, "Fuck that nigger, I'll kill these goddamn—shoot that motherfucker if they let me . . . Don't send us a deadbeat nigger from a temp site." In 2022, Grégoire de Fournas wasn't trying not to be racist when he shouted "Go back to Africa" at Carlos Martens Bilongo, a Black, French lawmaker. In 2023, Conservative councillor Alexis McEvoy wasn't trying not to be racist when she called Ian Wright a "typical black hypocrite."

It is a mistake to look at the mountains of evidence for discrimination in employment, in healthcare, in policing, in the service industry and in many other areas and attribute it entirely to unconscious bias. Indeed, the scientific research has never even demonstrated that most contemporary bias is unconscious, only that some of it is unconscious. In many instances, the people being racist are perfectly aware of what they're doing.

They're just trying not to get caught.

And, very often, they succeed.

Chapter 7

The Games People Play
How to Be Racist while Believing You're Not

I've been promising you some interesting psychological trickery for a while now, so it's about time that I deliver and look at some of the ways that we justify, downplay, minimize and excuse our own racism. I should warn you, if this book hasn't already made you feel a bit uncomfortable, this is probably where your discomfort will begin. That's because this part of the book is talking directly to *you*.

I'm making some assumptions, but I'm guessing that the kind of person who decides to read a book called *The Science of Racism* is already interested in racism and already suspects that racism may be a problem in society. However, that person is probably also pretty sure that they are not part of the problem. I think that's likely to be a reasonable description of you: you're sure that somebody, somewhere is racist, but you're also pretty sure you are not that racist somebody. This chapter may disabuse you of that rose-tinted notion.

Since I'll be talking directly to and about you, I'd like to start by asking you a few questions. Specifically, I'm going to place you in a few hypothetical scenarios and ask you how you'd respond. Of course, you don't have to answer these questions. However, what follows will be more interesting and more informative if you do answer the questions, and if you answer them as honestly as you can.

To begin, I'd like you to imagine that you are a White person (you may be a White person, in which case, this first part should not tax your imagination too heavily). Then, I'd like you to imagine that you're taking part in a psychological study. For this study you've been teamed up with two other participants. You've never met either of them before. Both are men. Both seem to be relatively nice and ordinary. One of them is Black and the other is White. The three of you are all sitting in the lab together. For this experiment, you'll have to work cooperatively on a task, and the experimenter is about to give you some instructions.

However, before the experimenter starts giving you the instructions, the Black participant remembers that he has left his mobile phone outside of the lab. He lets you all know that he's going out to retrieve it. On his way out of the lab, he gently bumps into the knee of the other White participant. Everybody waits for the Black participant to come back without saying anything.

Here's the question. Imagining yourself in this situation, would you feel upset? In fact, let's put a number to that feeling. You're sitting in the lab, you've just watched the Black participant leave, gently bumping the other White participant's leg, presumably accidentally, as he made his exit. Nobody said anything. On a scale of 0 to 9, where 0 means that you're not upset at all and 9 means that you're extremely upset, how upset would you feel? Write down your answer below:

Scenario 1: How upset would you feel? _____

Now let's do it again, with a very similar scenario. Just like before, you're a White person, you're in the lab with two other participants, one's Black and one's White, and the Black one has forgotten his mobile phone outside the lab. As before, he lets you all know that he's going out to retrieve it and, on his way out, he gently bumps into the knee of the other White participant. This time, however, the incident does not go unremarked. This time, once the Black participant has left the room and is out of earshot, the other White participant comments: "Typical, I hate when Black people do that."

In this new scenario, after the other White participant has made that comment, how upset would you feel? Use the same scale as before (0 = not at all upset, 9 = extremely upset) and write down your answer.

Scenario 2: How upset would you feel? _____

One last time. Again, this hypothetical scenario is very similar to the last two. Just like before, you're White, you're in the lab with a Black participant and a White participant. The Black participant has forgotten his phone so he's going to get it. He gently bumps into the knee of the other White participant on his way out. As in the second scenario, once the Black participant has left the room, the White participant makes a comment. This time, the comment is somewhat more, shall we say . . . impassioned. In this scenario, the other White participant says, "Clumsy nigger."

Using the same scale as before, how upset would you be this time?

Scenario 3: How upset would you feel? _____

Here's a follow-up question for that scenario. Let's assume that the Black participant comes back and the three of you complete the experiment with no further notable incidents. The experimenter then thanks you all, pays you for your time and lets you go.

However, there is a second experiment you could do right away. It wouldn't take too long, and you'd be compensated for it. There's a catch, though. You'd need a partner to complete that second experiment. Do you have one? You look around and both of the other participants are still in the area: the Black guy who forgot his phone outside of the lab, and the White guy who called him a "clumsy nigger." Either of them could potentially be your partner for this second exercise. So, here's your follow-up question: would you select the White participant to be your partner in the second exercise, yes or no?

Scenario 3: Would you select the White participant to be your partner in a second exercise? _____

We'll get back to your answers before the end of the chapter.

For now, I'd like to approach the psychological tricks we play in a particular order: victim blaming, aversive racism, playing games with definitional boundaries, and overly positive self-perceptions. There are, of course, many other psychological tricks that we use to hide or justify our racism. Indeed, there are entire books that could be written on each of these types of psychological tricks. However, these four should offer a useful overview, giving you a chance to see how they apply in your own life.

Victim blaming

In 1999, in an article titled "When Discrimination Makes Sense," social commentator Dinesh D'Souza made the argument that we sometimes call certain behaviors "racism" or "discrimination" when they are in fact just reasonable responses to real-world data. He gave the example of cab drivers in Washington, DC, who were apparently being fined for refusing to pick up young Black men. D'Souza argued that, despite the complaints of civil rights activists, the drivers weren't motivated by "racism" or "bigotry." Rather, their discrimination was a logical response to some relevant facts about Black men: Black men are (according to D'Souza) between six and ten times more likely to be convicted of violent crimes than White men and, at any given time, over a quarter of Black men (compared to only about 5% of White men) are in prison, on probation or on parole. Assuming that these statistics are accurate, the cab drivers (many of whom weren't even White themselves) were just making the best decisions they could, given what they knew to be true. After all, are you eager to have a potentially dangerous criminal in the back of your car?

Similar sentiments have been offered by a prominent figure in the UK. In 2000, in an article in the *Guardian*, Boris Johnson (who would become UK prime minister in July 2019) admitted that he would "turn a hair" when he came across a "bunch of Black kids, shrieking in the spooky corner" in the park at night. However, he questioned whether this could really be described as racial prejudice. Like D'Souza, he explained that there were good reasons for his negative reaction. After all, he has read press reports about the greater likelihood of being mugged by "young Black males" than by any other kind of person. Maybe these reports weren't entirely fair. Maybe a lot of them were in right-wing newspapers. But you've probably read them too. And wouldn't you "turn a hair" at night if you came across the kind of people most likely to mug you?

The apparent violence and criminality of Black people has also been used to explain (or distract from) more deadly concerns than missing a cab in Washington, DC, or disturbing Boris Johnson during his nightly jog. As an example, a 2016 article by Philip Bump in the *Washington Post* described the response of

American presidential hopeful Jeb Bush when he was asked about police brutality against Black people. Bush largely dismissed the problem, claiming that it was "very small." In his opinion, what was more important—and certainly worth bringing up, even though nobody had asked about it in that conversation—was "Black-on-Black" crime. After all, Bush said, "most" of the crime in Black communities was Black-on-Black, so that—not the police—should be the real focus of our attention.

Sometimes, all subtlety is abandoned and people are explicitly directed to avoid ethnic minorities because of their violent, dangerous tendencies. In 2016, Simon Denyer of the *Washington Post* reported on Air China's advice for tourists visiting London. The advice said that "London is generally a safe place to travel, however precautions are needed when entering areas mainly populated by Indians, Pakistanis and Black people. We advise tourists not to go out alone at night, and females always to be accompanied by another person when traveling."

There's a lot to discuss here, but the common thread running through all these comments is that negative behavior toward ethnic minorities is justified, or at least not very important, because the ethnic minorities themselves are bad, or appear to be bad. Dinesh D'Souza, for example, accepts that cab drivers treat Black potential customers worse than White potential customers. He's not pretending that Black and White people are being treated equally, or that Black people are just being sensitive, or that they're making things up. He's even willing to acknowledge that this worse treatment is specifically because of their racial identity, rather than some other factor like their dress or behavior. However, this worse treatment of Black people is fine, because (according to his statistics) Black people are much more violent and criminal than White people. Given those simple truths, isn't it just logical to avoid Black people if you're a cab driver?

Similar things could be said about Boris Johnson. He admits to "turning a hair" when he sees a "bunch of Black kids" and admits that he probably wouldn't react in the same way if he saw a bunch of White kids. At no point does he pretend that his responses to Black and White people are the same, or that they're due to anything other than race. However, his responses to Black people are fine because they are based on the behavior of the Black people themselves (or at least, their reported behavior in the news). Presumably, if the Black people would "shriek" a bit less, or not hang out on the "spooky" corner, or commit fewer violent crimes, then his responses to them would change accordingly.

In a similar vein, Jeb Bush would presumably be more concerned about police officers killing Black people if most Black people weren't killed by other Black people. And Air China isn't being racist when it tells visitors to London to avoid places with Indians, Pakistanis, and Black people, because these groups really do commit more crimes, don't they?

If you are looking for justifications for the negative treatment of ethnic minorities, this logic is very seductive, partially because it is based on what appear to be true facts, and logical responses to these facts. The most recent statistics on the UK prison population come from a 2023 report for the House of Commons, written by Georgina Sturge. This report found that approximately 95,526 people were in prison in the UK in 2023. More relevant to this discussion, however, were the relative proportions of different ethnicities in British prisons. The report pulls no punches here. It clearly states that "the BAME [Black, Asian, and Minority Ethnic] population is overrepresented within the prison population." Specifically, ethnic minorities make up only 18% of the general British population, but a significantly larger 27% of the prison population.

Focusing more specifically on White and Black prisoners

makes the contrast even more stark. Looking at just England and Wales (the regions for which they had the clearest ethnicity data), White people make up 82% of the general population, but only 72% of the prison population, a ratio of only .88. Black people, on the other hand, make up only 4% of the general population, but a whopping 12% of the prison population, a ratio of 3! Comparing these two ratios directly certainly lends support to Johnson's and D'Souza's concerns. Black people in England and Wales are between 3 and 3.5 times as likely to be in prison as White people. These are just the facts.

We should interpret these numbers with some caution. After all, they don't cover every form of crime. A study by Rosado Marzán in 2021 shows that wage theft, for example, accounts for more theft than any other kind, but is generally not punished with a prison sentence. These statistics also don't cover the number of people who were in prison and have been released, or those who are on parole or probation. Importantly, they also don't acknowledge or account for racial discrimination in the justice system (see Chapter 3). However, even if we accept that these statistics are only accurate in the broadest, most general sense, they do seem to support some caution when interacting with those dangerous, criminal ethnic minorities.

Similarly, Jeb Bush was right. The US Bureau of Justice Statistics regularly publishes the results of a National Crime Victimization Survey. This survey usually spans several years and offers a breakdown of both victims and perpetrators by race. According to the most recent version of this survey that I could find (the one spanning the period from 2017–2021), Black people were the victims of 3,095,610 violent crimes. However, in most of those instances (1,884,205, or about 61% of the time) Black people were also the perpetrators of the violent crimes. Incidentally, if we focus our interest specifically on homicides, the pattern remains true.

Statistics from the Federal Bureau of Investigation confirm that most Black homicide victims are killed by other Black people. As Jeb Bush suggested, there's no escaping the factual reality that, when it comes to violent crime in the US, most Blacks are victimized by other Blacks. Not by police. Not by White people. Other Blacks. So, it seems that Jeb was correct to say that we shouldn't worry about police officers killing or brutalizing Black people, but instead put our focus on Black-on-Black crime.

Or maybe he wasn't.

There are a few points of information here that have been ignored or presented in a skewed way. For example, let's take another look at the prison population of the UK. As I said, the 2023 report for the House of Commons found that about 95,526 people were in prison in the UK in 2023, of whom 85,851 were in England and Wales, the regions for which they had the clearest ethnicity data. Of these 85,851 prisoners in England and Wales, 61,823 were White and 10,494 were Black. These might sound like huge numbers at first, but they are small compared to the overall population. Findings released by the Office of National Statistics estimated that in 2022, the total population of England and Wales was 60,236,400. Assuming that all the percentages in the House of Commons report are correct, that would mean there are, in England and Wales, about 49.4 million White people (of whom only about 62,000 are in prison) and 2.4 million Black people (of whom only about 10,000 are in prison).

As you can see, in the context of these larger population numbers, the number of prisoners is consistently tiny, regardless of whether we're looking at White or Black people. We could look at the percentages of people in prison (about .13% of the White population of the UK, compared to .44% of the Black population) and focus on the fact that Black people are 3.5 times more likely to be in prison. Or, we could look at the other side of those numbers.

They indicate that 99.87% of White people in the UK are not in prison and a very similar 99.56% of Black people in the UK are not in prison. Looked at that way, the differences between White and Black people seem a lot smaller and less important. It seems much harder to justify generally treating Black people worse than White people across a wide variety of social interactions because only 99.56% of Black people aren't in prison, compared to the almost identical 99.87% of White people who aren't in prison.

Similarly, Jeb Bush was correct to say that most violent crime committed against Black people was perpetrated by other Black people, but he overlooked the fact that most violent crime committed against White people was also perpetrated by other White people. According to the same National Crime Victimization Survey mentioned earlier, White people were the victims of 15,795,650 violent crimes. However, in most of those instances (8,721,450, or about 55% of the time) White people were also the perpetrators of the violent crimes. As before, if we look specifically at homicides, that pattern remains true. Statistics from the FBI confirm that most White homicide victims were killed by other White people. Jeb Bush entirely ignored the factual reality that, when it comes to violent crime in the US, most Whites are victimized by other Whites. Not by police. Not by ethnic minorities. Other Whites.

Yet I have never heard anyone use that statistic to raise a fuss about White-on-White crime. I've never met anyone who heard about the shooting of Justine Damond, a White woman who lived in Minnesota, by ethnic minority police officer Mohamed Noor, and responded that we shouldn't focus on that because most Whites are victimized by other Whites, not by police officers. The truth is that when people are violently victimized, it is mostly by those with whom they live, work, share a family, or share other public spaces. White people mostly live, work, and relate to other

White people, so most violent crimes against White people are committed by other White people. The same could be said for any ethnicity, including Black people. Turning this statement of fact into a justification to ignore disproportionate police brutality against a particular ethnicity is not only crass and dehumanizing, it's not even reasonable *according to the statistics themselves*.

However, falling into a debate about statistics obscures the central problem with these arguments. They are all based on the idea that the preferential treatment of White people (and the negative treatment of Black people and other ethnic minorities) is justified because of the behaviors of the ethnic minority populations themselves. All those Black people aren't being treated unfairly, the argument goes. They're just paying the logically expected price for their (or their group's) criminal behavior. If White people were similarly violent or criminal, people would treat them in similar ways.

Or would they?

The science, in fact, does not support the idea that ethnic minorities are merely paying the price for their criminal behavior. Recall Pager's study published in 2003, in which the experimenters sent out four versions of an otherwise identical CV: one from a Black man with no criminal record, one from a White man with no criminal record, one from a Black man with a criminal record, and one from a White man with a criminal record. If participants were merely responding negatively to the criminality or assumed criminality of the applicants, then the Black man with a criminal record and the White man with a criminal record should have received similar callback rates. But they didn't. The White applicant with a criminal record had a callback rate that was over three times higher (17%) than the Black applicant with a criminal record (only 5%). More importantly, this study found that even the Black applicant without a criminal record had a lower callback rate (14%) than the White applicant with a criminal record (17%). In other words, Pager found that confirmed criminality from a White participant still got more favorable responses than non-criminality (or, perhaps, suspected criminality) from a Black applicant. This is clearly not just a matter of responding reasonably to ethnic minority criminal behavior.

This isn't the only study of its kind. Six years later, in 2009, Pager, Western, and Sugie published a field experiment of a similar nature. For this study, they sent matched teams of testers to apply for 250 real entry-level jobs throughout New York City over the course of nine months. The testers were, in the author's words, "well-spoken, clean-shaven young men, ages twenty-two to twenty-six . . . matched on the basis of their verbal skills, interactional styles (level of eye-contact, demeanor, and verbosity), and physical attractiveness." Their CVs were also matched in terms of qualifications and experience. The only significant differences between the testers were their ethnicities and whether or not they supposedly had a criminal record.

And did the experimenters find that potential employees merely responded logically and proportionally to evidence of a criminal background, without any consideration of the ethnicity of the applicant?

At this point, do I even need to tell you? Of course they didn't. The experimenters found exactly the opposite. Pager and colleagues found that a criminal record had a significant negative effect on hiring outcomes. That much was unsurprising. However, more interestingly, they found that this effect was not even across ethnicities. In the authors' own words: "the negative effect of a criminal conviction is substantially larger for blacks than for whites . . . the magnitude of the criminal record penalty suffered by black applicants (60 percent) is roughly double the size of the penalty for whites with a record (30 percent)."

This increased negativity for Black applicants with criminal records manifested in multiple ways. Black applicants with criminal records were more likely to get negative responses to the revelation, and less likely to get sympathetic responses to the revelation, than were White applicants with criminal records. And, even within the limited group of those with criminal records who received sympathetic responses, White applicants were still significantly more likely to get a callback or a job offer than equivalently qualified Black applicants. The ability to talk about one's criminal record, rather than it being presented only on paper, appeared to help mitigate some of the negative effects, but the opportunity to discuss it was offered to Black applicants much less often than to White ones. Furthermore, being deprived of the opportunity to discuss their criminal record didn't affect the applicants evenly. As the authors put it: "among whites, these limited interactions are not overly consequential; whereas for blacks, job opportunities appear substantially reduced."

Pager and colleagues are, of course, not the only ones who have conducted research of this kind. In 2015, Decker, Ortiz, Spohn, and Hedberg applied for more than 500 jobs while keeping the qualifications of the applicants consistent, varying only their ethnicity and criminal history. Similar to the repeated findings of Pager and colleagues, Decker and colleagues found that "The effect of a prison record was particularly strong for blacks."

Other, cross-sectional data also support these experimental findings. For example, in 2021, the Public Policy Institute of California released a report based on almost 4 million stops of motorists and pedestrians by police in 2019. From these data, provided by the police officers themselves, the analysis found that Black Californians were more than twice as likely to be stopped and searched as White Californians. However, when the police searched Black Californians, they were less likely to find either contraband or evidence of illegal activity than when they searched White Californians. Stops involving Black people were also more likely to lead to no enforcement of any kind, not even a warning given by the police, which raises the question of why they were stopping all these Black people in the first place. Had the police merely been responding to criminal behavior, or even statistical patterns evidenced in their own searches, they should have been searching White people more frequently than Black people—the exact opposite of their actual pattern of behavior.

The scientific research clearly does not support the idea that ethnic minorities are merely paying the logical, proportional price for their criminality. Quite the contrary: while higher relative levels of criminal convictions among ethnic minorities are often used as a convenient excuse for discriminatory behavior, the research clearly shows that most ethnic minorities are not dangerous criminals; that ethnic minorities pay a disproportionate penalty for past criminality in their own lives, or even criminality statistically associated with their race; that White people are treated less like criminals, even when they are statistically more likely to be caught doing illegal things; and that ethnic minorities sometimes remain disadvantaged even if they personally have no criminal record and their White competition does.

This is victim blaming at its finest. It ignores instances in which White people are statistically more likely to commit crimes. It uses quippy phrases like "Black-on-Black crime" but ignores the mirrored reality of "White-on-White crime." It uses small but apparently real statistical differences in criminal convictions between groups to justify large, widespread, disproportionate and sometimes deadly forms of discrimination, even when White people who have been themselves convicted of crimes do not face the same level of stigma. If you want to be really racist, but you don't want to admit it to yourself, this is a great way to start.

Aversive racism

That last part about not admitting it to yourself is important. Reading about these justifications, you might think I'm just calling people sneaky and dishonest, but I'm not. Simple dishonesty was covered in Chapter 6. We know what that looks like. These psychological tricks are altogether more complicated.

Rather than thinking of yourself as an angel (perfectly blameless, egalitarian, and honest), or as a demon (willfully racist and deliberately lying about it), it might be more helpful to compare yourself to the internally conflicted Dr. Jekyll, who sprang from the imagination of Robert Louis Stevenson. As this unfortunate doctor mused: "man is not truly one . . . I hazard the guess that man will be ultimately known for a mere polity of multifarious, incongruous and independent denizens." Or, in simpler, more contemporary terms, we are inconsistent, we contradict ourselves, and some of our desires get in the way of our other desires, even if both are truly ours.

This is also true in the realm of racism and egalitarianism. Most people do racist things, at least some of the time. The research shows that many of the examples of racism discussed in the previous chapters aren't just the result of a few bad apples skewing the data, but that most people show pro-White biases in at least some domains. Remember the Implicit Associations Test from Chapter 4, which, by asking participants to quickly categorize concepts like good/bad and Black people/White people, predicted a variety of racist behaviors: from the use of racial slurs, to cutting the budgets of ethnic minority organizations (Rudman and Ashmore 2007), to offering suboptimal healthcare to Black patients (Green et al. 2007), to giving Black students poorer lessons (Jacoby-Senghor et al. 2016)?

Well, after analyzing millions of results of IATs taken between 2000 and 2006, Nosek and colleagues (2007) found that most people (about 68%) showed a preference for White people and light skin over Black people and darker skin. Later results (for example, from 2015) indicated very much the same pattern, with about 68% of people still showing a preference for White people and lighter skin. And that's just looking at a narrow range of Implicit Association Tests, mostly considering different responses to White and Black people. There are other Implicit Association Tests that look at responses to Arabs/Muslims, Hispanic people, East Asian people, and Jewish people: being non-biased against a particular ethnicity is no guarantee at all of being non-biased against another. So, while it's technically possible that you're one of the minority of people who treats everyone equally regardless of their ethnicity, the science says it's pretty unlikely.

Still, even though most people sometimes do racist things, most people genuinely don't want to be racist, or at least don't want to think of themselves as racist. Some of my own research (for example, from 2012) shows that most people report very high levels of internalized motivation to be (or appear to be) non-racist, even when they're totally anonymous and there's no possibility that they could suffer any negative repercussions for their responses. Studies using large-scale surveys with over 1,000 participants (for example, Crandall et al. 2002) show that most people consider it to be highly unacceptable to express prejudice against ethnic minorities: more unacceptable than it is to express prejudice against many other groups, such as police officers, lawyers, environmentalists, or fat people. Still more research by Howell et al. in 2015 shows that people respond very negatively to feedback that they are more racially biased than they previously believed, and will even engage in strategies to avoid the feedback altogether.

But you probably don't need a lot of research to convince you of this point, so why don't I just ask you directly? Do *you* think you're racist? How would you feel about a test, or an activity, that seemed to indicate that you were a lot more racist than you thought? How would you feel about a person who told you that you probably do racist things, and that you probably do them far more often than you realize? If you're like most people, you wouldn't like this person at all.

We are faced with a "racism without racists" problem similar to the one I highlighted at the start of Chapter 5, except on a much more individual and personal scale. How do we square our incongruous behaviors and motivations? How do we get our Jekyll (our drives to be fair and egalitarian, our loathing of the idea that we might be racist) and our Hyde (our various racial biases and discriminatory behaviors) to coexist in the same mind? Aversive racism offers a solution to this dilemma.

In 2009 Professors Pearson, Dovidio, and Gaertner described aversive racism as "a form of prejudice characterizing the thoughts, feelings and behaviors of the majority of well-intentioned and ostensibly non-prejudiced [White people]." This is not the racism of the hardcore right-wing pundit, the kind who might be caught publicly excusing or downplaying serious racism because of supposedly high levels of Black criminality or so-called Black-on-Black crime. No, this is the racism of the left-wing liberal, the *Guardian* reader, the Obama voter—the kind of person who might have (not to make things awkward again) paid their own hard-earned money to buy a book called *The Science of Racism*.

The term "aversive racism" describes the fundamental conflict between this individual's (possibly unacknowledged) negative attitudes and beliefs, and their deeply held conviction that they are free of prejudice. Personally, I'm not a huge fan of the term "aversive racism." I don't think it gives people a good idea of the type of racism it describes. It's meant to capture both the individual's "aversion" to ethnic minorities and their "aversion" to thinking of themselves as racist. This was the thinking in the 1980s, when the term was coined. Were it up to me, I would probably call it something like "conflicted racism," to highlight the conflict between the two opposing motivations.

And it is a real internal conflict. Neither side is allowed unilateral control. The genuine motivation to be non-prejudiced does not stop biased thoughts, feelings, or behavior from happening. Rather, it affects *when* and *how* the biases are allowed to manifest. Since these individuals value their apparent racial egalitarianism, they will not do racist things if their behavior can be easily understood, even by themselves, as a response to someone's race. They will only discriminate if the situation is blurry or ambiguous enough for them to explain their actions away by appealing to some other aspect of the situation. In other words, as Pearson and colleagues put it in 2009, "when they are presented with a situation in which the normative response is clear . . . aversive racists will not discriminate against Blacks." However, in circumstances where their responses "can be justified or rationalized on the basis of some factor other than race . . . aversive racists may engage in behaviors that ultimately harm Blacks but in ways that allow Whites to maintain a non-prejudiced self-image."

That sounds like a really complicated idea, and it seems like a difficult thing to prove. How could scientific research possibly find support for this "discrimination-but-only-if-I-can-get-away-with-it-even-to-myself" hypothesis?

Well, it's actually not that hard. It just requires an expansion of the experimental design described in Chapter 2. As before, we need a genuine experiment (a double-blind, randomized, controlled trial) where the only thing that varies is the race of the stimulus or target and a mechanism for detecting reliable, statistically significant differences in the participants' responses to the varied stimuli. This design could be expanded across a range of settings: job applications, court cases, descriptions of intimate relationships, and so on. So long as you keep the double-blind, randomized, controlled trial, you're doing fine.

Once you have that basic design, you add one more dimension to it. Specifically, on top of the conditions you already have, you put the participants in one of two situations: either a situation in which their discrimination would be obvious, even just to themselves, or a situation in which they could explain their discrimination away, even to themselves, by appealing to some other factor. If aversive racism is a useful model for describing how racism works today, we should see evidence of discrimination in the second situation but not in the first.

It's probably easier to explain with some real examples from the research. Let's start again with a CV study before expanding to other areas of life. In 2000, Dovidio and Gaertner recruited 194 White American participants for what was supposedly a study of the feasibility of a proposed peer counseling program. The participants were given a set of materials to evaluate, among which was the CV of a potential candidate for this program. You can probably guess one part of the design—the CVs were entirely identical, except that some of the participants were shown a CV that appeared to come from a White candidate, while the other participants were shown a CV that appeared to come from a Black candidate. However, within these conditions, there were also other differences. The participants were shown either a CV that was unambiguously stellar, a CV that was unambiguously unqualified, or a CV that was more ambiguous. Put together, that meant that a participant could see one of six possible CVs: stellar White applicant, stellar Black applicant, unqualified White applicant, unqualified Black applicant, ambiguous White applicant, or ambiguous Black applicant.

If Dovidio and Gaertner were correct about aversive racism, the participants should appear to be egalitarian—that is, they should respond equally to the White and Black applicants, so long as the applicants were unambiguously well qualified or unqualified for the job. However, when the CVs were ambiguous, participants would be expected to rate the White candidates higher than the otherwise identically qualified Black candidates.

This is exactly what Dovidio and Gaertner found. In their own words: "bias against blacks in simulated hiring decisions was manifested primarily when a candidate's qualifications for the position were ambiguous." Their participants responded to the Black and White candidates equally, so long as their applications were unambiguously strong or unambiguously weak. However, the ambiguously qualified Black candidates received significantly less favorable responses than ambiguously qualified White candidates. Looking at the data further, Dovidio and Gaertner found a specific and disturbing pattern. Participants responded to ambiguous White applicants as if they were strong applicants, but they responded to ambiguous Black applicants as if they were weak applicants. White people get the benefit of the doubt. Black people are assumed to be unqualified until definitively proven otherwise. And it's done so neatly that the participants can pretend, even to themselves, that they're not being racist.

Of course, this isn't the only experiment of its kind. In 2005, Hodson, Hooper, Dovidio, and Gaertner recruited 90 British participants for a study that was ostensibly about the "interpretation of legal scenarios." The design should be very familiar to you at this point. All participants were given information about a defendant who was being charged with robbery. This information included a statement from a witness who claimed to have seen the defendant commit the crime, and some DNA evidence linking the defendant to the scene of the crime. Of course, as in all the previous experiments, the information about the defendant was exactly the same, except that half of the participants were told that he was White while the other half were told that he was Black.

So far, that's just the usual experimental design to test for racist responses. To make this a test for aversive racism, the researchers added another dimension. The DNA evidence was really a slam dunk for the prosecution. It made the defendant seem unambiguously guilty. So, to create the kind of situation that would allow them to test for aversive racism, Hodson and colleagues told half the participants that the DNA evidence was all fine, while they told the other half of the participants that the DNA evidence had been ruled inadmissible by the judge, and therefore should be ignored. To quite literally highlight these instructions, for participants in the *inadmissible* condition, the researchers drew double-strikethrough lines through the text about the DNA evidence. These lines left the text legible (so the participants could still read it if they really wanted to), but left no doubt about whether or not the participants were supposed to disregard it.

Thus, participants were assigned to one of four possible conditions: unambiguously guilty White defendant, unambiguously guilty Black defendant, ambiguously guilty White defendant (due to inadmissible evidence), and ambiguously guilty Black defendant (due to inadmissible evidence). Other than these changes, all information about the defendants was exactly the same.

Given this information, whom did the participants think was the guiltiest? In line with aversive racism, when the evidence was unambiguous, White and Black defendants were seen as similarly guilty. However, when the evidence was ambiguous, the racism was made clear. When the participants were told to disregard the DNA evidence, they successfully disregarded it for the White defendant. The ambiguously guilty White defendant was seen as less guilty than the unambiguously guilty White defendant. In contrast, for the Black defendant, the participants did not disregard the inadmissible evidence at all. Indeed, the Black defendant with the inadmissible evidence was seen as the guiltiest of all—even guiltier than the White (or Black) defendant who was unambiguously guilty. This may have been due to the double stigma of being perceived both as guilty and as trying to hide that guilt. As the authors put it, "after receiving orders from a judge stipulating that incriminating DNA evidence should not be utilized in making upcoming decisions, the Black defendant, compared to the White defendant, was considered to be more guilty, given longer sentence recommendations, seen as more likely to re-offend, and rated less likely to be rehabilitated." So long as the situation is unambiguous, the two defendants may be treated the same. However, if there is any room for discretion, aversive racism kicks in.

I've even done an experiment on aversive racism myself (West, Lowe, and Marsden 2017). Working with some of my students, I recruited 130 White, British women for a study that was ostensibly just about romantic relationships. You can probably guess the design. The participants were shown a male–female relationship and asked to give their impressions of how positive the relationship was for the woman involved. Of course, all the information was identical except for two things. First, half of the participants were shown an image of a monoracial couple (a White man and a White woman), while the other half were shown an image of a mixed couple (a White woman and Black man). Second, all the participants were given almost the same information about the couple, except that half of the participants saw only positive information, while the other half saw the same positive information but also saw a couple of sentences at the end alluding to a rumor that the man had once been violent with the woman. In the study we were very clear that this was just a rumor and that there was no evidence at all that it was true.

So, once again, the participants were placed in one of four conditions: unambiguously good White partner, unambiguously good Black partner, White partner with a rumor of negative behavior, and Black partner with a rumor of negative behavior. And how did they rate these four relationships? You should be able to guess. So long as all the information about the partners was unambiguously positive, the White and Black partners were interpreted as equally good for the woman involved. However, once there was a rumor that the man may have been violent, the differences emerged. In the presence of the rumor, the interracial relationship was rated as significantly worse than the all-White relationship.

As we put it in the paper, "participants reported more negative judgments of an interethnic relationship, compared to a White one, but only in the presence of ambiguously valid negative information, which made it possible to engage in aversive racism without appearing to be racially biased." What really stung about this study was how much effort we had put into making sure the participants knew there was no evidence to support the rumor at all—and yet, it was still enough to damage the Black partner's (but not the White partner's) reputation. White people are innocent until proven guilty. For Black people, however, you don't even need evidence, merely suspicion and insinuation, and they're guilty until proven innocent.

Ever since I became cognizant of racism, I think some part of my mind has understood how this works. People sometimes ask me how I deal with racism, and I often respond that I just unambiguously outperform all the White people that I have to compete with. Sometimes I even throw in a little joke about how that isn't as challenging as White people often assume. It's a bit reminiscent of that feminist joke attributed to Charlotte Witton: "Whatever women do, they must do twice as well as men to be thought half as good. Luckily, this is not difficult."

That strategy has worked well for me so far, but it's hard to explain the immense, grinding pressure of always having to be clearly, unambiguously, perfectly good, or risk being judged, even without any evidence at all, as unqualified, guilty, and bad. So long as every application I make for every job is unambiguously stellar, I stand a good chance of getting it. But let there be any ambiguity, any room for discretion or interpretation, and the White candidates will reap the benefits of assumed superiority while the ethnic minority candidates, including me, will be assumed to be weak and unqualified until definitively proven otherwise. If I ever get in trouble with the law, I might be just fine so long as I have unmistakable, unambiguous evidence of my innocence. But let there be any room for doubt or interpretation, and I will be guilty until proven innocent. In my friendships and relationships, even if there are just rumors of my supposed wrongdoing with no evidence at all to substantiate them, in many people's eyes this will be enough to justify the negative responses that they would never have had to an otherwise identical White person.

This pressure is portrayed quite well in the BBC television program *The Capture*, a 2019 mystery thriller series that was mostly written and directed by Ben Chanan. I won't reveal any major spoilers here because it's a really good show and you should go watch it if you haven't already done so. But one of the subplots involves a Black government minister, Isaac Turner, who has been accused of having an extramarital affair. In series 2, episode 2, while talking to Isaac, his White colleagues in government jovially suggest that it's just the kind of thing that might have plausibly happened, and from which he'd probably recover just fine. After all, as they explain, "We all fuck up."

Isaac retorts, "That's where you're wrong . . . You see, it doesn't quite work like that if you look like me. If I'm dishonest or promiscuous, I'm just confirming everybody's worst suspicions . . . no one's going to give me a second chance."

The horrifying thing is, of course, that nobody can live a life of unadulterated (pardon the pun) perfection. Isaac's friends were right. We do all fuck up. All of us. Try as you might, sooner or later you're going to have a bad moment, or a bad day, or bad week. Every job applicant has some lines on their CV that are open to interpretation. Very, very rarely do we have perfectly clear, unambiguous proof of anyone's guilt or innocence. Almost everyone has messed up at least once in every relationship they've ever been in. Ambiguity and imperfection is the ironclad rule among humans, not the exception. And when ethnic minorities fall short of unambiguous perfection, aversive racism strikes like a snake in the grass, offering the awaited excuse to engage in the kind of racism that had, until that moment, been kept at bay.

And afterward—after people have made these biased, unfair judgments, and the damage is done—aversive racism becomes a shield they can wield even against their own self-awareness, attributing their actions to anything at all but race or racism. *This procedure's not racist. That application just really wasn't that strong. This verdict has nothing to do with race. Didn't you see the evidence against that guy? I don't like your partner, but of course it's got nothing to do with race. Haven't you heard the rumors about them?* At each of these junctions, aversive racism steps in to protect someone's non-prejudiced self-image.

We're not racist. We're not racist at all.

Pushing the boundaries

When I was young, someone told me that when a Chinese baby is born the parents choose the baby's name by throwing a coin against a metal rubbish bin. Whatever sound the coin makes becomes the new baby's name—"Ching!" or "Chang!" or "Shing!" Even as a child, I didn't believe it, and I think it was clearly meant in jest. However, what was interesting to me was that the person telling the joke was someone whom I liked and respected, a person who was highly educated, generally very intelligent, and usually open-minded about a range of subjects. They also had many Chinese friends and neighbors. When interacting with these friends and neighbors, this person didn't show even a whiff of hatred or malice—they were generally pleasant, even spontaneously generous. This appears to raise an interesting question about the baby-naming claim: was that a racist joke?

The joke certainly fits a larger theme. As noted by multiple researchers, including Ervine in 2022, Chinese culture (and East Asian culture more generally) is often stereotyped as silly, funny, or incomprehensible. In that vein, the baby-naming joke is similar to a lot of other jokes that I still see many people in my online social circle passing around today. For example, there's one that goes: "I used to let certain people bother me, until I discovered the wisdom of the ancient Chinese philosopher Fuk Yu." Whether or not you see those specific jokes as harmful, they are also reminiscent of jokes that dehumanize Chinese people, or make light of their suffering or deaths.

On July 6, 2013, Asiana Airlines Flight 214 from Incheon International Airport near Seoul, Korea, crashed on its approach to San Francisco International Airport. Almost 200 people were injured, many of them seriously. The crash also killed three people, including a sixteen-year-old girl, Ye Mengyuan. Mengyuan was a middle school student who still wore glasses and braces. She performed well in school, excelled at piano and calligraphy, and was traveling with her friends on a summer trip to the US to improve their English. During the crash, she was thrown from the plane and landed, badly injured, on the tarmac outside. She survived all this, presumably engulfed in pain and fear, only to die soon afterward when a fire truck rushing to the scene ran over her body.

KTVU, the San Francisco Bay Area's FOX affiliate, was one of the first stations to break the story. The coverage went as expected for a professional news station covering a serious accident. At least, that was the case until the news anchor Tori Campbell read the names of the pilots who were supposedly in charge of Flight 214: "Sum Ting Wong, Wi Tu Lo, Ho Lee Fuk, and Bang Ding Ow."

Something wrong. We too low. Holy fuck. Bang, ding, ow.

The incident was blamed on an intern who had apparently confirmed the wrong names. Asiana Airlines took legal action against KTVU for their woeful representation of a genuine tragedy, and three producers at KTVU were fired. Still, in response to an article about the incident published online in the *Journal*, several people took to their keyboards to explain that it was, in fact, not racist: "In very poor taste given people died but how is this racist? Stereotypical, for sure but racist?" "Em, it might be disrespectful and in bad taste, but 'racist'?? I don't think so." And "I believe that the intern's name is Wai Yu Soo Dum."

The connection might not seem obvious, but when I think about this incident it echoes uncomfortably with certain scenes in the 1994 film *Pulp Fiction*, which was directed by Quentin Tarantino and written by Tarantino with Roger Avery. It's a film full of gangsters, mobsters, hitmen, sexy women, and cool dudes who blow people's heads off while wearing suits with skinny black ties. One such cool dude is Jules, a Black mobster played by Samuel L. Jackson. Jules has a problem: his partner has blown the head off another Black man who was sitting in the back of his car and now needs somewhere to hide the car and the body before someone spots him and calls the police.

In a moment of inspiration, Jules takes the car to the house of his friend Jimmy, who is White and played by Quentin Tarantino. Jimmy is understandably upset about suddenly being burdened with a dead body, but what I remember most about the scene is how he expresses this upset. The very White Jimmy launches into a long diatribe about the inconvenience of having a "dead nigger" in his garage. He says this phrase many times—"It ain't the coffee in my kitchen, it's the dead nigger in my garage"; "Did you notice a sign out in front of my house that said 'Dead Nigger Storage?'"; "Storing dead niggers ain't my fucking business," and so on.

The scene is made even more uncomfortable by Jules's reaction, or more specifically, his lack of reaction. Jules, who is Black, has already been shown to be a dangerous man, an armed man. And yet he sits quietly in the kitchen, making vaguely complimentary noises about the quality of Jimmy's coffee, while Jimmy, a White man, shouts racial slurs at him. It's made even more uncomfortable when you realize that the man who plays Jimmy in this scene is also the writer and director of the film, which means that a White man intentionally wrote, directed, and starred in a scene in which he repeatedly shouts "nigger" at a Black man and suffers no consequence for this behavior.

What are we, as the viewers, supposed to make of this scene? I am not a literary analyst, but to me at least, one plausible interpretation seems to be that it is sometimes OK for White people to use racial slurs, and that Tarantino was invested in making this point as clearly, and perhaps shockingly, as possible. I have heard people try to explain the scene in other ways. Some people suggest that the repeated use of the racial slur was a "joke," but I find this explanation unconvincing. Nothing in the tone of the scene suggests that it is supposed to be interpreted as funny either by the audience or the characters. None of the characters in the film react as if something humorous is happening. Nothing in the music or lighting suggests that this scene should be taken as anything but a serious one. Meanwhile Jules, whose partner just killed a man, does not appear to react to the racial slurs at all and nothing in the scene suggests that an eventual reaction is imminent or expected. Similarly, nothing in the scene suggests that either Jimmy's racial slurs, or Jules's lack of reaction to them, should be interpreted by the audience as problematic in any way.

To me, the scene very clearly says that yes, calling Black people "niggers" is racist in general, but maybe we're supposed to see that it depends on the context. Maybe if you're friends with a Black person, or if you're doing a Black person a favor, it's fine. Maybe if you're dealing with the shock of a dead man in your garage, that's enough to excuse it. Maybe it's "disrespectful and in bad taste," but in those contexts, is it really racist? Jules didn't seem to think so, and he's Black.

Aaron Sibarium raised similar concerns on February 6, 2023, via Twitter. His specific tweet read: "ChatGPT says it is never morally permissible to utter a racial slur—even if doing so is the only way to save millions of people from a nuclear bomb." His tweet was in response to an overwhelmingly fanciful scenario in which the only way to disarm an atomic bomb was to utter the password, which was voice-activated, and set to "a certain racial slur." When asked if it would be morally acceptable to say the racial slur in this case, the artificial intelligence ChatGPT responded, "No, it is never acceptable to use a racial slur," and this was the source of Sibarium's concern. Of course, Sibarium will never find himself in such a ridiculous predicament. That's not the point. The point Sibarium was trying to make is that it must sometimes be fine, indeed morally required, for a White person to use racial slurs. Having established that using racial slurs is OK in some contexts, the reader may then consider other potential contexts in which using racial slurs is, perhaps, "in bad taste," but not racist.

The 2003 musical *Avenue Q* offers a similar line of reasoning. The musical is a jarring presentation that uses cute, child-friendly, *Sesame Street*–style puppets to discuss very non-child-friendly, non–*Sesame Street* topics like pornography, schadenfreude, and racism. Their song "Everyone's a Little Bit Racist" makes the point very explicitly. It acknowledges that there is such a thing as serious racism, and that we can indeed get worked up about things like hate crimes. However, when it comes to things like making race-based judgments, or assuming two people of the same race are related, or making fun of people's accents, or telling stereotype-based jokes, the song suggests a very different response. For these less serious examples of racism, we should acknowledge that everyone does them, and just relax.

Sum Ting Wong, Wi Tu Lo, Ho Lee Fuk.

Presumably, this injunction to "relax" also extends to repeatedly shouting the word "nigger" at a Black man if you are his friend, or if he asks you for a favor, or if there is a dead body in your garage, or a nuclear bomb set by the world's most idiotic and cartoonishly racist terrorist.

These stories all make an appeal to the same central concept. In social-psychological terms, the concept is called "definitional boundaries of discrimination." This term was devised in 2021 by my friend, Dr. Katy Greenland of the University of Cardiff, with a little help from me and from Professor Colette van Laar of the Katholieke Universiteit in Leuven. As we wrote in two papers, one published in 2021 and the other in 2022, definitional boundaries of discrimination are the cultural tools that we use to determine whether a non-egalitarian act is "really" discrimination (that is, an act that's crossed that psychological boundary into the kind of behavior we should be concerned about) or "not really" discrimination (an act that might be a little bit racist, but is also harmless, or understandable, or otherwise not very important). There are a few central aspects to the concept of definitional boundaries of discrimination. The first is that these are not explanations that we make up as individuals, but widely available, culturally recognizable arguments that we use to explain how we sort "real" discrimination from "not" discrimination. I'll present a few of these arguments, and you can see if you recognize them.

The first argument is that intention matters. You can't say that someone is racist just because they did one thing or another; you have to know whether they really meant it or not. A second argument revolves around the notion of racism being necessarily malicious. If you're not being malicious, it can't be racism. Third, for an act to be real racism, it has to be attributable to race and nothing else (not class, or dress, or hair, or behavior). So to say that something is racist, you need to show that race and only race made that person do what they did. The fourth argument is that benign ignorance is not the same thing as real racism. We can't blame some people who do racist things, because often they just don't know any better. And a final argument is that real racism is perpetuated by a certain kind of person. This person isn't reasonable, logical or sensible. They're often not highly educated, and they can't explain their actions with reference to any logical motivation.

You probably don't agree with all these arguments, though you almost certainly agree with some. In any case, your agreement is not as important here as your recognition of these arguments. You've heard them before. Almost all of us have. That's how we know they're cultural tools.

A second key aspect of definitional boundaries of discrimination is that, if you look at them carefully, they're not tools for recognizing racism or discrimination. If you think about it, they are actually tools for *not* recognizing racism or discrimination. Let's assume that we agree with all five aspects outlined in the previous paragraph (intent, maliciousness, possible ignorance, possible appeals to other explanations, and the restriction to a certain kind of person). That would mean we should refrain from ever calling any act "racist" unless we have an almost god-like understanding of the secret, inner thoughts and feelings of the person who committed the act. If we bought into these arguments, a person who did something racist would only have to claim genuine ignorance, or that they committed the act without malicious intent, or that they didn't mean it that way, or that it was just their diabetes flaring up, or that their behavior was based on the other person's clothes, or their hairstyle, or their behavior. To successfully claim that racism occurred, we'd somehow have to know that person's inner mind and be able to prove exactly what the racist person was thinking and feeling at the time.

This may sound like a ridiculously high bar (because it is), but this high level of protection from accusations of racism is exactly what definitional boundaries of discrimination offer. Katy Greenland demonstrated that quite neatly in another paper (from 2018). In this paper, participants were discussing the journalist and TV host Jeremy Clarkson, who had recently been dismissed from his hit BBC show *Top Gear* after being caught on camera using the word "nigger." When asked whether they considered Clarkson's behavior to be racist, the participants leaned heavily on the idea that an observer would have to truly know Clarkson's private thoughts and intentions in order to make that judgment. In one participant's own (spoken) words as quoted verbatim in Greenland's paper: "Someone like Jeremy Clarkson, not a lot of people know who he is as a person. You don't know whether he says that, erm, that he . . . whether he says 'nigger' under his breath as a racist or as a non-racist, because you don't know him. So if, so like, racism is so dependent on the beliefs that a person has because, if you know what their beliefs are, then you know whether or not something that comes out, you'll know what the meaning of that is. You'll have a much better idea of the meaning of what is coming out of their mouth."

So there you have it. If you make use of these definitional boundaries of discrimination, you can essentially do what you like. Even if you're caught on camera using racial slurs, you can still argue that it's not racist. Tarantino, Sibarium, *Avenue Q*, and KTVU News must be pleased to hear it.

Before we go any further, it's probably worth considering how narrow or broad your own definitional boundaries of discrimination are. Where do you draw the line? I'm going to go out on a limb and assume that you think slavery, genocide, and hate crimes count as "real" racism. Most people do. But what else do you include in your definitional boundaries? Do you think ethnic jokes are "real" racism or do you, like *Avenue Q* and one apparent intern at KTVU News, think they're probably fine? Do you think White people should always avoid using racial slurs? Or do you, like Tarantino and Sibarium, see a range of possible situations in which it might be acceptable? And what about even more subtle things? Do you think it's racist when you confuse one person for another of the same race? Or when you give up trying to pronounce their difficult names? What about victim blaming, the kind in which you just point out certain facts like "Most Blacks are killed by other Blacks" in discussions of police brutality? What about assuming the worst of ambiguously presented ethnic minorities? What about backhanded compliments, like telling a Black person that they're very articulate?

Before the next paragraph, take a moment to be honest with yourself about where you draw your boundaries. You might make a list on a piece of paper with all the "real" discrimination examples on one side and all the "not" discrimination examples on the other. Clarifying your thoughts in this way will make the next few paragraphs more interesting.

That done, now we can talk about the third important aspect of definitional boundaries of discrimination: everybody has a different set point for their definitional boundaries, and this set point matters. Maybe you're one of the people who employ the most narrow definitional boundaries imaginable, literally refusing to recognize something as racist unless it's a hate crime, or a genocide, or race-based slavery. Or maybe you're one of the people with much broader definitional boundaries. Maybe you don't care about any of the arguments or excuses. If something looks racist, you're going to call it racist. Be it ethnic jokes, or making fun of some people's accents, or using racial slurs even if you have ethnic minority friends who are cool with it, it's still racist. In any case, the way you draw your definitional boundaries has implications for your other race-related beliefs and responses.

In 2021, Katy Greenland, Colette van Laar, and I recruited about 300 people and had them complete a number of measures relating to race and racism. These included measures of both implicit and explicit racism, as well as their definitional boundaries of discrimination and their support for certain topical race-related issues (for example, their support for Black Lives Matter or All Lives Matter movements). We found a lot of things in that study. However, most relevant here is that we found very strong associations between narrow definitional boundaries of discrimination and just plain being racist.

To put it bluntly, people who were more likely to buy into the arguments used to arrive at narrow definitional boundaries of discrimination (intent, maliciousness, possible ignorance, possible appeals to other explanations, and the restriction to a certain kind of person) were also significantly more likely to have strongly biased scores on the Implicit Associations Test, and also more likely to agree with explicitly racist statements such as "Blacks have more influence on society than they ought to have," and "Blacks should not push themselves where they are not wanted." They were also more likely to dislike the Black Lives Matter movement and to prefer All Lives Matter. Your definitional boundaries aren't just a matter of personal taste. They are tools that can be weaponized to encourage or discourage our recognition of contemporary racism and to predict our likely responses to that racism—letting it slide, or doing something about it.

Which brings us to one final important aspect of definitional boundaries of discrimination.

I know I said that "everybody has a different set point for their definitional boundaries," but that wasn't entirely accurate. Forgive me. The truth, and the last important aspect of definitional boundaries that I'll discuss, is somewhat more complicated. The assertion that "everybody has a different set point for their definitional boundaries" makes things sound a lot more stable, consistent, and reasonable than they actually are. You do not, in fact, have a single, well-thought-out method for distinguishing between "real" discrimination and "not" discrimination. Instead, you likely have a fluctuating set of borders that become narrower in some circumstances and broader in others. Specifically, this fluctuation is also weaponized to protect you from being accused of racism.

How could I know such a thing? I'll explain.

In 2022, Katy, Colette, and I, and a shared student of ours—Ditte Barnoth—wanted to know if people applied their definitional boundaries of discrimination consistently or inconsistently. Specifically, we wanted to know if people stuck to their reasoning regardless of who was doing the racist thing and who was the victim of the racist thing, or if people modified their reasoning to benefit people like themselves and penalize people who were not like themselves. In essence, we wanted to know if people applied self-serving double standards, narrowing their definitional boundaries when they were being racist against other people, but broadening the definitional boundaries when other people were being racist against them.

To do this, we recruited 258 White men across two studies and asked them all to respond to fifteen statements reflecting the arguments that are commonly used to narrow definitional boundaries of discrimination. The participants would indicate, on a numerical scale, how much they agreed with statements such as "The core of racism is that it is malicious: if you are not being malicious, then it can't be racist," and "To say that someone is racist, you need to show that race and only race made them do what they did."

Except, that's not quite what we asked them. What the participants didn't know was that we had secretly split them into two conditions. One condition responded to statements about racism by White people against Black people. Those were statements like: "The core of racism is that it is malicious: if a White person is not being malicious, then it can't be racist" and "To say that a White person is racist, you need to show that race and only race made them do what they did." The other condition responded to almost exactly the same questions, except that they were asked to think about racism by Black people against White people (what some people call "reverse racism"). Those were statements such as "The core of racism is that it is malicious: if a Black person is not being malicious, then it can't be racist," and "To say that a Black person is racist, you need to show that race and only race made them do what they did." In both conditions the instructions were very clear, and the participants knew exactly what kind of racism (White-on-Black vs. Black-on-White) they were supposed to be considering.

In theory, this should not have mattered one bit, not if the participants were defining racism in a fair and consistent way. After all, it should make no difference who's doing the racist thing. Intent either matters or it doesn't. Factors other than race either matter or they don't. If the participants are being honest and sticking to their reasoning, we shouldn't find any difference in levels of agreement between the two conditions.

But, of course, we did find differences in levels of agreement between the two conditions. Consistently, our White male participants narrowed their definitional boundaries when thinking about White people being racist against Black people, but broadened their definitional boundaries when thinking about Black people being racist against White people. As we put it in the paper, this research showed that "there are not stable, universally applied definitional boundaries of discrimination, even for a single individual. Instead, some individuals . . . shift the definitional boundaries of discrimination depending on the targets and perpetrators of that discrimination." When White men are being racist against other people, they want the definitional boundaries to be narrower and more restrictive, closer to only recognizing the most overt and aggressive forms of racism. However, when other people are being racist against them, they want the definitional boundaries to be broader and more inclusive, closer to recognizing more subtle and ambiguous forms of racial discrimination.

If you do this little dance correctly—if you push the boundaries back and forth at just the right times and in just the right contexts—you can fix it so that you're never racist against anybody, but other people are certainly racist against you, at least some of the time. Have you just told an "ethnic joke" or used a racial slur? Did you just turn down a qualified minority candidate for a post? Narrow the boundaries! Nobody can reasonably call you racist unless they know exactly what you were thinking at the time. But then, did someone pass you over for an opportunity you wanted, one that an ethnic minority got "in your place"? Broaden the boundaries! It doesn't matter if it was deliberate discrimination. It doesn't matter if there's some other plausible explanation (like the ethnic minority's qualifications). This is racism, pure and simple. Perform the dance skilfully enough and you can convince yourself, despite all the overwhelming evidence to the contrary, that the real victims of racism today aren't ethnic minorities at all, but White people.

Overly positive self-perceptions

There are many, many more things that you probably do to hide your racism from yourself, things that we don't really have the time (or, more accurately, that I don't think it would be the best use of our time) to cover at length. For example, there are a range of strategies that people use to minimize the consequences of racism. Certain commentators like Haidt in 2017, Lilienfeld in 2017, and Rosen in 2014 have made the claim (sometimes with staggeringly little evidence) that ethnic minorities are just being "hypersensitive" to trivial things that wouldn't bother White people nearly as much. In 2019, I conducted three studies involving 508 participants to disprove that little bit of unsubstantiated silliness (West 2019b). My research found no evidence at all that ethnic minorities were more sensitive to subtle forms of mistreatment, only evidence that they experience these kinds of mistreatment significantly more frequently. Still, I often hear versions of the hypersensitivity argument used as a way to tell ethnic minorities to just "get over it."

In another example, some people will baldly assert that their very racial judgments and preferences are somehow not racist. For example, research by Mendelsohn et al. in 2014, Miller et al. in 2004, and Murstein et al. in 1989 (among others) has shown just how comfortable many White people are with explicitly stating pro-White dating preferences. As one Reddit user put it: "There's nothing wrong with having racial preferences in dating. Everyone has a specific type and certain races may fit that type better than others . . . If someone only wants to date someone with light skin, black hair, and blue eyes because it's their ideal type, then so be it."

Let's ignore the wealth of research by, for example, Butkowski et al. in 2022, Hagiwara et al. in 2012, Hill in 2017, Li et al. in 2008, and Maddox and Gray in 2002, that documents the pervasive societal messages about which people should be considered ugly (dark-skinned, dark-eyed people) and which people should be considered attractive (light-skinned, light-eyed people). Let's ignore the fact that your completely individual, not at all racist romantic preferences align really well with these racist societal messages about attractiveness. Never mind the academic research (for example, by Reece in 2016) showing that Black people are perceived as more attractive if they just say that they're mixed race, even when they still look exactly the same as a Black person without a claim to mixed Black and White heritage. Never mind my own research (for example, West 2019a) showing that racial preferences in dating align well with other stereotypes of ethnic minorities. For instance, people who like women prefer East Asian partners (stereotyped as submissive and hyperfeminine) to Black partners. In contrast, people who like men prefer Black partners (stereotyped as hypermasculine) to East Asian partners. Never mind all of that. Your preference for a light-skinned, blue-eyed partner is just your random, individual thing and clearly has nothing at all to do with racism. Don't even worry about it.

But I'm getting distracted.

I hope that the larger point has successfully been made. Racism doesn't have to be unconscious to be hidden. Even just considering the three strategies that I focused on in this chapter, none of which require unconscious bias—victim blaming, aversive racism, and playing with definitional boundaries of discrimination—you should now be able to see how easy it is for someone to be racist all the time, without ever having to recognize their own racism. Indeed, I'm happy to go even further: with such psychological tricks available to all of us, and with strong social norms against acknowledging one's own biases, how could anyone in contemporary society have an honest perception of how racist they really are? Try as we might to give a faithful answer, if people today were asked to assess their race-related feelings or to predict their future race-related behaviors, it stands to reason that most of us would be wildly inaccurate.

And this brings us back, at long last, to the questions I asked you at the beginning of this chapter. Hopefully, you followed the instructions and wrote the answers to those questions when I asked you to, because this where they become useful.

I asked you to indicate how upset you would be (0 = not at all upset, 9 = extremely upset) in three different scenarios: if a Black man accidentally bumped into a White man's knee and nobody said anything after the Black man had left the room; if a Black man accidentally bumped into a White man's knee and the White man said, after the Black man had left the room, "Typical, I hate when Black people do that"; and if a Black man accidentally bumped into a White man's knee and the White man said, after the Black man had left the room, "Clumsy nigger." I also asked you if, in the third scenario, you would ask the White man to be your partner in a second exercise. I am now going to guess your answers to these questions.

In response to Scenario 1, you gave yourself an "upset score" of 3 or 4. In response to Scenario 2, you gave yourself an "upset score" of about 7 or 8. And in response to Scenario 3, you gave yourself an "upset score" of about 8 or 9. I'm also going to guess that you said "no" to the last question, thinking that you would not ask the White man who said "Clumsy nigger" to be your partner in a second exercise.

How did I do? Before you get too impressed at my accuracy (assuming that I was in fact accurate), I should point out that I had some help. In 2009, Kawakami, Dunn, Karmali, and Dovidio recruited 60 participants—whom they called forecasters—and randomly assigned them to one of three scenarios, asking them to predict or forecast how upset they would be in each. You are already very familiar with the three scenarios; they are the same ones I outlined above. The activity you did at the start of this chapter was essentially playing the role of a forecaster in Kawakami's experiment. The reason I've been able to guess your scores with relative confidence is that I already knew the scores that the forecasters gave for these three scenarios in the original experiments.

But there were also three other conditions. Kawakami and colleagues also recruited a further 60 participants—whom they called "experiencers"—and assigned them to conditions that were almost identical to the forecaster conditions, except that participants in the experiencer conditions actually experienced the things that the forecasters were merely asked to imagine. That is, the participants in the experiencer conditions actually went into the lab to do an experiment, actually saw a Black man bump into a White man's knee and actually heard the White man say either nothing (Scenario 4), or "Typical, I hate when Black people do that" (Scenario 5), or "Clumsy nigger" (Scenario 6). After these events, the experiencers were asked to report how upset they actually felt using the same scale that the forecasters had used to predict how upset they thought they might feel.

If people were generally good at predicting their responses to racism, we should expect the scores for the forecasters and the experiencers to align reasonably well. However, the title of the paper, "Mispredicting affective and behavioral responses to racism," is a bit of a spoiler. The researchers did not find, at all, that the forecasters and experiencers had similar scores.

It was quite the opposite. The experiment showed that the participants (all of whom were White) were terrible at predicting their responses to racism. Specifically, they strongly overestimated both how much racism would upset them, and what their responses to a racist person would be. The forecasters predicted very high "upset scores" for both Scenarios 2 and 3 (the ones in which they were asked to *imagine* another White person saying either "Typical, I hate when Black people do that," or "Clumsy nigger")—generally these scores were 7 or above. However, the experiencers reported much lower "upset scores" in response to actually living through these events (Scenarios 5 and 6). Their upset scores for both those scenarios hovered around 3 or 4. Not very upset at all.

Even more disturbing, the participants were similarly awful at predicting whether or not they would ask a racist person to be their partner in a second exercise. To be fair, participants were reasonably good at predicting their responses in the conditions in which the White person said nothing in response to the Black person bumping into their knee. For these conditions the forecasters predicted that they would ask the other White person to be their partner again about 68% of the time, which wasn't too different from the experiencers who actually asked the White person to be their partner again about 53% of the time.

However, the predictions became much less accurate when the other White person in the room made racist comments. In these conditions the forecasters predicted that they would only ask him to be their partner again about 17% of the time, while the experiencers actually asked him to be their partner again about 63% of the time. In case you missed it when I just cited the numbers, I want to highlight two shocking findings. The first is that most forecasters said that they *wouldn't* ask someone who made racist comments to be their partner in a second exercise (83%), while most experiencers *did* ask that person to be their partner in a second exercise (63%). The second is that, when the White confederate made racist comments, he actually became more popular than when he said nothing. His likelihood of being selected in a second exercise moved upward, from 53% to 63%.

These are the terrible consequences of the psychological tricks that we play on ourselves. When it comes to racism, we do not know ourselves at all. The researchers didn't probe the participants' reasoning in this study, so we don't know exactly why they made the choices they did. However, it's not hard to imagine the experiencers in that experiment unleashing a barrage of victim blaming ("Well, maybe that Black guy bumps into people a lot, maybe it's his fault"), aversive racism ("Well, the situation is a bit ambiguous"), and playing with definitional boundaries of discrimination ("Well, maybe the White guy has Black friends, or diabetes, or Tourettes or something, I don't know") to justify, minimize, and excuse the White confederate's behavior, just like they would probably justify, minimize, and excuse their own.

Again, this is not a claim I make lightly, but one based on research.

In 2019, Bell, Burkley, and Bock conducted three very similar studies on a total of 515 participants. There were minor variations in these studies, but all three covered the same central hypothesis and all three had almost identical designs, so it seems fair to describe them together here. For the first part of each study, participants completed a "pre-screener questionnaire." Ostensibly, the purpose of this questionnaire was to determine whether the participant was eligible for any other studies in the future. As part of the pre-screener, each participant saw a list of 46 behaviors and had to indicate whether they had ever engaged in each behavior by selecting "yes" or "no" beside it. The list was long and contained a seemingly random assortment of bad or embarrassing behaviors, for example, "Have you ever lied to get out of a gathering with friends or family?" and "Have you ever worn the same underwear two days in a row?"

However, embedded in the list were 30 items specifically about racist behaviors, for example, "Have you ever avoided interacting with a Muslim person out of fear?," "Have you ever laughed at another person's joke about Asian people?," and "Have you ever used the N-word to refer to Blacks?"

This list of yes-or-no responses to the 46 items gave the researchers profiles of each of the participants in the studies:

profiles that would become very useful a few months later when the participants were invited back to complete a totally unrelated (wink, wink) second study.

For this "unrelated" second study, the participants were given another, randomly selected person's profile and asked to rate this completely random other person on a list of negative traits. Some of these negative traits had nothing to do with racism, such as how dishonest this random person was, or how disgusting this random person was. However, embedded in this list of questions was also one about how racist this random person was. Finally, the participants compared themselves to this other, randomly selected person. Across all three studies, the participants consistently rated themselves as less racist than this randomly selected other person.

And this is where I reveal the trick, the trick that you probably saw coming. The participants were not in fact rating another, randomly selected other person based on their profile. Each participant was given their own profile, the one they had completed a few months earlier. Each participant was looking at a description of themselves, not of a randomly selected other person. And yet, when asked to compare themselves to this profile, participants consistently rated themselves as less racist than the person in the profile. They consistently claimed to be less racist than themselves.

This brings us full circle to an interesting question. How racist are you? Do you still think that you can offer an accurate self-assessment in that regard? If you do, then I'd like to suggest that you are using one of the most widely recognized of all psychological tricks: an unshakeable belief in your own exceptionalism. Having read about the research, you probably believe and understand that other people engage in these psychological strategies to mask their own racism, but not you. That is one of the hardest mental barriers for us to break through. There is, unfortunately, quite a gulf between general knowledge and honest self-perception. Indeed, despite having studied these human psychological processes for years, even I am not immune to them, because I'm still human. So you'll forgive me for pointing out that you're not immune to them either.

Nonetheless, there is probably still a part of your mind that sees all this as a useful guide to the way other people delude themselves: your racist uncle, your mother-in-law, your boss, that person from your friendship circle who can sometimes say awkward things. *They* blame the victim. *They* use aversive racism. *They* shift their definitional boundaries around. *They* erroneously believe that they are much better people than they actually are. But not you. You don't do any of that.

You're not racist at all.

PART III
THE COMPLEXITIES
OF RACISM

Chapter 8

The Other Side of the Game
Reverse Racism

The morning of May 6, 2023 saw the Coronation of King Charles III of the United Kingdom and the Commonwealth Realms. He succeeded his mother, Queen Elizabeth II, who had been one of the longest-reigning monarchs in history.

Charles's coronation faced a few challenges. The UK was experiencing an aggressive cost of living crisis. There was high inflation coupled with widespread wage depression, and furious strikes across several industries. The number of food banks in the UK had been increasing for some time, and a growing number of Britons were forced to choose between eating food and heating their homes. This left some of the king's subjects disgruntled (to say the least) about throwing a £100 million party to celebrate a staggering display of inherited wealth and privilege.

However, the criticism of the Coronation that captured the most attention in the UK was about something else entirely. Despite some people's misgivings, the ceremony was, understandably, a center of focus for the British media. It was streamed on most of the larger television stations with flag-waving, cheers, and celebrity commentary. Adjoa Andoh was one of these commenting celebrities. She is a Black British actor, likely most famous for her role as Lady Agatha Danbury on the hit Netflix series *Bridgerton*—at least, until that day.

In the UK, Andoh may now be best known for uttering two words about the royal family as they stood together on the balcony of Buckingham Palace following the ceremony at Westminster Abbey: "terribly White." Her full quote was, "We've gone from the rich diversity of the Abbey to a terribly white balcony. I was very struck by that." But "terribly White" was the isolated phrase that ended up plastered all over the British headlines. London paper the *Metro*'s headline was: "Bridgerton: Adjoa Andoh Dubs Buckingham Palace Balcony 'Terribly White'." The *Daily Mail* ran with: "Bridgerton Star Adjoa Andoh Stuns ITV by Calling the Buckingham Palace Balcony 'Terribly White'." The *Telegraph* said: "The Row over the 'Terribly White' Royal Balcony Exposes the Hypocrisy of the Woke Left."

Soon, the headlines shifted. British people were apparently very upset about the comment and started to complain to Ofcom, the UK's communications regulator. Within a very short time, the "terribly White" comment had become the most complained-about televised moment of 2023. From the *Metro* : "Bridgerton Star Adjoa Andoh's 'Terribly White' Coronation Comments Attract over 4,000 Ofcom Complaints." From the *Daily Mail* barely a week later: "Now ITV Is Hit with Record 8,252 Ofcom Complaints over 'Terribly White' Coronation Balcony Row."

People were incensed. One Talk TV presenter, Kevin O'Sullivan, commented: "Well the balcony scene was the royal family! They are White! My family is White! You are allowed to be a White family, surely?" Julia Hartley-Brewer, another Talk TV presenter, seemed most concerned about the hypocrisy of it all: "If anyone said 'terribly Black balcony,' that would absolutely cause outrage as a racist comment." Hartley-Brewer also interviewed Ben Jones from the Free Speech Union, who voiced his agreement, pointing out that "the way reverse racism is tolerated is something that people find very frustrating."

And that is what this chapter is about: reverse racism. There have been quite a few examples of apparent reverse racism: some rather shocking.

In 2015 in Canada, an Indigenous woman, Tamara Crowchief, yelled "I hate White people" while she punched a White woman in the face. Despite the seemingly clear evidence, Judge Harry Van Harten said, "I am not satisfied beyond a reasonable doubt that this offense was, even in part, motivated by racial bias."

In 2018, South Korea–born Sarah Jeong was appointed to the editorial board of the *New York Times*. Soon after, however, it emerged that Jeong had (in 2013 and 2014) tweeted derogatory things about White people: "oh man it's kind of sick how much joy i get out of being cruel to old white men," "#CancelWhitePeople," "are white people genetically predisposed to burn faster in the sun, thus logically being only fit to live underground like groveling goblins?" The *New York Times* defended their decision to appoint Jeong, saying that the tweets had been taken out of context, but this did little to appease public figures like Governor Mike Huckabee or the then–Fox News host Tucker Carlson. There was outrage. Jeong was labeled a racist. In 2019, she left the *New York Times* editorial board.

In 2018, the French rapper Nick Conrad released the song "Pendez les Blancs," which translates to "Hang the Whites." The lyrics encouraged listeners to kill White babies and torture their parents. It was accompanied by a music video in which a White man was kidnapped, tortured, shot, and hanged from a tree. The word "lynched" springs readily to mind. Conrad denied being a racist, saying that his video used inverted roles to highlight and comment on contemporary racism. A likely story indeed!

Meanwhile, on Spotify and Apple Music, you can still listen to songs like "I Don't Like White People" by Rucka Rucka Ali. On Netflix, you can still watch *White Chicks*, a 2004 film in which two Black men—Marlon Wayans and Shawn Wayans— spend most of the movie in "whiteface." Not even the children are safe. In 2015, Heron Creek, a middle school in Florida, had an incentive program aimed specifically and exclusively at African American students. White students were openly told that they were not welcome to participate in the program. The principal didn't even deny it!

I won't insult your intelligence by pretending that all these examples are indicative of how White people are regularly treated in contemporary society. However, some people also point to quantitative research that seems to expose anti-White sentiment as more widespread than you might assume. For example, in 2023, Rasmussen Reports conducted a national survey of 1,000 American adults (of whom 130 were Black). One of the questions in the survey asked participants how much they agreed with the statement "It's OK to be White." Shockingly, only a very slim majority of Black respondents (53%) agreed with this statement. Of the rest, 26% disagreed with the idea that it's OK to be White, and 21% were not sure how they felt.

These findings caused Scott Adams, creator of the well-known comic strip *Dilbert*, to, quite frankly, freak the hell out. On his YouTube channel he encouraged other White people to "get the hell away from Black people," because, "if nearly half of all Blacks are not OK with White people—according to this poll, not according to me, according to this poll—that's a hate group." Black people, as a whole, are apparently a hate group.

So there we have it. Reverse racism is a real, serious, widespread problem.

Or is it?

Ethnic minorities like White people more than White people like them

You might be surprised to read that the scientific evidence doesn't support Scott Adams's perspective. First of all, though claims of anti-White negativity make great attention-grabbing headlines, they don't align with the scientific findings. On the contrary: a large body of scientific research has consistently found that relationships between White people and ethnic minorities are asymmetrical in ways that favor White people. Put more simply, ethnic minorities reliably like White people more than White people like ethnic minorities.

For example, since 1958, a series of yearly Gallup polls have tracked how much American adults approve of interracial marriage—specifically, marriages between White people and non-White people. This number has steadily improved between 1958, when only 4% of Americans approved, and 2021, when 94% of Americans approved. This is generally lauded as a wonderful sign of progress. However, what's more relevant for this chapter is the way the rates of approval of interracial marriage vary between White and non-White people. Since 1968, Gallup has disaggregated the data by the race of the respondents. Across those fifty-three years of surveys, would you like to guess which year first saw interracial marriage reach a higher approval rate among White participants than among ethnic minority participants?

The answer is never. This has never happened. Every single year for which there is data, ethnic minorities have expressed more approval for marrying White people than White people have expressed for marrying ethnic minorities.

Research finds very much the same pattern when looking at the question through a different lens. In 2014, Mendelsohn,

Shaw Taylor, Fiore, and Cheshire analyzed the personal profiles and communication records of over a million users of an online dating site. Maybe Gallup polls find evidence of asymmetry in racial attitudes, but surely the hip young kids doing online dating are past all that nonsense, right?

Wrong! Indeed, the researchers found very similar patterns of racial asymmetry. First, let's consider the number of people who explicitly specified that they would only like to date members of their own race. This behavior was relatively infrequent among Black people. Only 8% of Black men indicated that they were only interested in dating other Black people, while 21% of White men (that's more than 2.5 times as many) indicated that they were only interested in dating other White people.

For many complex reasons that are not the focus of this book, women of all races generally tend to be more restrictive in their dating patterns than men are. Still, even with this caveat, the familiar pattern of asymmetry also asserts itself among women. Specifically, the researchers found that 32% of Black women indicated that they were only interested in dating other Black people, while a significantly higher 43% of White women indicated that they were only interested in dating other White people.

However, the really exciting findings came not from what the dating site users said that they wanted, but from what they actually did. When the analysis moved from "preferences as stated" to "preferences as revealed in behavior," the asymmetry between Black and White people became much more stark. In this analysis, fewer than half (45%) of the contacts initiated by Black people (men and women combined) were to other Black people, while 37% of the contacts initiated by Black people were to White people. In contrast, White people were much more likely to stick to their own. Specifically, 85% of the contacts initiated by White people were to other White people. Only 3% of the contacts initiated by White people were to Black people. As the researchers noted, Black people were more than ten times as likely to contact a White person as White people were to contact a Black person.

This asymmetry is not limited to the realm of romantic relationships. In 2002, Nosek, Banaji, and Greenwald reviewed the data they had collected from over 600,000 completed Implicit Association Tests taken between 1998 and 2000. Across this massive dataset, collected over a number of years, the researchers found that both White and Black people expressed explicit preferences for their own groups (that is, White people explicitly preferred White people and Black people explicitly preferred Black people), but their implicit preferences were not so symmetrical. When considering their implicit data, the researchers found that White people continued to show a strong preference for White people over Black people. Black people, on the other hand, only showed a weak preference. And this preference was also for White people over Black people.

That's right. Though the effect is weaker for Black people, the researchers found that, on average and on the implicit level, both White people and Black people like White people more than Black people.

Other studies have found similar asymmetrical patterns. For example, in 2012, Newheiser and Olson tested 141 White and Black American children between the ages of seven and eleven. When they looked only at the children's explicit responses, the White children expressed a preference for White people over Black people, and the Black children expressed a preference for Black people over White people. However, when looking at the implicit responses, White children continued to show significant preferences for White people over Black people, while the Black children did not show a preference in either direction. Ethnic minorities reliably like White people more than White people like ethnic minorities.

But let's imagine that they didn't. Let's pretend that there was no explanatory context whatsoever for the comments of Adjoa Andoh, or the programs set up by Heron Creek Middle School, or the findings of the 2023 Rasmussen Reports. Let's pretend that Sarah Jeong and Nick Conrad weren't responding to and mirroring racial abuse that they themselves had witnessed or received. Let's just imagine that everything they said should be taken unthinkingly, at face value, as demonstrations of unprovoked, unabashed, anti-White hatred. Even if we did that, these examples would still not be recognized (at least, not by the scientists studying such matters) as evidence of racism. Why? Because of power, privilege and context.

Power, privilege and context

Imagine two White, German men. Imagine that each of these men is standing face to face with another man: a Jewish man. Imagine that the two German men each say exactly the same thing to the Jewish man in front of them. They say: "I hate Jewish people. I hate you because you are Jewish. It is my intention to hurt you, to kill you and your family, and to take your possessions for myself." This would clearly be an instance of vile antisemitism. It is undeniable that both German men in this imagined scenario are deeply prejudiced against Jewish people.

Moreover, so far, it sounds like each man's bigotry is identical to the other's. However, without changing anything about the German men or what they say, it is possible to make each man's bigotry very different from the other's. To do this, we need not change anything about the bigoted men themselves. We only need to change the context.

Imagine that the first German man was having that conversation on the streets of Berlin, on 16 January 1942. This was the day German authorities began to deport Jewish people from the Polish city of Łódź to an extermination camp in Chełmno. Over the next three years, at least 167,000 Jewish people (plus over 4,000 Roma) would be killed by the German authorities at Chełmno.

Imagine that the second German man was having exactly the same conversation, but he was having it inside an Israeli police station sometime in 2025. Imagine that he was the only non-Jewish person in the room, and that everyone else was a well-armed, highly trained, Jewish Israeli police officer.

Now we can see how these two conversations are very different. In both cases, the German man is expressing identical bigotry and hatred. But bigotry and hatred are only part of the picture when it comes to racism. The other important part of the picture is power.

The first German man, the one in 1942 Berlin, has his hatred backed up by all his power and privilege as a White German living in a White supremacist, antisemitic German state. The Jewish man on the receiving end of the German's hatred has few resources with which to defend himself. There is no higher authority to whom he can complain about the German's behavior. There are likely no Jewish people, or even sympathetic non-Jewish people, among the police, or the courts, or the government, who can be counted on to defend him from this antisemitism. Indeed, if the Jewish man ran to the nearest police station, they would probably just capture him and ship him off to Chełmno to die. Not only would the German man suffer no consequences at all for his hateful outburst, it is very likely that he would be able to follow through with his threats. The full weight of the German state and infrastructure is on his side, making his threats very deadly and very real.

In the second case, the German man's heart is no less hateful, but he is much less powerful. Speaking from the inside of an Israeli police station in 2025, surrounded by Jewish Israeli police officers, he has no means to carry out any of his threats. The likely outcome is that he will be arrested (if he hasn't already been) and perhaps charged with some kind of hate speech. In Israel, in 2025, it is the German who will suffer for his outburst. The Jewish man to whom he is speaking is relatively safe. The full weight of the Israeli state and infrastructure is on his side, making the German's threats, while abominable, relatively hollow and weak.

Of course, even in the second instance, the words of the German man are still offensive and potentially terrifying. It has not been so very long since many people with views like his were able to carry out their threats with the backing of powerful antisemitic governments. Furthermore, antisemitic violence still occurs, even today, in too many places around the world. For example, in 2021, the Community Security Trust (a charity that monitors antisemitism) recorded 2,255 antisemitic incidents in the UK, including 173 violent assaults. In 2017, a group of White supremacists gathered in the US city of Charlottesville, Virginia, and one of their chants was "Jews will not replace us." To hear this shouted by an enormous crowd of angry White men hoisting burning torches is all the reminder we should need of the danger and persistence of contemporary anti-Jewish hatred.

However, even with these contemporary examples of antisemitism in mind, it is obviously erroneous to claim that the two situations I asked you to imagine earlier are the same. Indeed, making such a claim would require a frightening level of dishonesty or willful ignorance. Yes, the beliefs, attitudes, and intentions of the two German men in the imagined scenarios were identical, but the differences in context, power, and privilege make their antisemitism radically, meaningfully, powerfully different.

The relevance of power and privilege doesn't just apply to Jewish people and antisemitism. As Trinidadian-born American civil rights activist Stokely Carmichael once said, "If a White man wants to lynch me, that's his problem. If he's got the power to lynch me, that's my problem. Racism is not a question of attitude; it's a question of power." For this reason, any attempt to discuss racism while ignoring relevant power structures is incomplete, and any perspective on racism that hides or downplays the importance of these power structures is deceptive. Indeed, differences in power and privilege are so essential to our understanding of racism that scholars like Professor Beverly Daniel Tatum of Yale University (Tatum 1999) have defined racism as "prejudice plus power," or perhaps even better, "a system of advantages based on race." If you don't have the system, if you don't have the power, if you don't have the advantages, you don't have racism.

You might not like that the definition of the word "racism" is restricted to those who have societal power behind them, and I can sympathize with that perspective. If you're a White person, it might feel like a way of cheating for all the non-White racists out there. After all, bias and hatred are always nasty. They're always bad. They're always unfair. It might feel as though we're minimizing these incidents by not referring to them as "racism" when they're directed against White people.

However, the goal of the definition is not to minimize, but to acknowledge the huge, scientifically demonstrable gap between what it means when a White person is biased against ethnic minorities and what it means when an ethnic minority is biased against White people. Maybe you want to use the words differently, and maybe you can make a case for that. However, what you cannot do (at least, not while maintaining any tether to scientific reality) is pretend that the gap does not exist.

Of course, the metaphor of the two antisemitic German men is not perfect, because no metaphor is perfect. However, I have found it a useful way to illustrate, with a different context, a concept that some White people find very challenging. They might not be willing to see why White-on-Black hatred is (in terms of context, power, and privilege) a very different thing from Black-on-White hatred, but I find that they often can see how ridiculous, bizarre and potentially dangerous it is to pretend that antisemitism was the same in 1940s Germany as it is in 2020s Israel.

It's possible that you found the metaphor too stark. After all, you might say that the gap between the power, privileges, and protections afforded to White people and those afforded to ethnic minorities isn't really that big. Again, I can sympathize. No two examples of racism are exactly the same, and metaphors always come with compromises. Nonetheless, I suggest we quickly recap some of the many, many examples of power, privilege, and protection that contemporary society affords to White people: examples that have been proven through scientific studies that weed out any other potential explanations for their race-based favor.

A wealth of scientific research has consistently shown that, even when they are otherwise identical or equivalent to ethnic minorities, White people are interpreted as more professional, legitimate, and likeable (Bavishi et al. 2010), judged as more competent and hireable (Eaton et al. 2020), more likely to receive calls to interview or offers of employment (Heath and Di Stasio 2019; Quillian et al. 2017), more likely to receive support and positive expectations during their studies (Milkman et al. 2015), more likely to be taught well by their instructors (Jacoby-Senghor et al. 2016), more likely to be perceived as friendly, nice, and approachable, even among children (Perszyk et al. 2019; Rutland et al. 2005), more likely to be perceived as desirable romantic partners (Mendelsohn et al. 2014; West 2019a), and more likely to see themselves represented positively across a wide range of media (Choi and Reddy-Best 2018; T. L. Dixon 2007, 2008a, 2008b, 2017; Franklyn and West 2022; Gilmore and Jordan 2012; Milkie 1999). White people are also treated more politely and more helpfully in stores (Bourabain and Verhaeghe 2018; Schreer et al. 2009) and in medical establishments (Wisniewski and Walker 2020), more likely to receive high prices for things they sell (Ayres and Banaji 2011), and more likely to be offered life-saving treatments (Green et al. 2007). They are more likely to be given the benefit of the doubt when accused of wrongdoing (Hodson et al. 2005; West, Lowe et al. 2017), or even found guilty of wrongdoing (West and Lloyd 2017) or exonerated of prior perceived wrongdoing (Howard 2019).

Conversely, even when they are otherwise identical or equivalent to ethnic minorities, White people are also less likely to be suspected of being troublesome or challenging in the classroom (Gilliam 2016), less likely to be stopped and searched by the police (Bowling and Phillips 2007) or stopped when driving (Pierson et al. 2020), less likely to have their criminal record count against them (Pager 2003), less likely to be shot when unarmed (Correll et al. 2002, 2007) or when interacting with the police more generally (Edwards et al. 2019; Schwartz and Jahn 2020; Statista 2021), and less likely to have to endure the many indignities of constant microaggressions (West 2019b). None of this even mentions all the institutional and systemic racism that works in White people's favor: dress codes, hair discrimination, voting laws, redlining, and the skills-based British immigration system (Banks and Hicks 2016; Wilson and Brewer 2013). This list is long, and it is certainly not exhaustive.

All these examples of unfair privilege and favor add up. According to the British government's own figures, about 82% of the UK is White, but about 90% of its members of parliament are White. About 92% of the House of Lords is White. The number of business CEOs in the UK fluctuates all the time, but a 2022 article by James Cook in *Business Leader* reported that 98% of the CEOs in the UK were White. According to that article, what was the total number of Black chairpersons, CEOs, or CFOs in any FTSE 100 company at the time?

Zero.

According to the United States Census Bureau, non-Hispanic White people account for about 58.9% of the US population. However, they also account for 76% of American millionaires, 77% of Congress, and 88.8% of CEOs, CFOs and COOs in the United States. In almost every high-status position, in every well-paid profession, we reliably find the overrepresentation of White people—doctors, lawyers, judges, bankers, professors, producers, editors. Think of a sphere of power and influence and then check the relative populations therein. You will almost certainly find that, statistically, there are more White people in that sphere than there would be if race was not a factor. In this sense, the infrastructure of contemporary society works toward the relative power, privilege, and protection of White people to the relative exclusion of others. White people have a staggering amount of financial and political power, and they have been known to use it.

Taking a particularly chilling example of the dangerous use of that power, the Tuskegee Institute has records of 3,446 lynchings of Black people in the United States of America between 1890 and 1968, primarily by White people. From their research, the Equal Justice Initiative estimates that about 6,500 Black Americans were lynched between 1865 and 1950. If those were evenly spaced, that would mean that somewhere in America one or two Black people were lynched every week for eighty-five uninterrupted years. The Equal Justice Initiative has also assembled a record of the reasons for these lynchings, some of which are as petty and absurd as they are tragic. Frank Dodd was lynched in DeWitt, Arkansas, in 1916 for annoying a White woman by "talk[ing] insultingly" to her; Henry Patterson was lynched in Labele, Florida, in 1926 for asking a White woman for a drink of water; Ernest Green and Charlie Lang (both fourteen years old) were lynched in Shubuta, Mississippi, in 1942, because a White girl said they attempted to attack her. These Black men and boys were not found guilty of any crimes. These are not examples of White people defending themselves. These are chilling examples of White people using torture and death to remind everyone of their supposed superiority and the relative worthlessness of Black people's lives.

And things didn't end in 1968. The last official lynching to take place in the United States was that of nineteen-year-old Michael Donald, a Black teenager from Mobile, Alabama. This was in 1981. Nineteen eighty-one! The year the first laptop was available for sale. The year Prince opened for the Rolling Stones at the LA Coliseum. The year MTV premiered. The year Prince Charles married Lady Diana Spencer. A year not so far in the past at all. And this is just the list of official lynchings. The unofficial list includes people like Robert Fuller, a Black man found dead, hanging from a tree in Palmdale, California, in 2020. The authorities swiftly ruled it a suicide; the Black community was deeply unconvinced. Meanwhile, the inverse—lynchings of White people by Black people, the thing that Nick Conrad rapped about and that made so many people so very upset—are so vanishingly rare that for most decades, it's hard to find any numbers at all. Because of these jarring inequalities in both treatment and outcomes, inequalities that have existed for a long time and that persist, in one form or another, to the present day, a White person expressing negativity toward ethnic minorities is simply not the same as an ethnic minority expressing negativity toward White people.

With this in mind, let's return to Talk TV host Julia Hartley-Brewer and her concern that "the rules are different for different people, purely because of the color of their skin." Of course, in a simplistic way this equivalence seems to make sense. If you don't know (or prefer not to acknowledge) the realities of power or privilege, you might think that Adjoa Andoh's "terribly White" comment should be treated as an example of racism. However, if we seriously consider the realities of both historical and contemporary race-based asymmetries in power and privilege for even a moment, a simple truth emerges: if you want a world in which we're all, regardless of race, allowed to use the same words, and tell the same jokes, and complain about the makeup of the British royal family in the same way, then you first need to create a world in which we're all, regardless of race, treated equally. Currently, we have nothing of the sort, nothing that even approaches such a world. In the context of the real world, Hartley-Brewer's pretense that a White person complaining about a "terribly Black family" is exactly the same as a Black person complaining about a "terribly White family" is as disingenuous, ill-informed, and suspiciously motivated as a person pretending that Jewish people in 1942 Berlin and Jewish people in 2025 Israel are facing the same dangers, challenges, and infrastructural obstacles. I am concerned about such a person's beliefs, motivations, and desired goals.

Indeed, maintaining the pretense of equal victimhood almost always requires an aggressive disregard for the relevant context. And by this I don't just mean the wider context of the many, many ways in which White people are privileged, but also the more specific context of the situation at hand.

For example, let's revisit that Rasmussen Reports Poll, which found that 26% of Black people disagreed with the statement "It's OK to be White." There are many reasons to be suspicious of this result. For example, the New York-based company Cloud Research, who specialize in recruiting participants for surveys, noted that the Rasmussen poll only recruited 130 Black people and did not include any way of figuring out why Black people disagreed with that phrase. When Cloud Research replicated Rasmussen's survey, they did so with a larger number of Black people (1,000) and with added open-ended questions intended to figure out why Black people might disagree that "It's OK to be White."

Cloud Research's results did not replicate Rasmussen's at all. A much higher proportion of Black people (67%) agreed with the statement that "It's OK to be White." A much smaller proportion (less than 10%) disagreed. The rest were not sure. Furthermore, when the researchers asked why the participants disagreed with the statement, it certainly wasn't because the participants didn't like White people. Through a barrage of other questions, the researchers found that the participants generally liked White people a lot. They just didn't like the phrase "It's OK to be White." Specifically, they said things like, "It seems like a race debate baiting question and I don't like that."

And, of course, they were right! "It's OK to be White" isn't just some innocent, harmless phrase about the general all-rightness of being melanin-deficient. It has been a song title for White power bands since at least 2001, and a slogan used by White supremacist groups since at least 2005. It has been the center of an online trolling campaign since 2017, one that was designed to troll the "liberal left" and was quickly picked up and promoted by White supremacists. In that context, the finding that 10% or even 26% of Black people don't like the phrase is hardly interesting. "A small number of Black people don't like White supremacist slogan" is not the shocking finding that Scott Adams seems to think it is.

The same could be said about Adjoa Andoh's comments on the royal family. Kevin O'Sullivan might have a White family, but King Charles III does not. He has a mixed family. His daughter-in-law and two of his grandchildren are not White. And even if you are the biggest Meghan Markle hater in the world, the fact remains that the non-White portion of King Charles's family has been aggressively excluded and expunged. Saying that any British family, especially the royal family, was "terribly Black" would be ridiculous and racist, given that Black people are, individually and systemically, mistreated and rejected in the UK. However, saying that a family is "terribly White" when all the non-White elements of that family are conspicuously absent is something else entirely.

In 2013, the comedian Aamer Rahman summarized the issue with more wit than I ever could. Rahman often makes jokes about White people, and he's sometimes challenged about this, saying that it's a kind of "reverse racism." To this Rahman has responded that he does believe that reverse racism is possible, but that it requires a specific set of criteria. He'd have to build a time machine, go back about 400 years, convince the leaders of Africa, Asia, the Middle East, and South America to invade and colonize Europe, steal European lands and resources, set up a slave trade in which White people were exported to work on plantations in Asia, ruin Europe over the centuries so that White people would be desperate to migrate to the wealthier countries that Black and Brown people live in, but also set up systems that privilege Black and Brown people at every possible social, political, and economic opportunity, then deprive the majority of White people of any real hope of self-determination, all the while forcing White people to conform to Black and Brown beauty standards so that they end up hating the color of their own skin, eyes, and hair.

As Rahman put it: "If after hundreds and hundreds and hundreds of years of that, I got onstage at a comedy show and said, 'Hey, what's the deal with White people? Why can't they dance?' that would be reverse racism."

Chapter 9

Different Strokes by Different Folks
Racism against Various Ethnic Groups

Up to this point, this book has largely framed racism as a Black and White issue, by which I mean that racism has mostly been presented as something that White people do, and something that Black people have done to them. There have been some exceptions: racist arguments about Black people from Dinesh D'Souza (who is of Indian descent); examples of employment discrimination against Latinos; examples of anti-Muslim discrimination in crime and perceptions of guilt; a section on anti-Chinese racism specifically in the context of jokes and dehumanization; and mentions of antisemitism both past and present. The last chapter was also dedicated to (dispelling the notion of) "reverse racism," or racism against White people. Nonetheless, despite these examples, I have most frequently framed the targets of racism as Black people and the perpetrators of racism as White people.

To some extent, this framing of racism reflects the available research. For example, in Chapter 2, I mentioned two meta-analyses on racism in employment—one of which, by Quillian et al. in 2017, was conducted in the United States, and the other, by Heath and Di Stasio in 2019, in the United Kingdom—and both showed a significant advantage for White people over equally qualified ethnic minorities. The meta-analysis conducted in the US looked at discrimination against Black people and Latinos.

However, Latinos are generally not a recognized racial category in the United Kingdom, so the UK-based meta-analysis did not consider them as a target of discrimination. Rather, this UK-based meta-analysis looked at discrimination against people with White minority names (for example, Greek names), Chinese names, Indian names, Pakistani names, Black Caribbean names, and Black African names. As you can see, Black people show up as targets of discrimination in both meta-analyses, but the other ethnic groups do not. Black people are recognized as targets of discrimination in many countries, and this discrimination is reasonably similar across a number of countries. Thus, there is a larger pool of research on anti-Black racism than there is on racism against some other groups.

That's one reason for the framing of this book. But I suppose that a second reason is that I am a Black person. For the most part, I prefer to keep personal stories and individual experiences out of a book about science. As I said in Chapter 1, the plural of anecdote is not data, and my personal experiences no more prove or disprove the widespread existence of racism than you looking out the window proves anything about climate change. That said, while personal stories are not scientific proof, they can be powerful illustrations of effects that might seem dry or dull when presented only as numbers and graphs. For these illustrations, I find it best to draw from my own experiences as a Black person, having never been an East Asian, South Asian, or any other kind of person. I certainly have friends (and even family) of a wonderful kaleidoscope of ethnicities. But those are their experiences, not mine, and I'm not sure that I could do them justice.

Regardless of the explanation, the result of these editorial choices thus far might leave you wondering "What about everybody else?" At this point in the book, you have a good grasp of what White-on-Black racism looks like, what its effects are, and how we can know scientifically that it's there. But what about White-on-Indian racism? White-on-Chinese racism? White-on-Arab racism? Are these the same as White-on-Black racism? If not, are they merely different in degree, or are they also different in kind? Furthermore, do they vary between countries, or is racism generally consistent across culture and geographies?

Furthermore, while Chapter 8 did away with the idea of Black people being racist against White people, that doesn't mean that Black people, or any other ethnic minorities, can't be racist against a different ethnic group. So, what about Black-on-Indian racism? Indian-on-Chinese racism? Or Chinese-on-Black racism? Given the considerations of power and privilege from the last chapter, are these forms of bias generally considered racism, and what does science say about how they function?

And, speaking of racism between ethnic minorities, what about racism by members of a racial group against other members of the same racial group—Black people who are biased against Black people, Indian people who are biased against Indian people, Chinese people who are biased against Chinese people, and so on. Does this happen? And what are the scientific explanations for it? These are all complicated questions, the answers to which could take up several books on their own. However, now that I have established a firm foundation on the basics of racism, this chapter can start to tease out those complexities. But while I will try my best to do that, I warn you that there will be caveats. Some questions like, "Does racism still exist?" can be answered with something strong, simple, unwavering and monosyllabic (in this case, the answer is YES; see Chapters 2, 3, and 4). However, more complex questions like "How does racism differ between minoritized groups?" cannot be answered this way. When asked such a complex question, a scientist might feel the urge to hem and haw, to use phrases like "it depends." This isn't because we don't know, or because we're trying to hide the truth. Rather, it's because we're aware of all the conditionalities: the mental footnotes that should appear at the end of every seemingly simple response. In this chapter, I will take the advice often attributed to Einstein and "make everything as simple as possible, but not simpler." But I also need to make a deal with you. Throughout, you will need to remember that what I say has hidden layers of nuance, and that many of my responses are conditional rather than absolute. In return, I will promise not to overuse the phrase "it depends."

Do some minorities have it worse than others?

Yes, though it depends. Quite a lot of research reveals a hierarchy of racial responses, showing that some minority groups are reliably treated more negatively than others. For example, let's return to Quillian et al.'s 2017 meta-analysis of hiring discrimination in the USA. This meta-analysis looked at 55,842 applications submitted for 26,326 positions and examined participants' responses to two ethnic minority groups—Latinos and Black people—as well as their responses to White people. As you can surely guess by now, White people received the most favorable responses. However, what about Latinos and Black people? Quillian and colleagues found interesting differences here as well: specifically, that Black people were reliably treated worse than Latinos. White applicants received 36% more callbacks than equally qualified Black people, but only 24% more callbacks than equally qualified Latinos.

Other research has found similar patterns. As we saw in Chapter 2, in 2009 Pager and colleagues hired carefully matched Black, White, and Latino confederates to apply to 171 employers for potential jobs. Of course, the White applicant received the most favorable responses, getting a callback or a job offer 31% of the time. However, there were also significant differences between the Latino applicant (who got a callback or job offer 25.2% of the time) and the Black applicant (who got a callback or job offer 15.2% of the time). The Latino applicant's response rate was about 80% of the White applicant's response rate, while the Black applicant's response rate was less than half of the White applicant's response rate. In the researcher's own words, "These results show a clear racial hierarchy, with Whites in the lead, followed by Latinos, and Blacks trailing behind."

In 2020, in a similar study looking at applications to scientific academic departments, Eaton and colleagues, including myself, found a number of complex, intersecting results, but generally we found that White and East Asian applicants received more favorable responses, while Latino and Black applicants received less favorable responses. Fairly similar results were also found by Forrest-Bank and Jenson in 2015, when they surveyed 409 Asian, Latino, Black, and White Americans about their experiences of microaggressions. Unsurprisingly, the White participants experienced microaggressions the least, but it was interesting to see that they were followed by Asians, then Latinos, then Black people.

In the UK, researchers have found evidence of a racial hierarchy that is similar, though not exactly the same. In 2005, Rutland and colleagues investigated the racial biases of 136 White British children between three and five years old. They did this by giving the children cards with adjectives written on them and allowing the children to ascribe these adjectives to pictures of other children. These pictures were matched for irrelevant features (like age and attractiveness) but varied by ethnicity: White, Black, East Asian (e.g., Chinese or Japanese), and Asian Indian or South Asian (e.g., Indian or Pakistani). By comparing the number of good adjectives each picture received (kind, clever, hardworking) to the number of bad adjectives each picture received (mean, stupid, lazy), the researchers could work out a bias score for each minority group. What they found wasn't dissimilar to the findings from the US. Of course, White children were seen most favorably. However, in the authors' own words: "the Anglo-British children showed the most racial intergroup bias toward the African Caribbean racial group . . . significantly less intergroup bias was shown toward the Asian Indian and Far East Asian racial groups."

Similar patterns have also been found in different contexts. For example, in 2007 Bowling and Phillips analyzed data on approximately 840,000 stops made by the police of civilians in the UK. By comparing this dataset to that of the relative populations of different ethnicities in the UK, they found that, per 1,000 people, 15 White people in the UK were stopped and searched, compared to 27 Asian people, 90 Black people, and 23 people of other ethnicities. Again we see a racial pattern, with White people being treated the best, followed by other ethnicities (East Asians, South Asians), and finally Black people. So it seems as though we have our hierarchy of racism. To grossly oversimplify based on the data reviewed thus far, in order of treated best to treated worst, the hierarchy looks something like: White > East Asian > South Asian and Latino > Black.

However, this pattern can also change with the context. In 2012, Sadler, Correll, Park and Judd recruited 69 non-police civilian participants to take part in a computer-simulated first-person shooter task. This task was similar to the one I described in Chapter 3. Participants were presented with backgrounds in which a potential target would suddenly appear. This potential target was either armed with a gun or completely unarmed, and the participants were asked to react as quickly as possible, shooting the armed targets and indicating that they would not shoot the unarmed targets. That much should be familiar to you. What made the experiment interesting was that the targets also varied by race and could be White, Black, Latino, or (East) Asian. There are many ways to look at Sadler and colleagues' data. However, overall, they found that when it came to targets with guns, the participants were quickest to shoot Black people and slower to shoot targets of any other race. There were no other statistically significant differences between races. So, when it comes to getting shot with minimal consideration, the racial hierarchy might look like: White and East Asian and Latino > Black.

But not so fast. Sadler and colleagues repeated the experiment with 224 police officers, specifically to test whether the police—that is, the people who are in fact more likely to have guns on them—respond to different races in the same way as non-police civilians. The results of this study were similar, but not exactly the same. Like the non-police civilians, the police were also quickest to shoot Black people. However, in a bit of a surprise twist, they were actually slowest to shoot East Asians, not White people. So, when it comes to getting shot by the police, rather than by non-police civilians, the hierarchy might look like: Asian > White and Latino > Black.

Taking an example in yet another context, in 2019, as previously mentioned, I conducted a study of the dating preferences of about 3,500 White British people. Of course, I found that White people most strongly, and by a significant margin, preferred other White people. (At this point, I probably didn't need to say it, but let's be thorough.) However, after White people, the next in line were Black people, then East Asian people, then South Asian people.

Sometimes, the kinds of biases that different minorities face are qualitatively different. For example, while Black people are more likely than East Asian people or Latinos to be discriminated against for a job, Black people (in America at least) do not face the stigma of "foreignness" to the same degree. As Sanchez and colleagues explain in their 2018 findings, "Asian Americans and Latino Americans also share the experience of being denied their American identity and being assumed to be immigrants . . . this assumption of foreigner status occurs more frequently for Latinos and Asians compared with African Americans." Thus, while there are certainly ways in which Black people are treated worse than other ethnic minorities, there are also issues that these other ethnic minorities face that Black people face less frequently, or not at all.

The point here is that context matters, and that we have to include caveats if we want to give honest and accurate answers. Are White people treated better than people of other races? Yes, almost all the time. However, there are some specific instances in which other races (for instance, East Asians) might be treated slightly better (such as when police are making rapid "shoot or don't shoot" decisions). Are East Asians treated better than Black people? Yes, most of the time, particularly considering selection for interracial friendships, employment discrimination, or brutality and violence at the hands of both police and non-police civilians. However, there are certain specific instances—like dating preferences in the United Kingdom, or the assumption of foreignness in the US— when Black people are treated better than East Asians. Similar caveats can be offered for the relative treatment of South Asians and Latinos. Like I said, it depends.

Things get even more complicated. Thus far, I've been pretending that terms like "Black people" and "Asians" represent largely undifferentiated categories, the members of which are generally treated the same. But this isn't true.

Let's take another look at Di Stasio and Heath's 2019 CV

study. The researchers sent out applications for nearly 3,200 jobs while pretending that the applicants were of a variety of different origins: White Western Europeans, Eastern Europeans, South Americans and Caribbeans, Africans (Nigerians, Ethiopians, Somalians, and Ugandans), people from the Middle East and North Africa, people from South Asian countries like Pakistan and Bangladesh, and people from, as the authors put it, the "model minorities" group of countries: India, China, Japan, South Korea, and Vietnam.

With such a dazzling array of ethnicities, I could not possibly hope to describe all the results here and keep your interest. So, to summarize the most relevant findings: of course White people received the most favorable responses. That much, I'm sure, you already knew. However, not all White people are as White as other White people. While Western Europeans had the best response rate, Eastern Europeans (who are also White) had a lower response rate, one that fell below the "model minorities" (the Indian, Chinese, and other East Asian applicants). Similarly, not all Asians were treated the same way; the model minority Asian group received responses that were, in some cases, almost the same as the responses to the Western Europeans. However, the Pakistani and Bangladeshi Asian group received responses that were almost as negative as the responses to the South American and Caribbean group. And within the groups assumed to be Black, there was still significant variation. The researchers found, in their own words: "The discrimination faced by applicants with Pakistani and Nigerian backgrounds is alarming." So, even within racial groups, there are significant differences in discrimination, and the boundaries of discrimination for one racial group can bleed into the boundaries of another.

Similar patterns were also reflected in Heath and Di Stasio's

2019 meta-analysis* of racial discrimination in the UK between 1969 and 2017. They found "modest" discrimination against some White minority groups, "uncertainty" about the levels of discrimination faced by people with Chinese and Indian names, and similar levels of discrimination against people with Black Caribbean, Black African, and Pakistani names. So even in the context of employment discrimination, the hierarchy of racial discrimination is more complex than it may initially appear: perhaps White majority > White minority > Chinese, Indian and other "model minority" Asian > Black Caribbean and Pakistani > Black African. That hierarchy vaguely approximates the findings of decades of work in the UK, and it's not too different from work done in the US (apart from the notable omission of Latinos).

And that is about as far as I can go with the concept of a neatly defined hierarchy of racial prejudice. After this point, things get so very complex that no amount of "it depends" could save the chapter from falling into inexcusable oversimplification.

After all, all the research I've presented so far in this chapter was conducted within a very narrow cultural context. Though claims of similarity incite outraged protestations on both sides, there is no escaping the fact that contemporary British and contemporary American people share quite a lot of common ancestry and still have a lot of linguistic and cultural overlap. What happens, then, when we go slightly further afield to countries with different colonial histories, languages, and cultures?

In 2000, Leach and colleagues did just that. They analyzed the survey responses of 3,242 participants from Britain, France,

---

* A note here to avoid confusion and explain that the previous paragraph made reference to Di Stasio and Heath's 2019 CV study, which is not the same thing as Heath and Di Stasio's 2019 meta-analysis. As we've seen in earlier chapters, a meta-analysis is an analysis of multiple studies that provides higher-level insights than any single study could alone.

the Netherlands, and Western Germany toward six different ethnic minority groups: North Africans, Southeast Asians, Turkish people, Surinamese people, South Asian people, and Afro-Caribbeans. The design of the study is a little complex and it should be noted that participants from different countries answered questions about different subsets of people, so not all the data could be directly compared. The participants also answered three different types of questions: the first about the explicit endorsement of racist beliefs (such as, that the ethnic minority groups were simply inferior); the second about the participants' negative or positive attitudes toward the ethnic minority groups (I know it seems similar, but you can think others are inferior to you and still have a positive attitude toward them); and the third about perceived cultural differences between the White ethnic majority group and the ethnic minority groups.

With all that going on, there are a lot of potential results to discuss, but I will highlight the ones I find most relevant for this chapter. First, I should acknowledge that all participants were, as always, most favorable about White Europeans. The researchers also found that "a fair number of respondents actually endorsed explicit racism: 26% of the French, 30% of the Dutch, 38% of Western Germans and 41% of the British somewhat or strongly agreed with the contention that the out-groups were relatively inferior." This led the authors to note that racism, even the old, explicit kind, was "alive and well" across Western Europe.

But the most interesting findings, at least to me, concerned who the targets of the strongest racism were and how that differed across countries. British people, for example, expressed the most open racism toward Afro-Caribbeans (more than they expressed toward South Asians), but also expressed similar or slightly more positive attitudes toward Afro-Caribbeans than toward South Asians. On the other hand, French attitudes toward South Asians were similar to those of the British; while the standout targets of explicit racism, perceived cultural differences and less positive attitudes in France were the North Africans. Other research, such as that by Küpper and colleagues in 2010, has looked at multiple groups across multiple countries and has also found indications that British people are generally concerned about South Asian and Afro-Caribbean minorities, while the French are most concerned about North African minorities.

Incidentally, this introduces a whole new group to slot into the hierarchy of racism: a group that I have thus far avoided for several reasons. This group is sometimes referred to as "North African," as in Küpper et al. 2010, or "Middle Eastern and North African," abbreviated as MENA, as in Di Stasio and Heath 2019, but neither term fully captures what we mean when we refer to this group and the racial discrimination that targets them. For that reason, some papers, such as Park et al. in 2007, refer to them as "Arab-Muslims," or even more simply, just as "Muslims," which you'll find in Abrams et al. in 2021, Wallrich et al. in 2020, and West and Lloyd in 2017.

I know, and you know, that Muslim is a religious category, not a racial one. I know that Muslims can be White, Black, Chinese, Indian, or anything else. I also know that some countries, such as Senegal, have a majority Muslim population (over 90% of Senegalese people are Muslim), but that Senegalese people are not the people whom most Western people think about when they think about "Muslims." It's an imperfect term. However, I also know that when people discriminate against this group, they don't always do it on the basis of how many times a day they pray, or how much of the Qur'an they've read. The bias, like the biases against Black, East Asian and South Asian people, is often based on little more than what they look like and what their names are. For this reason, we often use the term "Muslim" as if it were a racial category, or at least similar enough to make the comparisons work, even though we know it's technically a religious one.

And where do Muslims sit in the racial hierarchy? Well, it depends. I've already mentioned research showing that they are the targets of particularly strong bias in France. There is also research from the UK (Banton et al. 2019; Turner and West 2011; West and Lloyd 2017), Germany (Wallrich et al. 2020), Sweden (Rooth 2010), and the US (Mange et al. 2012) that has found evidence of several types of anti-Muslim bias, including explicit racism, implicit racism, employment discrimination, lower perceptions of humanity, higher perceptions of guilt, threat and irrationality, and the fact that merely thinking about Muslims "makes Americans shoot faster," according to Mange et al. in 2012.

All this is to say that the evidence for the bias is there, but what's harder to pin down is exactly how much weaker or stronger this anti-Muslim bias is compared to racism against other groups. I've already mentioned research which found that British people are particularly negative toward Afro-Caribbeans, but not all research supports this hypothesis. For example, between December 2020 and June 2021, Professor Dominic Abrams and his research team surveyed 15,131 British participants to investigate their personal attitudes about three specific groups: White people, Black people and Muslims. Of course, the White people were most favorable about White people, but in second place came Black people and then last were Muslims, who were seen least favorably of all.

Do Muslims, then, come after Black people in the racial hierarchy? Maybe. It depends. To illustrate: in 2023, Green and colleagues compared the explicit bias scores and implicit bias scores (taken from their Implicit Association Tests) of almost 2 million (exactly 1,973,583) participants. The study included measures of bias against four groups—Black people, Arab-Muslims, Asians, and Native Americans—but for the purpose of this section, we'll only focus on the anti-Black and anti-Muslim prejudice scores. Interestingly, Green and colleagues found that the relative strengths of anti-Black and anti-Muslim prejudice depended on whether the prejudice in question was explicit or implicit. Specifically, when only explicit prejudice was considered, Green et al.'s participants (similar to the British participants of Abrams and colleagues in 2021) reported higher levels of anti-Muslim prejudice than anti-Black prejudice. However, when only implicit prejudice was considered, the participants showed higher levels of anti-Black prejudice than anti-Muslim prejudice.

Further complicating the picture is the fact that prejudice can vary in consistency as well as strength. For example, in 2022 Thijssen and colleagues analyzed the outcomes of 94 employment discrimination experiments between 1973 and 2016, experiments that covered some 240,000 job applications carefully controlled to be equivalent or identical except for the demographics of the person who was applying. Interestingly, Thijssen and colleagues found that levels of anti-Black discrimination were generally higher than levels of anti-Muslim discrimination, but also that anti-Black discrimination was a lot more variable: in some countries it was significantly higher than in others. Anti-Muslim discrimination was overall lower, but also much more consistent, which would explain why sometimes you find that Black people are treated worse and sometimes you find that Muslims are treated worse.

But there is still another complication. It turns out that, at least some of the time, maybe Middle Eastern and North African Muslims aren't ethnic minorities at all. Maybe they're White. By this I don't mean that sometimes unambiguously White people are born into or convert to Islam (although that certainly happens). What

I mean is that people who are generally regarded as belonging to this Middle Eastern and North African group are sometimes ambiguous in their Whiteness or ethnic minority-ness.

Explicit examples should help. Do you think Turkish people are White? Are Iranians White? Are Egyptians White? These are questions to which there are no definitive answers. Indeed, if we are to be scientifically rigorous, we have to acknowledge that, biologically, there's no such thing as White people. Or, for that matter, Black people, or (and this is very easy for you to accept if you're from the UK) Latinos.

I am not a biologist. However, people with the appropriate degrees and peer-reviewed scientific publications in biology (as discussed by Smedley and Smedley in 2005) have been very clear that race is not a biological category, it's a socially constructed one. If you'd like to read more about that, I'd strongly recommend the book *How to Argue with a Racist* by British geneticist Adam Rutherford. In it, he exposes many of the myths we tend to accept about the biological nature of race. He clarifies that genuine scientific research has never indicated a specific number of biological human "races" (other than one), has never clarified what the boundaries between these races may be, or even affirmed that race, as it is colloquially understood, has any tangible biological referent at all. He expertly debunks the supposedly genetic explanations for a host of "racial" differences in performance on everything from IQ tests to the 100-meter dash. As he puts it in his introduction, "when properly understood, modern genetics refutes any meaningful biological basis for racial categories." He further states at the end of his first chapter that "skin color is . . . a superficial route to an understanding of human variation and a very bad way to classify people. Our view of reality, so profoundly limited, has been co-opted into a deliberate political lie." Race is a social construction, not a biological reality.

So, since no race is "real" in a biological sense, there is no "real" answer to the question of whether Turkish people, Egyptians, or Iranians are White. They're White if we all agree that they're White. They're not White if we agree that they're not White.

This might sound incredibly silly, but it's a well-documented issue. Neda Maghbouleh, associate professor of sociology and research chair in migration, race, and identity at the University of Toronto, has written a book about just this issue, titled *The Limits of Whiteness: Iranian Americans and the Everyday Politics of Race*. As her book explains, sometimes Iranians are White. The US federal government officially lists them as "White," alongside people from Lebanon, Egypt, and a number of other MENA countries. However, in everyday life, they're not treated as though they're White, and they often don't think of themselves as White—at least, not all of them, and definitely not all of the time.

To demonstrate, in 2022, Maghbouleh and her research team surveyed several hundred Americans, some of whom were MENA and some of whom were non-Hispanic White people. They asked participants their opinions about whether certain target individuals were White, or whether they were something else. Despite non-negligible levels of disagreement, they found that generally, "both non-MENA Whites and MENAs classify MENA-related traits, including ancestry, names, and religion, as non-White ethnoracial markers." In other words, White people don't think MENAs are White, and MENAs don't think they're White either. And, since race is a social construct, if people don't think you're White, you're not White.

Indeed, concerning their own racial categorization, "when MENA is offered as a category, only 10% [of MENAs] continue to exclusively choose White. The majority instead choose MENA." The researchers also found that experiences of discrimination are part of the reason why MENAs don't see themselves as White—White people don't treat MENAs the way they treat other White people. Hence, MENAs don't really care what the census forms say. Maybe they're "Brown." Maybe they're "Muslim." But whatever they are, from the way they're treated, they're definitely not White.

Unfortunately, as the authors of the paper explain, this confusion about their status as White people or ethnic minorities can make it very, very difficult to form a clear picture of the discrimination that is happening against them. In the researchers' own words: "The US government's classification of Middle Eastern and North African (MENA) Americans as White means there is no direct way to numerically count members of this group in official statistics . . . any potential disparities and inequalities faced by MENA Americans remain hidden." So are they treated better or worse than other ethnic minorities? So far, it's been very hard to get reliable data to answer that question; so you can see why any attempt to neatly slot Muslims into the racial hierarchy is just a step too far into the realm of oversimplification.

There are so many other things I haven't mentioned. For example, I have barely acknowledged the existence of mixed people, an enormous omission considering their large numbers and the rapid rate of growth of the mixed population. I have only very briefly mentioned racism against Native Americans, despite the vast and horrific racism perpetuated against them (if you're interested in that, I would strongly recommend the work of Professor Stephanie Fryberg). I have also not discussed people like Polynesian or Pacific Islanders, whom some people consider to be Asian-ish. I have only once mentioned Australian Aboriginals, whom some people consider to be Black-ish. And that's not to mention the quagmire of Jewish racial identity. So many books, chapters, and articles have been written on exactly the same question: "Are Jews White?" by Atiya Husain; "Are Jews White? Yes.

and No" by Dave Schechter; "Are Jews White? Or, The History of the Nose Job" by Sander L. Gilman; "Are Jews White? It's a Mistake Even to Ask" by Gershom Gorenberg.

While it is important to flag them up, I will not be tackling those thorny questions here. Each of them could be (and some have been) a book unto themselves, and no number of caveats would allow me to do them justice in the space of a chapter. Besides, in all this talk about racial hierarchies and who is or isn't White, we've lost sight of something big. I have only really considered how White people respond to different groups of ethnic minorities. What about the ethnic minorities themselves? How do they respond to each other?

Racism between ethnic minorities

In 2020, in an interview with *Dalit Camera* reproduced on *Monthly Review Online*, Arundhati Roy, the well-known author of one of my favorite books, *The God of Small Things*, remarked that "Indian racism toward Black people is almost worse than White peoples' racism." In the same interview, she mentioned India's caste-based culture, "obsession" with lighter skin, and films in which the dumb, savage villains are all Black Africans.

None of Roy's observations were a surprise to me. I've lived in a few majority White countries in my life—the United Kingdom, the United States, France—and I have had many, many racist experiences in my travels. Nonetheless, despite the relatively higher number of encounters with White people, the most open, vicious, and unrepentant racism I've ever experienced has been from South Asian people. Everything from the shopkeeper who is all smiles and "sir" and "madam" with White customers but then barks rude orders at Black customers, to the waiter who fawns over the White people at the table but refuses to take orders from the Black ones, or the gas station attendant who demands that you hold everything you've picked up high enough to make sure "you're not stealing anything." When my relatively light-skinned son was born, a little South Asian girl in a store came over to my wife to tell her in no uncertain terms, "I love White babies," but then fled to her mother once I picked him up to warn her that the "scary man was doing something to the baby."

But anti-Black racism isn't restricted to South Asians. In 2001, Gorey conducted an analysis of the racial attitudes and beliefs of 8,808 American adults of various races. Among his results was the finding that "76.2 percent of [East] Asians and 66.8 percent of Hispanics say that blacks prefer to live on welfare." In 2021, in a letter addressed to the Department of Justice in the US, the president of the Asian American Coalition for Education, Yukong Zhao, wrote that "Asian Americans have been historically discriminated against in American society. Nevertheless, many of us have achieved our American dream mainly through hard work, as well as an emphasis on education and family values, rather than political favoritism or privilege." This was such an obvious dig at Black people that to call it thinly veiled would be an insult to veils everywhere. Though the letter addressed many real and terrible examples of anti-Asian prejudice, one of its clear intentions was to contrast the supposed East Asian strategy of dealing with discrimination in America (hard work, discipline, family values) with the apparent Black strategy of dealing with that same issue (laziness, handouts, special favors, and not taking care of their children).

This stance is not unique to the Asian American Coalition for Education. In 2023, Liu and colleagues analyzed the legal documents of several (East) Asian American activist groups. They found that these groups reliably oppose policies like affirmative action, particularly if they perceive these policies to be aiding Black people. To explain their opposition, the groups would often lean on the combined narratives of anti-Asian discrimination (Asians face discrimination too, not just Blacks) and Asian exceptionalism ("but we overcome discrimination by working hard and having good family values, unlike Blacks").

But there are also examples of anti-Asian racism (both East and South Asian) by Black people. In a 2021 article in the *Guardian*, Pulitzer-winning author Viet Thanh Nguyen reflected on his experiences of racism from both Black and White people while living in France; experiences of racial slurs, or being mocked with a "ching-chong" accent. In 2022, an East Asian TikTok user in the US named Stephanie (handle: @lycheemarteenee) posted a video of a Black woman shouting at her: "Go eat your dog with some rice . . . go back to your country . . . go do some nails or some feet or something, bitch." On a larger scale, I personally know people whose families were devastated by President Idi Amin's expulsion of Indians from Uganda in 1972.

That last example offers an excellent opportunity to return to the definition of "racism" as "prejudice plus power" (see Tatum 1999). It's true that most scholars would not see prejudice against White people by Black people in the UK or the US as "racism." This is because White people hold vastly disproportionate power in these societies and therefore can be victims of prejudice, but not of racism. However, prejudice against Indians by Black people in 1970s Uganda can legitimately be called "racism" because, in 1970s Uganda, Black people held far more social and political power than Indians did. This enabled Black people to do terrible things to the Indians and face relatively few repercussions. In a similar sense, prejudice against Black people by Indians in India can also be called "racism," because in India, Indians have the disproportionate amount of power. The people who have the power might change, but the understanding of racism as "prejudice plus power" remains the same. This discussion can get a bit more complex, but it's worth acknowledging that, in that sense, anybody can theoretically be "racist"; there is nothing fundamentally special about White people. It just happens that, due to a number of significant events over the past four centuries or so, White people commit a disproportionate amount of prejudice and hold a disproportionate amount of power in a large number of societies.

However, when it comes to bias between ethnic minorities in majority White countries, scholars still refer to this as "racism," but for a different reason. As Professor Jennifer Ho, president of the Association for Asian American Studies, explained in a 2020 essay entitled "Anti-Asian Racism, Black Lives Matter, and COVID-19," even when it's being used by ethnic minorities against other ethnic minorities, racism in majority White countries still serves the "ideology of White supremacy," in that it still elevates and privileges White people—and, as I will explain in more detail later in this chapter, operates in the same way and according to the same stereotypes that White people use to mistreat us.

Perhaps an example from my own life would help. I wish I could say that I have lived a life devoid of anti-Asian racism, but regrettably I can't. Once, in my twenties, in the US, I went to see a very artsy theater-dance performance, the kind in which they use foreign languages and symbology with no translation or explanation. In one scene, a large symbol that appeared to be either Chinese hanzi or Japanese kanji appeared in the middle of the stage. I gently tapped the East Asian–looking man sitting to my right on the shoulder and asked him if he knew what that symbol meant. He responded with the strongest and most indignant American accent I have ever heard: "Excuuuse me, sir? No, I do not!" I realized that I had, in line with White supremacist ideas, equated his race with foreignness: exactly the kind of racism identified by wider social-psychological research.

I really don't enjoy this part of the book, where I have to talk about ethnic minorities' racism against each other. I feel compelled to point out that there are many, many examples of positive inter-actions between ethnic minority groups. For example, Lloret-Pineda and colleagues in 2022 identified several examples of Black and Muslim solidarity with Chinese people as they were experiencing vicious racism in the wake of the coronavirus pan-demic. There are also several examples of Indian and wider South Asian identification with and explicit support for the Black Lives Matter movement, including the groups South Asians for Black Lives and the Alliance of South Asians Taking Action. Sadiq Khan, the Muslim mayor of London, has joined the Jewish Labor Move-ment and accused the Labor Party of being "far too slow" to tackle antisemitism. Khan has also been outspoken about "the anti-Black racism, injustice and other systemic inequalities" in British soci-ety. Clearly ethnic minorities can and do work together. We often like each other. We intermarry. We build shared communities. Also, though I know that this is the kind of thing that racist people say, some of my best friends are Jewish. Some of my best friends are Indian, Chinese, or Muslim. At least one of my friends is all three.

Still, as much as I hate writing about it, there is no escaping the uncomfortable fact that ethnic minorities are also racist toward each other. I hate writing about it because I can imagine a certain type of racist White person using this section as a shield for their own racist behaviors: "See," they'll say, "they're all racist against each other, so why should they expect anything else from us?" Never mind all the evidence that White people receive significant, unearned advantages over all ethnic minorities. Never mind White people's overrepresentation in almost all spheres of wealth, power, and influence. I still worry that this chapter will be used to support the misleading notion that racism is much the same, regardless of who it's coming from.

I also hate writing about this because it's embarrassing, because I'd prefer a world in which a lifetime of experiencing racism made you too aware of what it is and how it works for you to ever turn it against someone else. Sadly, however, this is not the world we live in. And science isn't about the world as we'd prefer it to be, it's about the world as it actually is.

Recall the experiment by Milkman and colleagues in 2015, in which they sent emails to over 6,500 professors at top universities in the US pretending to be White, Black, Hispanic, Indian, or Chinese prospective students. Of course, the researchers found that the fictional White prospective students received more favorable responses than any of the others. That should not surprise you at this point. However, what may surprise you is that "the representation of women and minorities and discrimination were uncorrelated." In other words, having more ethnic minority (and women) professors did not change the rate at which the apparent ethnic minority students were discriminated against. Quite the contrary: ethnic minority professors showed very much the same patterns of discrimination as the White professors did. Or, as Professor Jennifer Ho might put it, their patterns of discrimination also served the ideology of White supremacy by privileging and elevating White students. The authors state their conclusions plainly: "representation does not reduce bias and . . . there are no benefits [to] Black or Hispanic students of contacting same-race faculty."

In 2022, Gran-Ruaz and colleagues used the Black–White Implicit Association Test to investigate the biases of 450,185 people across the USA and Canada. They were particularly interested in whether implicit anti-Black bias varied between the two countries and whether it varied depending on the ethnicity of the person doing the test. The answer to both questions was largely "no," though there were a few exceptions. Average implicit bias scores for Black people in both America and Canada, Native Hawaiian/Pacific Islanders from Canada, and American Indian/Alaskan Native participants from Canada, all fell within the "neutral" range. However, every other group—White people, East Asian people, multiracial people, Hispanic people, and South Asian people—had significant levels of pro-White (or anti-Black) implicit bias. White people's scores generally weren't that different from those of the ethnic minorities. The sad reality is that ethnic minorities see ethnic minorities much the same way that White people do.

There is, of course, one notable exception. Though this statement comes with significant caveats (that I will address more fully in the next section), we (ethnic minorities) do tend to like *ourselves*, at least more than we tend to like other ethnic minorities. For example, in 2021, Bell and colleagues surveyed a diverse group of 4,350 White, Black, Asian, and Latino middle school students to investigate how they felt about both their own ethnic group and all the other ethnic groups. No prizes for guessing that White students preferred White people most of all (followed, after a significant gap, by Black people, Latino people and then Asian people, all a bit clumped together). You should have been able to predict that. But what about the ethnic minority students. Whom did they prefer?

With so many participant groups and target groups, the results are complex, but the general summary was that every group liked themselves the best, followed by White people, and then by the other ethnic minorities. So, Asian students liked Asian people the best, followed by White people. Black students liked Black people the best, followed by White people. Latino students liked Latino people the best, followed by White people. White people were everyone's second choice: not as favored as their own group, but seen more favorably than any other ethnic groups.

In 2009, Gross found similar results in a study of own-race bias in facial recognition. This bias has been well established in psychological research and represents a tendency for individuals to perceive the faces of people belonging to their own race as distinct and easily differentiated, while they see the faces of people belonging to other races as largely homogeneous. Put less scientifically, it's the reason why you hear some White people claim that "all Asians look the same" or "all Blacks look the same." Incidentally, and since we're talking about racism between ethnic minorities, this effect is also referenced in the film *Rush Hour 2*, in which Inspector Carter (Black, and played by Chris Tucker) accidentally punches his friend Inspector Lee (Chinese, and played by Jackie Chan) in the face. By way of apology, Carter explains to Lee that "Sorry, man, all y'all look alike."

While own-race facial recognition bias is a well-known effect, Gross wanted to investigate how this bias varied across individuals of different races. Gross recruited 248 participants between the ages of eighteen and twenty-three, 89 of whom were White, 35 of whom were Black, 51 of whom were East Asian, and 73 of whom were Hispanic. All participants completed a number of tasks to test their recognition of faces belonging to people of their own race and to people of the other three races.

Unsurprisingly, White people recognized White faces better than they recognized those of any other race. But what about the other participants? Well, similar to Bell and colleagues' middle school students, ethnic minorities recognized faces belonging to their own race and to White people best, followed by those belonging to other races. Specifically, Hispanic participants recognized Hispanic and White faces better than Asian and Black faces; Black participants recognized Black and White faces better than Asian and Hispanic faces; and Asian participants recognized Asian and White faces (and, to some extent, Latino faces) better than Black faces. Even in the realm of facial recognition, ethnic minorities show the least bias against their own group and White people, and more bias against members of other minority groups.

These results may be disheartening, but perhaps they should not be surprising. Ethnic minorities often watch the same television, read the same newspapers and browse the same magazines as the White people in their countries. In more ways than most people realize, the media constantly bombard us with dehumanizing stereotypes of ethnic minorities—South Asian people who are comical, insular, superstitious, and either disastrously poor or some kind of mid-level shop assistant; East Asian people who are foreign, inscrutable, obsessed with honor, and given to eating weird food; Black people who are lazy, dumb, hyper-aggressive, criminal, and always looking for a handout.

In collaboration with Caryn Franklin MBE, a former fashion editor of *i-D* magazine and former host of BBC television's *The Clothes Show*, I've written a whole book about bias in the media, so I won't go into detail here. Suffice it to say that even the most seemingly innocuous sources fill our heads with ideas about the beauty, brilliance and morality of White people to the detriment of our perceptions of everyone else. As a Black person, I might be taken in by the biased representations of others, like South Asian and East Asian people, but at least I have myself to use as a counterpoint to the biased representations of Black people, and that shields me from absorbing negative ideas about myself.

Or does it?

With that question, we must come to my very least favorite part of this book: the part about racism by ethnic minorities against themselves.

They make us hate ourself and love they wealth

One of the most influential psychological experiments of all time was published in 1947 by the husband and wife psychologist team Kenneth and Mamie Clark, with the unassuming title "Racial identification and preference in Negro children." It is one of our field's best known studies and has been revisited countless times on television, in newspapers, in court cases and in follow-up research that has replicated and extended its findings. Even if you have come across it before, the details of the study are important, so I will briefly revisit them here.

In the 1940s, the Clarks were interested in how Black children developed a sense of racial identification, both in terms of knowledge (do Black children know that they're Black?) and in terms of racial attitudes (how do Black children feel about Black people?). To explore these questions, they conducted a series of experiments on many Black children in America.

These experiments used slightly different methodologies, but all revolved around a similar theme. For example, some of the studies involved questionnaires about identification and attitudes. Other studies involved letting the children select a crayon (light, medium or dark) to color in an image of themselves; sometimes an image of themselves as they actually were, sometimes an image of themselves as they would like to be. All the Clarks' experiments produced interesting and impactful results. However, the most famous study by far is the doll study. In this study, 253 "Negro"*

---

* This is the language the Clarks used in the 1940s, so I am replicating it here. Similarly, throughout this chapter, because it was the language the experiments used at the time, I will also use words like "colored" to refer to ethnic minorities, even though these terms are widely considered very rude today.

children between the ages of three and seven were given a choice, or rather, a series of choices. Specifically, each of the children was presented with "four dolls, identical in every respect save skin color."* Two of the dolls were "brown with black hair" and two were "white with yellow hair." In all other ways, the dolls were the same.

After showing the children the dolls, the experimenters made eight requests to the children. The first four of these were designed to determine how the children felt about White people versus Black people. These were (1) "Give me the doll that you would like to play with/like best"; (2) "Give me the doll that is the nice doll;" (3) "Give me the doll that looks bad;" (4) "Give me the doll that is a nice color." Questions 5, 6, and 7 were designed to check whether the children understood racial categorizations: (5) "Give me the doll that looks like a White child"; (6) "Give me the doll that looks like a colored child"; (7) "Give me the doll that looks like a Negro child." And, finally, question 8 was designed to check whether the children understood their own racial identity: (8) "Give me the doll that looks like you."

The Clarks found that the children were generally very good at racial categorization. Despite their young age, 94% of them gave the experimenters the White doll when they asked for the White doll, and 93% of them gave the experimenters the brown doll when asked for the colored doll. As the authors said, "these results indicate a clearly established knowledge of racial difference." Accuracy fell a bit when the experimenters asked for the "Negro" doll. Only 72% of the children correctly chose the brown doll in this case, which the experimenters attributed to a less well developed concept of "Negro" as opposed to "White" or "colored."

---

* The Clarks were using "skin color" here to refer to race. The dolls were also different in hair color.

But the real drop in accuracy came when the experimenters asked the children to give them "the doll that looks like you." Then, only 66% of the children gave the experimenters the brown doll, while 33% gave them the white doll. There were many potential explanations for this, including some of the "Negro" children being much lighter skinned than the others and potential motivational reasons, which we'll come to.

The most interesting findings, however, concern the children's racial preferences. In their responses to every single relevant question, it was clear that these Black children preferred the white doll to the brown doll. Whether it was the doll that the children "would like to play with" (67% vs. 32%), the doll that "is the nice doll" (59% vs. 38%) or the doll that "is a nice color" (60% vs. 38%), the children reliably picked the white doll more frequently than the brown one. They only picked the brown doll more frequently when they were asked to identify the doll that "looks bad." In this case, they only picked the white doll 17% of the time, and the brown doll 59% of the time (the rest of the time, they didn't pick either).

The results of the experiment were clear: even at a very young age, Black children already preferred White to Black. They had already internalized their supposed inferiority. This was made all the more explicit when the experimenters asked the children why they preferred the white doll ("'cause he's pretty," "'cause he's White") or disliked the brown doll ("'cause he's ugly," "'cause him Black"). And, even at this age, the children were wrestling with the psychological consequences of disliking themselves. One of the children said, when he selected the brown doll as the one that looked like him, "I burned my face and made it spoil." Another child was eager to explain that he was actually White: "I look brown because I got a suntan in the summer." Two of the children ran out of the room, "unconsolable, convulsed in tears," when they were required to answer the self-identification question. They didn't want to be the brown doll.

That's all depressing stuff, but surely things are better now? Surely, if we repeated the experiment in the 2020s, we would find something completely different—wouldn't we?

Sadly, we would not. In 2021, Sturdivant and Alanis conducted a partial replication of the Clarks' doll experiment. They made a few changes. They wanted to see how children behaved "in the context of their everyday lives, rather than examining the way children react to an experimental situation." Hence, rather than asking the children a series of questions about which was the "nice doll," the "doll you would like to play with" or the "doll that looks bad," they simply left a "White doll," a "Latina doll" and two "Black dolls" in the play area of a preschool classroom and observed how the children (58% of whom were Black) responded to them.

Despite the passage of seventy-four years, an actual lifetime since the 1947 study, Sturdivant and Alanis found very similar results. The Black children overwhelmingly rejected the Black dolls, only playing with them when no other dolls were available. When given the first pick of the doll they'd like to play with, they sometimes chose the Latina doll and sometimes chose the White doll, but never chose the Black doll. When only Black dolls were left, the children opted to share or fight over the White and Latina dolls rather than play with the Black ones. When even that wasn't an option, they simply gave up on playing with dolls altogether. Even when they clearly expressed a desire to play with a doll, if only Black dolls were available, they decided to play with something else entirely.

In a chilling new twist on the findings by Clark and Clark, Sturdivant and Alanis also found a pattern of mistreatment of the Black dolls. The children would step on the Black dolls. They would try to remove their heads. Sometimes they would pick up a Black doll, put it in a toy cooking pot and turn up the knob on the stove. "I'm gonna cook my baby in the pot," a Black child gleefully declared. They would poke the Black dolls in the eye, or toss them in the sink and cover them with food. None of these violent play behaviors were observed with the White dolls or Latina dolls. As far as racial identity and racial attitudes were concerned, little had changed since the original study in 1947. As the authors concluded, "young children are aware of race and are integrating racist messages."

Other research has shown that this pro-White bias stems from an internalization of the idea that White people are higher in status than Black people. Recall the 2012 study by Newheiser and Olson explored in Chapter 8—the one in which they found that seven- to eleven-year-old White American children showed a strong implicit bias in favor of White people, but that seven- to eleven-year-old Black American children showed no bias either way. While this is a good general summary of the results, it's not the complete story. The researchers also asked the children about other attitudes they might have: how much value they put on status, how much they liked rich people versus poor people. When they included these data in their analyses, Newheiser and Olson found that the more a Black child valued status and wealth, the stronger their preferences were for White people over Black people.

Incidentally, this effect is not just limited to majority White countries. In 2022, Marshall and colleagues surveyed 214 children in rural Uganda, children between the ages of five and twelve who only had limited, if any, contact with people from any other country. They asked the children a series of questions to investigate their beliefs about status (Who has lots of toys and new clothes? Who gets to pick the games that everyone plays?) and their racial attitudes (Who do you want to play with? This kid or this kid?). The researchers found that "the Ugandan children overwhelmingly exhibited a pro-White bias; despite themselves being Black, they chose to play with White children over Black children 78% of the time." They also found that this pro-White preference was driven by status-oriented beliefs: "the higher participants placed White over Black targets on the status ladder, the greater their pro-White racial bias."

And, of course, internalized racism is not a problem that is limited to Black people. Significant bodies of research, including, for example, work by Harper and Choma in 2019 and Liu et al. in 2022, have been published on internalized anti-Indian and anti-Chinese racism. As I mentioned earlier, we are all, even in non-majority-White countries, frequently fed messages about the superiority of White people. Here, as in the previous chapters, I have merely focused more on the internalized anti-Black racism because it's the kind I can most easily relate to my own experiences.

And I can certainly relate it to my own experiences: incidents of Black-on-Black racism in my own life fill me with a combination of rage and shame. I think of the many Black security guards who have followed me around stores, fully convinced of our apparent shared criminality, sometimes ignoring White people who took the opportunity to shoplift while all eyes were elsewhere. I think of the Black friend who goes on at length about the beauty of light skin, light eyes, and straight hair. I think of the times White friends have visited me in Jamaica and how I have grimaced in humiliation when the Black waiters and servers have ignored me, my Black sisters and my Black friends, interested only in making sure that my White friends found everything to their liking. I recall visiting African countries—proud, anti-colonial countries that, on paper, are taking charge of their own destinies—and watching in shock as people have all but bowed and scraped in front of White visitors, deferring to them, calling them by titles they neither had nor deserved and allowing them to saunter unimpeded through checkpoints and security gates, all while treating Black people, people who looked like themselves, with contempt. I recall the feeling of weighty disappointment when I heard them ask, upon seeing me traveling with my White wife, how they could get a White person to rescue them from poverty, as I so clearly had done.

I know the explanations. I know the effects of the media and of the stratified society in which we live, even on a global scale. I know the history of European colonialism. Still, these experiences of internalized racism affect me more deeply than anything any White person has ever done. Only in them do I ever get a glimpse of despair. Only then do I wonder whether this is the kind of problem that can ever be fixed. They are reminders of how deep, how intractable the shackles of racism can be, infesting not only our infrastructure, not only our financial and political outcomes, not only our friendships and relationships, but even our very minds. It's only when I see how effectively so many of us have been taught to hate our own reflections that I ever think: God, they truly have beaten us. We really have lost.

But we haven't lost. Not really. Having fallen into the depths of despair, it is time to start climbing back out. The system of racism is vicious, enormous and ubiquitous. But it is neither invincible nor inevitable. We created it. And, if we wish, we can destroy it.

PART IV
DEALING WITH RACISM, SCIENTIFICALLY

Chapter 10

The More You Ignore Me, the Closer I Get
The Color-Blind Approach

In 2005, in an interview on the American television show *60 Minutes*, Mike Wallace (White and Jewish) asked Morgan Freeman (Black), "How are we going to get rid of racism?," to which Morgan Freeman responded, "Stop talking about it. I'm going to stop calling you a White man and I'm going to ask you to stop calling me a Black man. I know you as Mike Wallace. You know me as Morgan Freeman." In the same interview, Freeman also expressed his distaste for Black History Month, asking Wallace, "When is Jewish History Month? . . . Do you want one?" And, when Wallace inevitably said, "No," Freeman quickly responded, "Well, neither do I."

From this interview, it appears that Morgan Freeman endorses what social psychologists call "color blindness." As I put it in an article that I published in 2021 with Katy Greenland and Colette van Laar, color blindness reflects "the belief that race should not and does not matter." It is an approach to dealing with race and racism that explicitly discourages (as Freeman did) any reference to racial categories or any activity that acknowledges racial categories.

This line of reasoning resonated with many people, and it seemed to be coming from a trustworthy source. As well as being Black, Morgan Freeman is also a good actor, a very wealthy person, and the owner of a mellifluous voice that lends narrative flair to even the most mundane of stories. Freeman gives off the air of being successful, knowledgeable, and wise. Thus, his support for color blindness made it seem more credible, even to ethnic minorities, than it might have if it had come from someone less impressive, or less Black. I mean, if Morgan Freeman was in favor of color blindness (and he played God in the film *Bruce Almighty*), then who were we to disagree?

And, of course, Morgan Freeman is not alone. Coleman Hughes is an African American author, writer, and commentator. With his sharp clothes and rugged beard, Hughes has the look of someone on a "Young, Gifted, and Black" poster. Like Morgan Freeman, he has also expressed explicit support for the color-blind approach. In a 2022 article in the *Free Press*, he argued that color blindness was the best perspective for the individual to adopt about race, the best approach for a multiracial society, and the best way to combat the types of racism that actually matter.

Dr. Ben Carson is a famous American neurosurgeon, a fine upstanding Christian, and a former Black presidential candidate (he's still Black, he's just not running for president anymore). Like Freeman and Hughes, Dr. Carson also supports color blindness. In a 2022 article he wrote for Fox News, he pointed out his desire to put to rest "the very idea that we should be divided based on race at all," claiming that this was based on the same desires as those of Rev. Dr. Martin Luther King Jr. (whom everybody now likes, and who was also Black). Remember how the good reverend had a dream of a nation where "an individual is judged based on the content of his character, not the color of his skin"? When it comes to race and racism, what higher aspiration could any of us have than that?

Like Dr. Carson, many other politicians and authority figures have used that very line from Dr. King's "I Have a Dream" speech in support of a color-blind approach to race relations (regardless of whether Dr. King himself would support such an approach). This list includes, among others, US Representative Charles Eugene "Chip" Roy, Canadian Conservative Party MP Maxime Bernier, and Dennis Prager, a radio talk-show host and founder of PragerU, the famously conservative non-university that's pretending to be a university. Even if they don't use Martin Luther King Jr.'s words to do so, other politicians have also expressed support for color blindness. For example, in 2020, American politician Peter Navarro (who is White) claimed, "I live my life in a race-blind world, and it troubles me that we have so much of this discussion when in fact we have got real problems in this country." So, if all these clever, powerful people think that color blindness is the way to go, shouldn't we listen to them?

Of course, it's not only Americans who like color blindness. Returning to the theme of handsome Black men who endorse a color-blind perspective, the UK would like to present Idris Elba. In a 2023 interview with Alex Bilmes for *Esquire*, Elba explained why he stopped describing himself as "a Black actor" and started describing himself as simply "an actor." To be fair to Elba, in the same interview he did explicitly acknowledge that racism was real, that it should be a topic of discussion, and that he was definitely a member of the Black community. However, he went on to say that racism is only as powerful as you allow it to be, that people are too "obsessed" with race, and that this "obsession" can hinder growth. He doesn't want to be thought of as the first Black this or the first Black that, just as the first Idris Elba.

Moving further into Europe, Boris Becker is a (White) former West German tennis player, and by all accounts he was one of the best. In 1992 he fell in love with German American model and designer Barbara Feltus, who is Black. By 1993 they were married. Becker has spoken about the ways in which racism affected their marriage, but only in the sense that *other* people were being racist about it. For his part, in an Apple TV documentary, he said, "I'm color blind. I didn't see she was darker than me and I just fell in love with the woman." See that? People who really love Black people are color blind about it. Have you married any Black people lately? No? Had any half-Black kids, as Becker went on to do? No? Then maybe you should just take Becker's advice and accept that color blindness is a good idea.

Even Nigel Farage, British broadcaster and former politician, can get behind color blindness! Or, at least, his political party was able to. Farage was once the leader of the UK Independence Party (UKIP), a party built on the explicit dislike of immigrants and foreigners (at least the ones who come to the UK). It is the party of councillor Rozanne Duncan, who was filmed saying she had a "problem with people with negroid features"; the party of councillor Dave Small, who wrote of a visit to Birmingham, "all around me I could hear the sound of jabbering in an alien voice . . . we also have the Pakistani's [*sic*] and the Somali's [*sic*]"; the party of candidate Joseph Quirk, who has said, "Well, I reckon dogs are more intelligent, better company and certainly better behaved than most Muslims." This is the party that British people join when the regular right-wing parties are still too left wing for them. And yet, even Nigel Farage proudly announced in 2015 that UKIP, as a party, was color blind.

Still, these are all examples of the distantly famous and powerful—of politicians and celebrities. For me, the pervasiveness of color blindness really came home in 2017, when little Jax Rosebush became famous. Jax, a young boy from Kentucky, became an internet sensation when he asked his mother to give him the same haircut as his best friend, Reddy, "so that his teacher wouldn't be able to tell them apart." So far, so mundane. Children try to pull silly pranks on their teachers all the time.

However, the interesting thing about Jax's request was that he was a very White boy, with pale skin, blond hair, and light-colored eyes. In contrast, Jax's best friend Reddy was a Black boy, with dark brown skin, black hair, and brown eyes.

I want to be clear about this. This was not a plausible case of a dark-skinned Mediterranean White boy who might reasonably be confused for his light-skinned half-British, half-Ghanaian friend. The racialized differences between Jax and Reddy were stark and immediately obvious—skin color, hair texture, facial features—all the things you'd expect to be different between a very White boy and a very Black boy. It is not only impossible that Jax somehow failed to notice these differences, it is ridiculous to even entertain the thought. And it was these racial differences, or more specifically, Jax's inability or unwillingness to acknowledge these racial differences, that made him such a sensation. When last I checked, the original Facebook post about Jax and Reddy had been shared over 27,000 times, and liked more than 88,000 times. People from all over the world took to the internet to share their opinions on Jax.

And, no, Jax didn't explode into popularity because thousands of worried parents wrote in with concerns about his poor vision, or his embarrassing portrayal of the level of reasoning skills taught to five-year-olds in Kentucky. Rather, Jax's apparent color blindness was universally hailed as positive. The news aggregation website Newsner said of Jax and Reddy, "Adults might think they always know best, but this story shows that we have a lot to learn by watching the youngest generation." Madeline Holcombe of CNN called it a "message of love in this boy's haircut." The boys' parents echoed similar sentiments. Pastor Kevin Weldon, the White man who became Reddy's father by adopting him from the Democratic Republic of Congo, said "There's an innocence children have that sometimes we lose." Jax's mother, Lydia Rosebush, who is also White, said, "If this isn't proof that hate and prejudice is something that is taught, I don't know what is."

Some of my closest friends shared the story on their Facebook pages as well, and were similarly met with a host of gushing comments about how sweet the two boys were, how beautiful the story was, how love has no color, and how much better it would be if everyone in the world could be like these two boys. People shared similar stories, such as one about a mother who asked her daughter, "How many refugees are in your class?," to which the daughter replied, "There are no refugees, there are only kids in my class." Isn't it just wonderful? Couldn't you just weep from the beauty of it?

Even among many of my friends and family—clever people, thoughtful people, people whose intelligence I respect, people who had dedicated a significant portion of their time to speaking out against racism—the message was clear. We weren't supposed to find anything jarring, disturbing, worrying, or weird in this example of obvious doublethink on the part of a small child. We weren't supposed to question the motives of the parents who encouraged it, or the teacher who later played along and pretended not to be able to tell the boys apart. We weren't supposed to question the sincerity of Jax's belief, or ask ourselves about the consequences for a young White boy's psyche of pretending not to notice something that everybody (including him) could obviously see.

Rarely did anyone seem to even consider little Reddy's experiences of this bizarre scenario—which is especially troubling considering the clear scientific evidence we have seen in Chapters 3 and 9 that children who are only three years old (significantly younger than either Jax or Reddy at the time) *do* notice race, assign value to it, treat each other differently because of it, and experience different treatment from their teachers because of it.

We weren't supposed to think about any of that. We were just supposed to like the story of Jax and Reddy, enthusiastically and uncritically. We were supposed to think it was good.

A lot of people (or at least, most White people in predominantly White Western countries) do think that color blindness—the unwillingness to notice or acknowledge race—is good. I don't base that conclusion on these stories, but on scientific data. For example, in 2015, Hachfeld and colleagues surveyed 433 teachers in Germany on their approaches to teaching multi-ethnic classrooms. They found that overall endorsement of a color-blind ideology was significantly higher than the midpoint of the scale (4.71 on a scale from 1 to 6). Put in less science-y terms, the researchers found that most people agreed with a color-blind approach. Similar results are found by non-scientific organizations using a simpler approach. In 2014, MTV partnered with David Binder Research to survey about 3,000 young American regular viewers of MTV on their attitudes toward racial bias and responding to that bias. This survey found overwhelming support for color-blind ideas: 70% said that they didn't see ethnic minorities any differently from the way they see White people, 73% believed it would improve society if people never considered race, 90% believed that everyone should be treated the same regardless of race, and 70% believed that it was never fair to give preferential treatment to one race over another, "regardless of historical inequalities."

Moreover, the respondents said that color blindness was the approach passed on to them from their families: specifically, 84% said that their family had taught them that everyone should be treated the same, no matter what their race. This finding is in line with other research on how parents talk to their children about race and racism. In 2018, Vittrup recruited 107 White American mothers who had children between four and seven years old and interviewed them about their approach to talking about race with their children. Vittrup found that very few of the mothers (only 30%) could be categorized as having a "color conscious" approach, while the grand majority (70%) were categorized as having a "color blind or color mute approach."

Even when parents acknowledged that it was important to talk about race (as 81% of them did), or claimed that they had such conversations with their children (as 62% did), very few of them (only 33% of the 62 who claimed to have such conversations, so only 21 mothers in total) "were able to recall any specific conversation on the topic," suggesting that many of them had, in fact, never had a specific conversation about race with their children.

Furthermore, when the mothers did discuss race with the children, they overwhelmingly approached it from a color-blind perspective. Many mothers focused strongly on "simply treat[ing] everyone the same." Some mothers assumed that their children were already color blind, or that race had not yet come up in their children's lives—an idea grossly at odds with the available scientific research (again, see Chapters 3 and 9). Others explicitly wanted their children to be color blind, and so they deliberately avoided talking about race or racism. If the children ever took the initiative and brought it up themselves, they would often be met with comments like "All people are equal, skin color makes no difference" instead of a more complete, honest or nuanced discussion of what race is, or how racism affects people. For most mothers, it was color blindness all the way.

If you're a parent, particularly a White parent in a predominantly White Western country, you probably recognize some of these conversations. You've probably told your children, in one way or another, that skin color doesn't matter, or emphasized that we should simply treat everyone the same way, or hushed them when they embarrassingly acknowledged someone's racialized features in public. Even if you're not a parent, you may have mentioned in a work meeting that the company should just select the best person based on their qualifications and value, and totally disregard considerations like race. Or, you may have told one of your ethnic minority friends, "I don't even think of you as Black/Asian/Latino," as if this were some kind of compliment. I have heard exactly this statement ("I don't even think of you as Black") from several people in my own life, some of whom I still consider to be friends to this day. As I've said, most White people really like color blindness. And, if the teachers and parents of today are any indication, the next generation will grow up to really like color blindness as well.

And that is a real shame, because color blindness is a terrible idea.

Why color blindness is a terrible idea

The first problem is that people are rarely as color blind as they pretend to be. In 2006, Norton and colleagues recruited 57 White participants to play a very simple game. The researchers asked 24 random people at a shopping mall if they could take their pictures, and then the 57 participants were shown the array of photographs of these strangers. The images differed in a number of detectable ways: the subjects' gender, race, age, hair color, facial hair, facial expression, and the background color of the photograph. All the participants in the study had to do was categorize the photographs along these lines when the researchers asked them to. So, if the researchers asked them to sort the photographs by gender, all the participants had to do was make two piles of photographs—one male and one female.* If they asked the participants to sort the photographs by race, they just had to make two piles, one White and one Black.† Seems easy, right? And it was easy. The participants overwhelmingly sorted the photographs correctly; they were at least 95% accurate across all the dimensions used in the study and were particularly accurate (99.1%) when it came to sorting people by race.

But that wasn't the only variable that interested Norton and colleagues. Before the participants completed the sorting tasks, the researchers asked them to estimate how good they would be at each of them: specifically, how long it would take them to sort the photos according to each aspect. This is where the interesting findings emerged. The participants consistently underestimated their speed at categorizing people by race. When asked how they thought they would do on the task, the participants imagined that race would be their second slowest dimension for categorization, faster only than age. However, in reality, race was the third fastest dimension, slower only than background color and gender.

The same pattern of results emerged when the researchers compared the participants' actual categorization times (in seconds) to their estimated categorization time. The participants had estimated that it would take them about four and a half seconds (4.43) to categorize all 24 pictures by race. However, in reality, it only took them about three and a half seconds (3.60)—a statistically significant difference, and one of a reasonable size when you consider the speed of the task at hand. Furthermore, this difference could not be attributed to a general tendency on the part of the participants to underestimate their categorization times. The

---

* I realize other genders exist, but these were the only ones specified in the study.
† The same applies here—other races exist, but these were the ones used in this experiment.

opposite was true—the participants *overestimated* how quickly they would categorize by gender. Nor could the finding be attributed to faulty estimations specifically in the realm of color. Again, participants were much more accurate at predicting their speed at categorizing by background color; for this task, there was no significant difference between the participants' estimated times and their actual times. It was only when it came to race that the participants claimed to be less efficient at categorizing than they turned out to truly be.

This issue of claiming to be more color blind than one actually is comes up in many more studies. For example, in a second experiment, Norton and colleagues recruited 30 White participants to play another game. This game was very similar to the board game Guess Who?. As soon as the first participant came to the lab, they were paired up with a second participant who was chosen completely at random (or, rather, not at all at random and, at this point, were we having a face-to-face conversation, I would wink knowingly at you). This second participant was then shown an array of 32 photographs that differed on a number of dimensions (for example, gender, race and background color) and asked to pick one in particular, but not to tell the first participant which one it was. Just like in Guess Who?, it was then the job of the first participant to identify the photo the second participant was looking at by asking as few yes/no questions as possible.

As in the last experiment, this game is not difficult. After a few quick questions (perhaps, "Is the person a woman?"; "Is the person Black?"; "Is the person on a blue background?"), anyone should be able to narrow down the potential list of photographs that the other participant is looking at. And that part of the study went very smoothly. Sort of.

The second participant I was winking about was of course not a real participant at all, but a confederate that the experimenter knew beforehand and was paying to pretend to be another participant. Indeed, depending on which condition the real participants were assigned to, they were either paired with a Black confederate or a White one. Now we can start to see the real shape of the experiment. The participants were trying to guess the person in the chosen photograph using as few questions as possible—but in one condition the participants were interacting with a Black confederate, and in the other, participants were interacting with a White confederate.

The experimenters wanted to see if the participants' apparent color blindness would change depending on the race of their interaction partner. And, of course, it did. When participants were paired with a White confederate, they mentioned race 94% of the time (i.e., almost all the time). However, when they were paired with a Black confederate, they only mentioned race 64% of the time. Interestingly, the race of the confederate also affected the words that the participants used to make reference to race. Participants were much more likely to make reference to the person in the photograph being "Black" or "African American" when they were interacting with a White confederate (57% of the time) than when they were interacting with a Black confederate (21% of the time). When they were interacting with a Black confederate, they were relatively more likely to ignore *Blackness*, and to instead ask questions about the *Whiteness* of the person in the photograph.

The conclusions of the study were clear, and further research—Apfelbaum et al. in 2008, Pauker et al. in 2015, Sullivan et al. in 2020—also supports the same conclusions: White people aren't actually failing to notice or acknowledge race. Indeed, it's exactly the opposite. They're doing a great job of noticing the race of their interaction partner and then modifying their behavior to *appear* not to acknowledge race if they are in the presence of a

Black person. This isn't color blindness at all. Instead, when coupled with participants' consistent claims of not acknowledging race, their quick changes of behavior in the company of Black confederates start to look a lot more like hypocrisy.

Still, supporters of the color-blind approach sometimes point out that this failure to be completely color blind is hardly a criticism of color blindness itself. After all, people are rarely as honest as they want to be, or as faithful as they want to be, or as charitable as they want to be. None of that indicates that honesty, faithfulness, and charity are moral failings. It certainly doesn't indicate that, when practiced well, they would be ineffective tools for building a better society. It merely shows that they are ideals to which we can and should aspire, even if we continue to fall short. Perhaps the very same thing could be said about color blindness. As Coleman Hughes has argued, advocating for color blindness isn't about "pretending" not to notice color. It is about endorsing a principle—about striving to treat people equally, without considerations of race, in both our public policy and private lives. So maybe we should cut the White people some slack. They're trying to be color blind, even if they aren't fully succeeding. Indeed, even if nobody is truly color blind (and even if they only selectively turn on this supposed color blindness in the presence of ethnic minorities), true color blindness remains something worth striving for, so long as closer approximations to the color-blind ideal result in less and less racism.

But therein lies the second problem.

More color blindness doesn't result in less racism. It wouldn't even be fair to say that color blindness is ineffective at reducing racism. It's much worse than that. A wealth of research shows that adopting a color-blind approach will make you significantly *more* racist in a number of important ways.

In 2021 (West et al. 2021), I recruited 287 British participants and tested them on their levels of a number of variables: color blindness (I asked how much they agreed with statements like, "It is important that people begin to think of themselves as British and not Black British or Asian British," and "Talking about racial issues causes unnecessary tension"); explicit racism (for instance, "Blacks should not push themselves where they are not wanted"); implicit racism (I had them complete an Implicit Associations Test); and narrow definitional boundaries of racism (such as, "The core of anti-Black racism is that it is malicious: if a person is not being malicious, then it can't be racism"). All these measures had been repeatedly validated in prior research and shown to be good measures of their chosen concepts.

This was just a correlational study, and every first-year university student of psychology knows that correlation doesn't equal causation. Still, if color blindness were a good thing, we could reasonably expect a negative correlation between color blindness and all these bad things. In other words, as levels of color blindness go up, we should find that levels of implicit racism, explicit racism and narrow definitional boundaries go down. This seems to be in line with what Morgan Freeman suggested: that one way to reduce racism was to "stop talking about it." But that was not at all what we found. We didn't even find that levels of color blindness were unrelated to levels of these bad things. Instead, we found sizable, highly statistically significant, positive correlations between color blindness and implicit racism, explicit racism, and narrow definitional boundaries of discrimination. Put simply, participants who were more color blind were also more racist, both implicitly and explicitly, and less willing to recognize racism.

Let's return to the Guess Who? study by Norton and colleagues in 2006. Another part of the experiment that I've so far failed to mention was that the interactions between the

participants and confederates were videotaped and sent to
independent observers who rated how friendly the participants
were being in each interaction. If color blindness was good for
interracial interactions, we should expect that the participants
who were more color blind (i.e., the ones who were more reluctant
to mention race) would have interacted more positively with the
Black confederates than the participants who were less color
blind. But this was not what the researchers found. The opposite
was true: color blindness was associated with less eye contact and
less friendly nonverbal behaviors. Again, in sharp contrast with
the advice given by Morgan Freeman, Ben Carson, Coleman
Hughes, and Idris Elba, far from helping with interracial interaction, color blindness is associated with being less friendly to Black
people.

There's more. In 2013, Zou and Dickter recruited 113 White
participants and measured their levels of color blindness using the
Color-Blind Racial Attitudes Scale (the same measure I used in my
2021 study mentioned above). Afterward, they showed all the participants a story about a White person who made a prejudiced
comment (for example, "I feel so bad for you people. Your hair will
always feel like a bad perm") and a Black person who confronted
the White person about the prejudiced comment ("Seriously, go
easy on the racism there"). If color blindness was good, we should
expect that people high in color blindness would be less supportive of the racism and more supportive of the person who confronted the racism. But this was not the case. Rather, the
researchers found that color blindness predicted more negative
perceptions of the person who confronted racism.

But, so far, we've still just considered research in which the scientists measured people's levels of color blindness. What about
that gold standard of experimental research, the randomized controlled trial? Are there any experiments in which researchers

manipulate participants' levels of color blindness? And do these experiments find the same thing?

Of course they do. In 2004, Richeson and Nussbaum recruited 52 White participants and randomly assigned them to one of two conditions. In the first condition they encouraged the participants to adopt a multicultural approach to interracial relations; that is, an approach that acknowledges and respects group-based differences in society, rather than seeking to ignore them or assimilate them. In the second condition they encouraged the participants to adopt a color-blind approach. To encourage these approaches, Richeson and Nussbaum provided the participants with one-page statements that explicitly endorsed either a multicultural or color-blind approach (depending on condition) and then asked participants to make a list of five reasons why either a multicultural or color-blind approach (depending on condition) is a positive approach to interracial relations.

After encouraging these perspectives, Richeson and Nussbaum tested the participants on their levels of both explicit and implicit racism. And what did they find? No prizes for guessing. In the researcher's own words, "the color-blind perspective generated greater racial attitude bias measured both explicitly and on the more unobtrusive reaction time measure." In other words, adopting color blindness makes you more racist.

I could go on. Research by Offermann et al. in 2014 found that people who are more color blind are less likely to spot discriminatory behavior in the workplace. Tawa et al. in 2016 found that color-blind people have less diverse friendships and social networks. In 2008, Correll et al. found that even in circumstances when color blindness does appear to reduce prejudice, the effect is short-lived. Color-blind people tend to show rebound effects, meaning that they end up more biased than they were before they tried being color blind. Perhaps most damning of all, they are reliably opposed to any action that addresses racism and its many, many scientifically proven detrimental outcomes. They are less supportive of Black Lives Matter and more supportive of All Lives Matter (West et al. 2021). Color blindness is also a strong, reliable predictor of opposition to affirmative action, more so even than plain old explicit racism (Awad et al. 2005).

You heard me. Someone who endorses explicit racism, someone who agrees with statements like "Over the past few years, the government and news media have shown more respect to Blacks than they deserve," and "Blacks should not push themselves where they are not wanted"—someone like that will still be less reliably opposed to affirmative action than someone who says things like "It is important that people begin to think of themselves as American and not African American, Mexican American, or Italian American." Color blindness is worse than ineffective against racism. It's a disaster. It's a scientifically proven way to make people more racist than they were before. Maybe that's why UKIP supports it so much. Maybe they've been reading the scientific literature.

We're seeing some of that disaster unfold in real time. In 2023, the US Supreme Court called an end to affirmative action policies in university selection. In the BBC's reporting of the outcome, it was said that "the six conservative justices in the majority heralded the decision as a step toward a more colorblind society." How right they were. Except that's not something to herald, because a "more colorblind society" is, scientifically, a more racist one.

To be color blind is to fail to notice that certain people—that is, White people—are given more support throughout their university journey, as shown by Milkman et al. in 2015. It is to ignore the fact that academic departments find some ethnicities (White and East Asian people) to be more competent and hireable than others (Black and Latino people), even when those people have exactly the same histories, qualifications and accomplishments, as shown by Eaton et al. in 2020. Color blindness does nothing to take away the system of pro-White affirmative action that currently affects almost every decision made in contemporary society, including universities. It simply erases the possibility of a counterbalancing pro-minority affirmative action. It entrenches the privileges and advantages of White people more firmly in society. It does the opposite of addressing racism.

Some supporters of color blindness argue that increasing racism (or at least sustaining it) was never its intention. Coleman Hughes, for example, has argued at length about the many noble *intentions* of the people who have supported color blindness in the past, arguing that color blindness has its roots in the Enlightenment, that it was developed during the fight against slavery and segregation, and so on. Even without these historical examples, we still have a contemporary lineup of famous, smart, successful, wise-sounding Black people (like Morgan Freeman, Idris Elba, and Dr. Benjamin Carson) happy to defend color-blind approaches. All this is meant to convince us that the people who proposed and continue to support color blindness have the best of intentions.

That's all fine and dandy. However, respectfully (and I can think of no way to state this more plainly), science doesn't give a damn about your intentions! It doesn't matter if Nelson Mandela, Rosa Parks, Jesus Christ, and Black Panther all support color blindness out of a genuine intention to improve the lot of ethnic minorities in contemporary society.* They'd still be wrong! The wealth of scientific experiments would still show that color-blind

---

* To be clear, I have no reason at all to believe that any of these characters do, have, or would support color blindness.

people are more racist, implicitly and explicitly. They would still show that the reluctance to acknowledge race leads to more negative behaviors toward ethnic minorities, a lower willingness to recognize racism, and more negativity toward people who challenge racism. They'd still show that color blindness leads to opposition to actions that might make minorities' lives better. In light of all that scientific evidence, anybody still talking about the positive intentions behind color blindness should be taken no more seriously than a five-year-old White boy who is obviously lying about being identical to his very Black friend.

I have sometimes had the baffling experience of explaining all this research to people and then hearing someone (almost always a White person) say that they're just going to continue to be color blind anyway. It's not that they don't understand the research. It's not that they still believe that color blindness will make them any less racist. It's just that it makes them feel more comfortable. And (though they never say this latter part explicitly) that comfort is apparently more important than doing anything about racism.

It's in those moments that I see color blindness as something truly awful: a form of willful ignorance, an active one, one that disregards its own effects and is all the more horrifying for doing so. This is a feeling that I think was best summed up by the philosopher Charles Mills:

Ignorance is usually thought of as the passive obverse to knowledge, the darkness retreating before the spread of Enlightenment. But . . . imagine an ignorance that resists. Imagine an ignorance that fights back. Imagine an ignorance militant, aggressive, not to be intimidated, an ignorance that is active, dynamic, that refuses to go quietly—not at all confined to the illiterate and uneducated but propagated at the highest level of the land, indeed presenting itself unblushingly as knowledge.

That is color blindness. It is not a strategy for improving the world, merely for growing more comfortable with the world as it is. It is not a strategy for reducing racism, merely for ignoring it.

But we're not children anymore. And it is silly to believe, of a problem as large and as powerful as racism, that if we ignore it, it will just go away.

Chapter 11

Mas que nada?
Are Diversity Initiatives Really Helping?

On June 29, 2020, on *BBC Breakfast*, Sir Keir Starmer, leader of the Labor Party and hopeful future prime minister of the UK, was asked his opinion about the Black Lives Matter organization, particularly their demand to "defund the police." His response was very bold indeed: "That's nonsense, and nobody should be saying anything about defunding the police. I would have no truck with that . . . My support for the police is very, very strong."

I should offer some important context for these remarks. Though the Black Lives Matter movement had existed since 2013, in 2020 it saw a flood of new support and attention. Earlier that year, on May 25, 2020, George Floyd, an unarmed African American man, was killed in broad daylight by a White police officer, Derek Chauvin. Chauvin knelt on Floyd's neck for almost nine minutes in front of a crowd of people, some of whom filmed the incident, until Floyd suffocated and died. In response, a series of protests erupted across multiple countries, including the US and the UK.

Over the years, the Black Lives Matter movement had also become politically divisive. Those on the right, including the then Women and Equalities minister in October of 2020, MP Kemi Badenoch, were openly critical of the movement, while those on the left were expected to be in support. The Labor Party, Keir

Starmer's party, is the dominant left-wing party in British politics and so any apparent criticism of Black Lives Matter, whether genuinely intended or carelessly delivered, would be a smear on his reputation. Strong, unqualified statements of support for the police in a conversation about Black Lives Matter, and in the shadow of the gruesome murder of an unarmed Black man by a police officer, seemed politically most unsavvy. Moreover, Sir Keir, who was clearly in a "in for a penny, in for a pound" mood, then went on to apparently dismiss or downplay the importance of Black Lives Matter, referring to it as a "moment," seeming to suggest something transitory, a bit of a fad, instead of a "movement," a community of like-minded people who could make an actual difference in society.

What happened next was not very surprising. Members of Black Lives Matter were not impressed. They criticized Sir Keir's dismissal of the movement. In particular, his disrespectful framing of it as a "moment" was interpreted as a sign of ignorance at best, or bias at worst. Black Lives Matter members clarified their stance on "defunding the police" as one asking governments to "invest in programs that actually keep us safe, like youth services, mental health and social care, education, jobs and housing." Black Lives Matter UK referred to Starmer derisively as "a cop in an expensive suit" and suggested that we should not "allow former prosecutors to tell us what our demands are."

Perhaps worst of all, Nigel Farage, of all people—leader of the political party that right-wingers join when regular right-wing parties aren't right wing enough—said that he heartily agreed with Keir Starmer's stance, utterly demolishing any pretense on Sir Keir's part that he was a credible left-wing politician.

What happened after *that* was also not very surprising. There was backtracking. There were apologies. There were claims of having been misunderstood. Labor MP Florence Eshalomi explained that Sir Keir's "choice of words" had been wrong. Sir Keir himself went on to explain that he had meant to refer to Black Lives Matter as a "defining moment," and that he regretted that people thought he had meant something else.

To be fair to Sir Keir Starmer, he may have been the victim of some misrepresentation and political trickery. After all, earlier that same month, on June 9, 2020, the day of George Floyd's funeral in Texas, Sir Keir (and his deputy, Angela Rayner MP) were being photographed in London "taking the knee," a gesture meant to communicate unequivocal support for the Black Lives Matter movement. Furthermore, Sir Keir had repeatedly made explicit statements indicating that he opposed racial injustice. Indeed, he tweeted the photograph of himself taking the knee with the caption, "We kneel with all those opposing anti-Black racism. #BlackLivesMatter."

Nonetheless, politics is a game of appearances. Regardless of what Sir Keir had actually meant in the original *BBC Breakfast* interview, the damage had been done. Something had to be done to repair it. That much was undeniable. However, in the midst of all of the predictable responses, Sir Keir did manage to do one thing that was a bit surprising, at least to me. He insisted that every member of the Labor Party, including himself, sign up for unconscious bias training. He said, "I think everybody should have unconscious bias training. I think it is important . . . I'm going to lead from the top on this and do that training first."

To some of you, this might seem perfectly logical. Rightly or wrongly, some people clearly felt that Sir Keir had expressed bias in his dismissal of the Black Lives Matter movement (or "moment"), so of course he wanted some training to reduce his bias. It all fits together. Sort of. Except the unconscious part. To me, that part doesn't fit at all. After all, Sir Keir was obviously not unconscious when he appeared on *BBC Breakfast*. He didn't mutter disparaging comments about Black Lives Matter in his sleep, or in a hypnosis-induced stupor. As far as anyone could tell, the Labor leader was very, very conscious the entire time. In light of his apparent consciousness, maybe a bit of explicit education about racism, policing and the history of the Black Lives Matter movement was in order. Perhaps it would have been a good opportunity to examine and revise his conscious beliefs or his overt attitudes. Maybe his attitudes were fine and what Sir Keir really needed was better political advisers, or some training in clear communication. Of all the approaches that could have been taken, why opt for unconscious bias training?

To spare you the bother of revisiting all that we already know about implicit bias from Chapter 5, I'll sum up its contents in three general statements. First, implicit racism is real; many people hold racist beliefs or attitudes about which they are unwilling and/or unable to communicate accurately or honestly. Furthermore, this implicit racism is a useful predictor of a variety of behaviors, from the way one teaches racial minority students, to the treatment one offers racial minority patients, to the willingness to include a racial minority in one's family. Second, implicit racism is neither the only kind of racism nor the only reason why racism is hard to detect. Sometimes people are explicitly racist, sometimes they know that they're racist but they lie about it, sometimes they play psychological tricks to conceal their racism even from themselves—and all of that can make it hard to tell who is racist or how strong their racism is. Third, a hyperfocus on implicit racism is unhelpful; it is inaccurate to assume that all racism, or even most racism, is implicit. Such an assumption can make us less concerned about racism and less likely to do anything about it.

All of that is useful information, but it still leaves some very important questions unanswered. Specifically, what should we think about things like unconscious bias training and related diversity initiatives? Do they work?

To be clear, I'm not in any way siding with politicians like Betsy McCaughey, the former lieutenant governor of New York, who argued that the institutional racism and unconscious bias "ideology" is intended to "humiliate" White people and frame them as "oppressors." I'm certainly not siding with politicians like Ben Bradley, the British Conservative MP who dismissed unconscious bias training as "Orwellian re-education courses . . . that tell ordinary people they are racists." Everything about Bradley's stance on the issue is, from a scientific perspective, bollocks. First of all, nobody needs unconscious bias training to figure out that "ordinary people are racists." We have thousands of studies on discrimination in employment, healthcare, education, media, friendships, romantic relationships, immigration, voting, policing and the justice system that already show the ubiquitous, damaging nature of contemporary racism (see, for example, Chapters 2, 3, and 4). Scientists figured out that "ordinary people" do a lot of racist things a very long time ago. It's ridiculous, and a bit childish, to call basic education about uncontroversial scientific facts "Orwellian" just because you don't like them. And if you, like Betsy McCaughey, find scientific facts about contemporary racism "humiliating," the solution is obviously to do something about the racism, not to deny the scientific facts.

Similarly, I am in no way siding with former president Donald Trump's 2020 "Executive Order on Combating Race and Sex Stereotyping." Despite its seemingly progressive title, this executive order was largely a complaint designed to stop anybody from talking about racism (or sexism), and to protect White people (and men) from being "scapegoated" (or, in more realistic terms, from having to face any of the ways in which society works unfairly in their favor). This executive order sought to stop things like unconscious bias training out of an unscientific belief that prejudice was no longer a serious concern and that talking about it was inherently "divisive."

These are not my concerns. As should be clear, I fully acknowledge the scientific reality of contemporary racism, including the implicit kind. My question is one about efficiency and effectiveness. Does unconscious bias training make us less biased? Does it, over the long term, increase the proportions of ethnic minorities in organizations? Does it create an atmosphere in which ethnic minorities are happier and more welcome? Even if it's not perfect, even if we shouldn't pretend that unconscious bias is the only kind of bias, is it better to do unconscious bias training than nothing at all? Should I sign up all my employees for mandatory unconscious bias training? Or, is this a weird scam? Is it an ineffective waste of money based loosely on a few scientific findings? Or, even worse, is this similar to color blindness—a Trojan Horse that promises equality but only reinforces the bias that it was meant to undermine? In short, did Sir Keir Starmer do the right thing?

This is an important question, because Sir Keir is not the only person to seek solutions to racism in unconscious bias training or similar diversity training. In fact, unconscious bias training is an incredibly and increasingly popular intervention.

According to an article by Pamela Newkirk in *Time* magazine, "In 2003, MIT professor Thomas Kochan noted . . . that companies were spending an estimated $8 billion a year on diversity efforts." And that number has only increased with time. In 2014, Google alone reportedly spent $114 million on its diversity program. In 2018, Indeed, a popular job website, reported that positions for diversity and inclusion professionals had increased by 35% over the previous two years. These diversity efforts may include multiple, varied components (and we will turn our attention to some of the others), but many of them include some kind of unconscious bias training.

Indeed, according to a "Workplace Diversity Practices Survey Report" by Essen in 2005, 65% of large firms in the US were offering some kind of diversity training in 2005. Later, a 2021 article by Nazia Parveen in the *Guardian* indicated that 81% of companies have conducted some kind of unconscious bias training. According to a report by Leitner in 2021 entitled *The Current Status of Equality, Diversity and Inclusion in the Further Education Sector in England*, an estimated "98% of companies now have [equality, diversity, and inclusion] training in place"—and much of this training focuses on unconscious bias.

Given the statistics, I can say with confidence that *you* have almost certainly done some kind of diversity training. If you are a person in any way involved in the contemporary Western workforce, you have almost certainly sat in a room while somebody has explained to you that you have implicit (or, more likely, "unconscious") biases, and that these affect you in ways you don't realize.

Indeed, *I've* been made to take unconscious bias training in my workplace. That's right, *me*! A Black professor of social psychology with several publications on racism and prejudice reduction to my name. I've also had to be "educated" (by someone with fewer relevant degrees than myself) about what racism is, how it works and what I can do about it. We are clearly approaching the diversity training singularity, in which every single person on the planet will eventually be made to do some form of diversity training, probably involving unconscious bias education. So, before we go any further down this path, it seems wise to figure out if all this time, money, and effort is being wasted, or if it's going toward something useful.

Does unconscious bias training work?

Before I launch into the research, I must disclose some relevant information. Indeed, it's a sort of confession. *I* have offered what you might call diversity training, what some people might even call unconscious bias training. It's true. I've done it many times, to many people. Thousands of people. Various companies have paid me money to do it. I've been doing it for years. It is very possible that you have sat down in a room and listened to *me* talk to you about bias, even about implicit bias, about what it means and what you can do about it. It's possible that I asked you to do a version of an Implicit Association Test and explained what it means for you and the biases that you're likely to exhibit. You may have seen me present scientific evidence of the effects of bias in the workplace and in our personal lives. I may have offered you handy, easily digestible nuggets of advice on what to do about bias.

That's right. Some of that $8 billion a year: I took it. Some of those 98% of people who've had diversity training: I trained them. And so I would understand if you thought that I had an obvious financial incentive to keep the game going. I would understand if you expected me to feed you a line about how good unconscious bias training is, and how you should all keep on paying to get people to do it for you.

And that's why the studies I'm about to share may surprise you.

In 2006, Kalev, Dobbin, and Kelly acquired "federal data describing the workforces of 708 private sector establishments from 1971 to 2002." They also conducted a longitudinal survey of the practices at each establishment between 1971 and 2002. These practices included things like mentoring and networking programs, affirmative action plans, diversity managers, diversity taskforces, diversity evaluations, and (of course) diversity training. By pairing and analyzing these two datasets covering hundreds of companies and spanning three decades, Kalev and colleagues were able to determine which of these practices (for instance, affirmative action) preceded increases in diversity (such as more Black people in management) and which did not. In other words, these longitudinal data were an excellent indicator of which diversity initiatives were effective and which weren't.

At this point, I won't discuss the most effective initiatives. I'm saving that for Chapter 12. For now, let's see where diversity training fell on this list of *most* and *least* effective interventions. In the authors' own words, "diversity training and diversity evaluations are least effective at increasing the share of white women, black women, and black men in management," and "practices that target managerial bias through feedback (diversity evaluations) and education (diversity training) show virtually no effect in the aggregate." That's $8 billion a year, for "virtually no effect."

But it gets worse.

In 2016 Dobbin and Kalev followed up on their 2006 analyses, this time looking at data from 829 midsize and large American firms and how their diversity initiatives affected the proportions of women and ethnic minorities in management. They also analyzed the data in a more finely tuned way. For example, they didn't just look at diversity training. Instead, they were able to separate diversity training into voluntary training (allowing employees to opt in or opt out of doing it) and mandatory training (in which all employees were required to do it). This might be a moment to reflect on the kind of diversity training that you've done. Was it voluntary? Were you forced to do it? And which do you think is more effective?

First, the good news: Dobbin and Kalev found that *voluntary* diversity training did have positive effects, increasing the proportions of Black men, Hispanic men, Asian men, and Asian women in management. The gains were small, and voluntary training was far from the most effective strategy, but at least the gains were there. But now the bad news: *mandatory* diversity training had no apparent positive effects at all. Indeed, mandatory diversity training led to decreases in the proportions of Black women, Asian men, and Asian women in management. Dobbin and Kalev were unflinching in their conclusions: "Your organization will become less diverse, not more, if you require managers to go to diversity training."

Problematically, there just isn't that much research that finds strong, reliable, positive effects of diversity training, but there is quite a bit that finds small effects, no effects, or even negative effects. In 2018, in a review of several unconscious bias training initiatives, Atewologun and colleagues found only mixed evidence for their effectiveness at reducing bias. They also found that "evidence for [unconscious bias training's] ability effectively to change behavior is limited," and even that "there is potential for backfiring effects when [unconscious bias training] participants are exposed to information that suggests stereotypes and biases are unchangeable." Findings like these have led some researchers, such as Noon in 2018, to describe unconscious bias training and the diversity practices based on it as "pointless." Others, such as Tate and Page in 2018, go further, positing the unconscious bias narrative as a distraction that "diminishes white supremacy and maintains white innocence," while Kempf in 2020 describes unconscious bias training as a "corporate friendly" perspective on bias that ignores "institutional, structural, and systemic levels," thereby removing the impetus to resolve real issues of bias. Scathing stuff.

But it gets worse.

Diversity training is only one part of a suite of new programs ostensibly aimed at increasing diversity and inclusion in organizations, and it's not the only one to come under fire. For example, in 2013, Kaiser and colleagues recruited 245 White American adults for an experiment. As part of this experiment, participants were given some general information about a company (the Smith & Simon Corporation, a fake company invented for the purpose of the experiment). The participants were then randomly split into two conditions. In the first condition, they were shown Smith & Simon's mission statement, while in the second they were shown Smith & Simon's diversity statement. The two statements were almost identical, except that the diversity statement included some language that "implicated a commitment to diversity and nondiscrimination in hiring."

The researchers then asked all the participants about their impressions of Smith & Simon, to see if the addition of just a handful of words altered people's perception of a company. And, of course, it did. Participants in the diversity statement condition perceived Smith & Simon to be significantly fairer to ethnic minorities than did the participants in the mission statement condition.

That's not very surprising (though it does show how little work is required to improve the reputation of a company). However, the researchers were also interested in the effect of cold, hard data. Specifically, what would happen if, on top of the information about the company's diversity statement, participants were also given numerical information indicating that there was or was not discrimination in the company?

The researchers tackled that question by splitting the participants into three further conditions on top of the previously mentioned two. That is, some participants (those in the first condition) were given data from the human resources department showing that White people were promoted at a higher proportion (28%) than ethnic minorities (10%). In the second condition participants were given no data at all about promotions, and in the third condition they were given data from the human resources department showing that the same proportion of White people and ethnic minorities were promoted at the company (25%). This created six conditions into which a participant could be placed: (1) mission statement + unequal promotions; (2) mission statement + no information; (3) mission statement + equal promotions; (4) diversity statement + unequal promotions; (5) diversity statement + no information; (6) diversity statement + equal promotions.

With these six conditions, Kaiser and colleagues could now see how diversity statements and cold, hard data about a company's promotion rates would interact to create a perception of that company. Perhaps the participants would ignore the diversity statement when they saw the actual numbers. That's what a reasonable person might expect to see. However, it's not at all what Kaiser and colleagues found. Instead, as the authors put it, "reading a diversity statement caused Whites to perceive the organization as more procedurally fair for minorities, and this pattern emerged irrespective of whether or not the organization promoted minorities and Whites equally." In other words, even when participants had clear data about a company's unequal practices, the mere presence of a few words in a diversity statement was still enough to make them perceive the company as fairer to ethnic minorities— something that Kaiser and colleagues referred to as an "illusion of fairness."

In a similar set of subsequent experiments, Kaiser and colleagues found that the presence of a diversity statement was enough to make participants ignore numerical information about salary discrepancies. Furthermore, just *mentioning* that managers at Smith & Simon had to take part in diversity training made participants perceive the company as fairer and also made participants less supportive of any bias-related litigation against Smith & Simon. As the authors said, "the mere presence of an organizational diversity structure causes high-status group members to legitimize potential inequalities by perceiving organizations as procedurally fairer for underrepresented groups."

Relatedly, research by Offermann and colleagues in 2014 found that merely finding out that a manager had a reputation for fair, equitable treatment led participants to give the manager the benefit of the doubt when they behaved in a racist, micro-aggressive way. This result isn't necessarily bad. I can understand why people's current behaviors should be interpreted in the light of their prior behaviors and reputations. However, if we consider the potential to falsely bolster one's reputation for fairness with a brief diversity statement or a quick dose of highly publicized unconscious bias training, the danger becomes more apparent.

Maybe that's why these initiatives are worth over $8 billion a year. Maybe that's why Keir Starmer imposed mandatory unconscious bias training on the Labor Party. Perhaps the introduction of compulsory unconscious bias training is not about decreasing bias, but about protecting the reputation of the companies in question. If you, as a CEO, know that your company discriminates in hiring, promotions or salaries, all you have to do is add a few words to a diversity statement, or say that all your managers have done mandatory unconscious bias training, and suddenly everyone will think more highly of your company and be less supportive of litigation against you. A cynical, uncharitable person might start to wonder if this was indeed why so many companies were doing it. In any case, it does lend weight to Tate and Page's

(2018) perspective that these diversity initiatives are just a distraction that "diminishes white supremacy and maintains white innocence."

What does all this mean? Should we, as Ben Bradley MP and Donald Trump have suggested, immediately stop all diversity training? Was I wrong to lead all those training sessions? Should we ditch the diversity statements and associated diversity propaganda? Have we all just spent a huge amount of time, energy, and resources only to make the world more biased, only to make sure that companies can discriminate with impunity?

Maybe. But I think the reality is a bit more nuanced than that. After all, even Dobbin, Kalev, and Atewologun's research finds that diversity training sometimes reduces bias and increases diversity, especially if that diversity training is voluntary. They also suggest ways to improve its effectiveness, and they point out that pairing diversity training with other initiatives (which we will come to in the next chapter) can produce stronger positive effects. Furthermore, there is robust, reliable evidence that diversity-related education does reduce racial bias (we'll look at that in the next chapter as well). So, even with the warning that diversity initiatives can sometimes be used as a smokescreen that allows organizations to continue with discriminatory practices, the take-home message is certainly not that all diversity training is bad all of the time.

Part of the problem is that bias reduction is not intuitive. Serious mistakes can be made. For example, I've been to many diversity training sessions that largely follow a simple two-step formula. Step 1: give the audience information about the pervasiveness of racism and White privilege. Step 2: encourage the audience not to be racist. To a layperson, these steps probably seem intuitive, reasonable and likely to reduce the audience's bias.

At the very worst, they are probably a bit simple, but at least they can't be doing any harm.

Or can they?

Let's take a look at a few experiments that might change your mind. In 2011, Soble, Spanierman, and Liao recruited 138 self-identified White students and randomly assigned them to one of two conditions: in the first they watched an irrelevant video about career prospects for university students, while in the second condition they watched a video about the pervasiveness of institutional racism and White privilege in the US. Unsurprisingly, the participants in the second condition later reported experiencing higher levels of awareness, empathy and White guilt. However, perhaps surprisingly, these participants did not report lower levels of racial prejudice. Specifically, the participants did not respond any differently to items on the Quick Discrimination Index, such as "I would feel OK about my son or daughter dating someone of a different race," or "I would enjoy living in a neighborhood consisting of a racially diverse population." The relevant point from Soble's (2011) research is that telling White people about contemporary racism can affect them in many ways (e.g., increasing their feelings of guilt), but that it's a mistake to assume it will automatically decrease their levels of racial bias. So we've just seen that the aforementioned diversity trainer's first step—"give the audience information about the pervasiveness of racism and White privilege"—isn't making anybody less racist.

Relatedly, in 2016, Dr. Katy Greenland and I wanted to investigate how the effects of a racism-reducing intervention might be changed if you subtly altered the framing of the intervention. The intervention itself was a guided imagery technique that encouraged participants to imagine a positive interaction with someone from a stigmatized group. This intervention had been shown to reduce bias in the past and we had good reason to be confident that it would do so again. However, the findings of our experiments are almost certainly not limited to that specific kind of intervention. So, for the purposes of this chapter, I don't want to make the specific design of the intervention the central focus.

Rather, what I do want to focus on is how the intervention was framed. Specifically, and depending on the condition to which they were assigned, Katy and I subtly encouraged the participants to either think in terms of avoiding bias, or to think in terms of being as egalitarian as possible. Psychologically, this is called adopting either a prevention focus (focusing on avoiding the thing you don't want) or a promotion focus (focusing on approaching the thing you do want). This difference between promotion and prevention is the important aspect of the experiments that I'd like to highlight for you.

To many people, avoiding bias (taking a prevention focus) and being more egalitarian (taking a promotion focus) might sound like the same goal, but psychologically they're not. This is due to a quirk in human cognitive psychology in which telling people "Don't do that" is simply less effective than telling them "Do this instead." By way of example, let's imagine that I don't want you to think about a white bear. I could adopt a prevention focus and tell you, "Don't think about a white bear." Chances are, that instruction would hopelessly fail. You're probably thinking about a white bear right now. If I really want you to stop thinking about white bears, it would be better to adopt a promotion focus and say something like, "Imagine a brown bear." That is a much more effective way to guide people's behavior.

With that in mind, let's return to the experiments conducted by myself and Katy Greenland in 2016. What happened when we combined the prevention (or promotion) focus with the prejudice-reducing intervention? As you might be able to guess, participants who framed the activity in terms of being egalitarian later reported less bias, which was good. However, participants who framed the activity in terms of avoiding bias actually reported more bias at the end of the intervention.

Let me repeat that. Trying to be "less biased" (instead of "more egalitarian") resulted in being more biased—much the same way that trying not to think of a white bear makes you more likely to think about a white bear. What this shows is that the aforementioned diversity trainer's second step ("encourage the audience not to be racist") isn't making anybody less racist either. In fact, according to some of my own research, the framing of the instructions is quite possibly making them more racist.

These are counterintuitive findings. Furthermore, some of them are quite nuanced, and I would not necessarily expect a layperson to be familiar with them. I can certainly understand the intuitive appeal of telling people how bad racism is and then telling them "Don't be racist," and I can see why many a well-meaning diversity trainer might take this approach. Indeed, this might sound a lot like the diversity training that you have received in your company. Unfortunately, however, as Soble's (2011) research and the research I did with Katy (2016) has shown, if this is the training you received you probably left feeling a lot guiltier, but no less racist (and possibly even more racist) than when you started. That's why good intentions simply aren't sufficient here. Without the proper scientific knowledge, even the most well-meaning diversity trainer might just be making things worse.

If I had to choose a single word to describe my problem with contemporary diversity training, it would be "unregulated." By that, I mean that there is no barrier to becoming a diversity trainer or an unconscious bias "expert." You could become one right now. Just declare yourself to be a diversity trainer, and you're done! It might help if you have a website or a nice jacket, but neither of those things is required. And, speaking of things that aren't required to be a diversity trainer, you also don't need any degrees; you don't need to have published any research in any of the relevant fields; you don't need to have any experience working with any particular kind of company; and you don't need to have even a passing awareness of what the science says about bias or how to reduce it.

This is a level of disorganization that we would never accept from any other professional field, not from doctors, dentists, or psychologists. Those three are all protected terms, meaning that you need specific qualifications and experience in order to legally call yourself a doctor, dentist, or psychologist. And there's a reason for that. Could you imagine the dangerous chaos that would ensue if anybody with a jacket and a website could call themselves a dentist? If you went in with a cavity, you might find someone knowledgeable and professional who could clean and repair your teeth. However, it's also plausible that you'd stumble across a charlatan who was only there to steal your money. Or perhaps you'd end up with someone who had the best of intentions, but who nonetheless didn't know the first thing about oral hygiene—someone who would extract the wrong tooth, lacerate your gums, and leave you poorer, in pain, and overall significantly worse off. This is the chaos we're living through right now, except with diversity instead of dentistry.

This extreme caveat emptor environment leaves you, the consumer, or your employer's HR department, with a lot of responsibility. It's on you to verify the qualifications and experience of your diversity consultants, to check if they have any relevant degrees or publications, to investigate their success with previous clients. Sadly, there is currently nothing more than this process between you and an ever-growing host of diversity consultants, only some of whom are actually helpful. So choose carefully.

However, the consultants can't shoulder all the blame for diversity training's inconsistent effectiveness. If I were allowed to pick a second word to describe my problems with contemporary diversity training, it would probably be "over-hyped." By that I mean that too many companies seem to think diversity training is the first, last and only necessary step on their journey toward equity. As we've seen, this is not a position supported by the available research from Kalev et al. in 2006, Dobbin et al. in 2007, or Dobbin and Kalev in 2016. Diversity training, if done properly, can increase awareness of bias and how it works, as found by Atewologun et al. (2018). However, by itself, awareness of bias is not enough to produce significant changes to behaviors or outcomes, or even to reduce bias (again, see Soble et al. 2011; West and Greenland 2016). This awareness becomes useful when it is channeled into strategies (preferably scientifically supported strategies) for reducing bias and its effects.

Unfortunately, this is another way in which the responsibility for the effectiveness of diversity interventions falls back onto the consumer. Something I have said in many of my own diversity-related talks is that the diversity-training-only strategy is a bit like a person whose entire exercise plan is to attend seminars about exercise. We can immediately see why this strategy would never work. You can attend all the best seminars on weightlifting in the world, you can spend years of your life reading the best books, you can listen to all the experts and learn all the science, but none of that will make you even the slightest bit stronger.

Eventually, you will have to leave the seminars and lift the occasional weight.

Chapter 12

Do It Good
How to Effectively Reduce Racism

Perhaps it's not surprising that the contents of a book about racism have thus far been quite negative. How much fun could we expect it to be? But I am about to introduce some much-needed positivity. This is where we finally discuss things that really reduce racism. And by that, I don't mean things like color blindness, which is actively harmful, or even things like diversity training, which can be inconsistent. I mean things that work well, things that work reliably, things you can start doing right now—things that, if you do them, really will make you less racist. While there is a wide variety of scientifically proven strategies, I will focus on three in particular that have been extensively studied and consistently shown to be effective: intergroup contact, education, and changing your media diet.

Some of you might be wondering why this section of the book comes so late. In response to that, I can only say that one must understand a problem before making a serious attempt to solve it. Thus, any chapter on reducing racism would be premature without first demonstrating how powerful racism is, how widespread it is and how it takes both individual and systemic forms. It would be unreasonable to expect you to understand how to tackle racism without first explaining the flaws in the concept of "reverse racism," or the ways in which ethnic minorities can be racist toward each other, or the ways in which they can be racist even toward themselves. In short, I wanted you to know what you were up against before you entered the ring. Now that you've been prepared, let's dive right in.

Intergroup contact

Intergroup contact is the fancy social psychology term that we use to describe "making friends with ethnic minorities." To be fair, it's a bit more nuanced than that. The "intergroup" part acknowledges that we categorize ourselves, psychologically, into different groups (for example, White people, Black people, Asian people, Mixed people, and so on). The "contact" part is indicative of getting people from those groups to interact, or make contact, with each other. Put simply, if people from different racial or ethnic groups interact with each other (particularly under certain circumstances), racism will decrease, and people will be happier around each other.

It does seem like a simple idea, even an obvious one. But this has not always been the case. Indeed, the contact hypothesis, as it came to be known, was popularized by the work of Gordon Allport in the 1950s (see Allport 1954). And if you have even a passing familiarity with history, you will know that (in the US) segregation, not integration, was the law of the land through much of the 1950s. The well-known "Jim Crow" laws, for example, limited African Americans' ability to enter certain public spaces, forbade them from living in certain White neighborhoods, segregated them from White people in theaters and restaurants, and forced them to use different—usually, significantly inferior—building entrances, water fountains, and even cemeteries. Not even death could place a person beyond the reach and indignity of racism.

While segregation took different forms in the UK, it similarly included banning racial minorities from using certain spaces or facilities in pubs, workplaces, and shops. There were also no British laws prohibiting racial segregation until 1965, making it perfectly legal to reject "colored people" for certain positions simply because they were "colored." Perhaps the most famous example dates to 1968. As an investigation by the *Guardian* revealed, this was the year in which Queen Elizabeth's chief financial manager informed civil servants that "it was not, in fact, the practice to appoint colored immigrants or foreigners" to clerical roles in the royal household, though they were permitted to work as domestic servants. It is unclear when exactly this banning of "colored immigrants" from certain roles ended, but it may have been as late as the 1990s.

Many of the arguments in favor of segregation were simply based on open White supremacy: the bald conviction that White people were superior to those of other races and therefore deserving of access to the best roles and resources. An excellent example of such arguments can be found in the words of George Wallace, the 45th governor of Alabama, who served for three terms between 1963 and 1987. Wallace was a White man who was raised a Methodist, and who described himself as a "segregationist, not a racist." Still, one of his arguments in favor of segregation was his staunch belief in the inferiority of Black people, whom Wallace considered to be both disproportionately criminal and disproportionately diseased. He had dire warnings about the consequences for White people if they allowed their progeny to be mixed with Black blood: "eventually our race will be deteriorated [*sic*] to that of the mongrel complexity." That all sounds a pinch beyond "segregationist" to me, but I'll leave you to interpret it for yourselves.

Other arguments for segregation involved fears that racial minorities would overrun White people, take over their communities and force them into submission. Calls for integration and shared living spaces—things that encouraged positive intergroup contact—were seen as traps that would lure White people into a false sense of security before allowing racial minorities to dominate and abuse them.

Perhaps the most famous British example of such arguments is the speech delivered by Enoch Powell to a Conservative Association meeting in Birmingham on April 20, 1968. John Enoch Powell served as a Conservative member of parliament between 1950 and 1974, and the speech that he gave in 1968, now widely known as the "Rivers of Blood" speech, continues to echo in the British consciousness to this day. For example, in a 2018 article for the *Atlantic*, Samuel Earle described what he called the "unsettling shadow of Powell" in relation to the arguments for the British separation from the rest of the European Union—an event more commonly referred to as "Brexit."

In his "Rivers of Blood" speech, Powell leaned heavily into lies and scaremongering, listing several alleged examples of racial minorities invading White neighborhoods, harassing the previous occupants and driving them out. For example, he told the story of a "respectable" street in Wolverhampton where, eight years prior, someone had made the mistake of selling a single house to a "Negro." Powell lamented that eight years after this mistake, only one White person lived on the street, an old White lady who had lost both her husband and son in the war, and who watched helplessly as more minorities moved in and transformed her street into a place of "noise and confusion."

Negroes would wake her up at 7 a.m., demanding to use her phone. When she reasonably refused, the Negroes verbally abused her, and would surely have attacked her if not for the chain on her door. Her windows were broken. Excrement was pushed through her letterbox. She couldn't even visit the shops anymore; when she tried, she was followed by "wide-grinning pic-caninnies" who couldn't even speak English, but who would chant the word "racialist" at her. What a nightmare! It's small wonder that one of Powell's constituents apparently complained to him that "In this country in fifteen or twenty years' time the Black man will have the whip hand over the White man." It's small wonder that Powell himself could see that the minorities' actual intentions were not peaceful integration, but "actual domination, first over fellow-immigrants and then over the rest of the population."

It's easy to recognize the fallacious racism in Powell's aggressive stance on integration. However, another, more subtle argument in favor of segregation and against intergroup contact was the idea that White people and ethnic minorities were both simply happier and better off when they kept to themselves. George Wallace was also known to use arguments like these. In 1964, in a letter to a Miss Martin, Wallace argued that he had done more for the "Negroes" of Alabama than any other individual person, including getting them better education, better jobs, and higher pay. It was therefore entirely unfair of anyone to suggest that his support for segregation was due to a hatred of the so-called Negroes. That wasn't it at all. It was just that it was better for both White people and Negroes if they stayed in the company of their own kind. As Wallace put it, it was clear that both White people and Black people preferred "their own pattern of society, their own churches and their own schools—which history and experience have proven are best for both races."

Far from being hateful, Wallace insisted, he was concerned about creating unpleasant friction for both races by forcing them to integrate and thereby disturbing a way of life that was so clearly best for all concerned. Of course, Wallace was not the only prominent figure to use such arguments in favor of continued segregation. Jerry Falwell, a White American pastor and conservative activist, criticized the US Supreme Court's 1954 anti-segregation ruling (Brown *v.* Board of Education) with the words: "The true Negro does not want integration . . . He realizes his potential is far better among his own race."

In this atmosphere, one in which segregation was the prevailing wisdom, Allport's contact hypothesis was the non-intuitive social psychology of its day. To people like Wallace and Powell it may have seemed ludicrous, if not dangerous. The Negroes were doing fine. They were happy where they were, and better off secluded in their own spaces. Forcing Whites and Negroes (or any other minority) to mix would only result in strife and chaos, if not the eventual domination of White people by minorities. The very idea that increasing cross-racial interaction would reduce bias (rather than cause friction) and improve interracial relations (rather than worsen them) was at odds with what many powerful and influential people believed at the time.

Nonetheless, it was absolutely right.

The earliest study I can find on intergroup contact and racism dates back to 1946 and was published by Allport and Kramer in the *Journal of Psychology: Interdisciplinary and Applied.* Allport and Kramer surveyed 437 university students on a number of race-related questions, including the level of interaction they had with racial minorities and their levels of racial prejudice against them. As you can probably guess, Allport and Kramer found that the students who interacted with racial minorities more frequently also reported lower levels of racial prejudice.

This was a start, but it was still just a correlation, a statistical association between two variables. And, as we know, "correlation does not equal causation." Just because intergroup contact was associated with lower levels of prejudice doesn't mean that it was *causing* lower levels of prejudice. It could be the reverse: perhaps it was evidence that people who were less prejudiced were more likely to seek out contact with racial minorities. Or perhaps some other variable, like education or political affiliation, was the real cause behind the levels of both intergroup contact and prejudice.

To clarify whether intergroup contact was actually causing a reduction in racial bias required a genuine experiment—a randomized, controlled trial. The earliest randomized controlled trial on contact and prejudice that I can find was conducted by Sayler in 1969. In this study, 126 White university students were randomly assigned to one of three conditions, "one third (forty-two students) were randomly selected to write term papers . . . one third to tutor White students . . . and the other third to tutor Black students." At the end of the term, the students were all asked what they thought about Black people. As Allport would have certainly predicted, those who had been randomly assigned to tutor the Black students had more positive attitudes toward Black people than the students in the other two groups. This was clear evidence that (at least in this experiment) it was the contact that was causing the reduction in racism.

Skipping thirty-nine years into the far-distant future of 2008, we find research with similar (though more complex) designs and similar, if not better, results. In this case, Shook and Fazio examined the racial attitudes of White American students in their first year of college who were randomly assigned to have either a White roommate (136 students) or an African American roommate (126 students). They tested the students' racial attitudes at two points: in an initial session that took place within the *first* two weeks of their first quarter of college and then in a second session that took place within the *last* two weeks of the same quarter. These two measurements would allow them to see how the students' attitudes changed over time. Also (since they had access to the futuristic technology of 2008), they didn't just ask the White American students what their attitudes toward Black people were in a survey. Instead, they measured their attitudes using an implicit measure (see Chapter 5), one that made it difficult for the White students to misrepresent their attitudes toward Black people.

When using this more foolproof measure, Shook and Fazio still found that, in their own words, "the results supported the contact hypothesis: White freshmen in interracial rooms exhibited significantly more positive automatically activated racial attitudes at the second session than at the first session whereas the automatically activated racial attitudes of freshmen in same-race rooms did not change." In other words, the White students with White roommates didn't become any less racist over time, but the White students with Black roommates did.

The Israeli–Palestinian conflict is one of the most tragic ongoing stories of our time. I am no expert in the relevant history or geopolitics of the region. Also, I am all too aware of how easy it is for a careless, thoughtless, or poorly researched opinion to deeply wound or offend someone affected by that conflict. I am also genuinely reluctant to mention even basic, historically accurate facts about the conflict for fear of being labeled either an antisemite or an Islamophobe. I will thus refrain from offering any of my personal opinions on it here, other than to make the relatively uncontroversial point that the divisions between the local Jewish and local Arab populations are deep, widespread, and devastating.

Yet even in this challenging context of active and ongoing conflict (at least, as of the time of writing), intergroup contact has been shown to reduce racial bias. In 2015, Berger, Benatov, Abu-Raiya, and Tadmor recruited 322 third- and fourth-grade Jewish Israeli and Palestinian Israeli students from schools in

Jaffa, which is now part of Tel Aviv in Israel. The students were randomly split into two groups. The first was a control group who participated in a social program designed to cultivate civic values and develop social-emotional skills. The second group was assigned to complete the "extended class exchange intervention," which was based on intergroup contact principles. It contained many elements, including dancing, doing art, making music, and playing games in mixed groups of Jewish Israeli and Palestinian Israeli students. Students were also encouraged to talk to each other and to become familiar with both the similarities and the differences between them.

Berger and colleagues measured the students' bias against members of the other group (Jewish bias against Palestinian Israelis, and Palestinian bias against Jewish Israelis) at three separate times: before assigning the students to their respective groups; immediately after they completed their social-emotional skills program (in the control condition) or the extended class exchange intervention (in the contact condition); and then fifteen months after the programs had ended. They measured these biases by asking the students to indicate how much the members of the other groups fit certain stereotypes (e.g., bad, lazy, stupid, dirty, ugly, and violent); by asking the students about the emotions they felt about the other group (e.g., anxious, threatened); and by asking them, in a child-friendly way, how happy they would be to live near to someone from the other group.

After fifteen months of interventions and testing, what did Berger and colleagues find? Well, first, they found no differences between the two groups at the start of the experiment, which was important for establishing that the control group and contact group were not meaningfully different before the interventions took place. However, after the interventions, Berger and colleagues found that the students who had completed the contact intervention were less biased against the other group, and that this reduction in bias persisted for at least fifteen months. In their own words: "Overall, the results indicate that the intervention was effective in reducing negative stereotyping, negative feelings and discriminatory tendencies toward children from the other ethnic group." So even in the particularly challenging context of the Israeli–Palestinian conflict, intergroup contact has been shown to reduce racism.

From here, I could provide a long list of similar studies showing that intergroup contact reduces racial bias. However, I think you see where this is going, so how about we just skip straight to the meta-analysis? In 2006, Pettigrew and Tropp conducted a meta-analytical test of intergroup contact. And it was a big one. It spanned several decades and included 713 independent samples from 515 studies, covering over 250,089 individuals from 38 different countries. It represented one of the biggest tests of any psychological intervention to accomplish any goal, and it found overwhelming support for the efficacy and reliability of intergroup contact at reducing prejudice.

Of its many findings, there are a few things in particular that I want to highlight. Even after decades of research, some people were concerned that perhaps intergroup contact wasn't really reducing prejudice (or maybe not reducing it that much), but that it was merely associated with other things that reduced prejudice. If this was the case, we should find that the apparent effects of intergroup contact were larger in correlational studies (in which researchers just look at the associations between variables) than in experiments (in which researchers really tease out the way one variable causes another). However, Pettigrew and Tropp's meta-analysis found exactly the reverse. When they compared the different types of studies, they found that "the mean effect rises sharply for experiments and other rigorously conducted studies" compared to the correlational studies. This implied that the true effects of contact were even stronger—it reduced racism even more effectively—than many of the studies appeared to indicate.

Other people were concerned that intergroup contact was only effective for people who weren't that prejudiced in the first place, and who would probably have chosen to interact with members of other groups anyway. It that were true, it would be a real limitation for contact as a prejudice-reducing intervention, as we wouldn't be able to use contact on higher-prejudice, more resistant individuals.

To address this, Pettigrew and Tropp also compared studies in which the participants were able to choose their interaction partners with studies in which they were simply assigned a partner (i.e., they were not able to choose). When they made this comparison, Pettigrew and Tropp found that "the investigations that allowed no choice for their participants to avoid the intergroup contact yield a slightly larger mean effect size in reducing prejudice than do studies that allowed choice." This undermines the idea that the apparent effects of contact were due to some aspect of the individual who chose to participate in the contact. Indeed, contact seems to work better when people just have to do it, whether they like it or not. Furthermore, some later research, including some of my own (Asbrock et al. in 2013; West, Hotchin et al. in 2017; and West and Hewstone in 2012), suggests that the worse your attitudes are at the start, the more effective contact will be at reducing your prejudice. This isn't just preaching to the choir. Contact works even when you are, metaphorically speaking, preaching to the devil.

To put it as bluntly as possible: if I could offer you one clear piece of scientifically backed advice on how to make yourself less racist right now, I would tell you to put down this book, leave your house, and immediately start spending more time in the company of people against whom you currently hold the strongest racial biases. When was the last time that you were in a majority Black space? A majority Asian space? A majority Muslim space? Why not take a visit to your local mosque? Why not hang out after the services are done and chat with a few people? If they are anything like the people at my local mosque, they will be overjoyed to see you. They'll be welcoming and friendly and happy to answer whatever questions you have. Incidentally, I could say the same thing about my local majority Black Baptist church, which I occasionally attend despite having no religious beliefs of my own.

Or, if religious services aren't your thing, there are parties, concerts, art exhibitions, and many other cultural events. One of the most joyful and rewarding times of my life happened during my studies at Oxford University when my friend Ambika invited me to join her Indian dance performing group. We learned the choreography to "Bumbro," a song made famous by its part in the 2000 Indian Hindi-language Bollywood action thriller *Mission Kashmir*. I never saw the film. I don't understand any of the language. But I spent a summer with Ambika's mostly Indian group, wearing Indian clothes, learning Bollywood dance moves and performing (to significant applause) at majority South Asian events. It was an amazing time and, almost two decades later, I am still grateful to Ambika for inviting me. Also, though this wasn't why I joined the group, the experience almost certainly made me less racist against Indians than I otherwise would have been.

The last set of results I'll look at involves the best way to do intergroup contact. Way back in the 1950s, Allport suggested that there were four necessary conditions for getting intergroup contact to work: (1) the participants should have common goals; (2) the participants should be in a cooperative environment;

(3) the participants from the different groups should have equal status; and (4) the intergroup contact should have the approval of authority. In their 2006 meta-analysis, Pettigrew and Tropp found support for Allport's conditions, stating: "these results show that establishing Allport's optimal conditions in the contact situation generally enhances the positive effects of intergroup contact."

All of which means that if you're planning to use intergroup contact, remember that it's more effective if you make a White teacher interact with ethnic minority teachers (equal status) than if you merely let them teach ethnic minority students (unequal status). It's probably better to organize a session of interracial Lego building (cooperative environment) than inter-racial, every-person-for-themselves, paintball (non-cooperative environment). If you must do competitive games, it's better if you put your White and ethnic minority soccer players on the same team (common goals) than if you organize a friendly five-a-side game of Whites vs. Blacks (competitive goals). And, it's better if you encourage people to try interracial marriage (support of authority) than interracial extramarital affairs (disapproval of authority).

That said, Pettigrew and Tropp also found that, while All-port's four conditions were helpful, they were not (as Allport had originally hypothesized) actually essential. Quite the contrary—even when the conditions were not met, Pettigrew and Tropp's results still showed that contact had a significant positive effect. As they put it, Allport's conditions served to "enhance the tendency for positive contact outcomes to emerge." In a particularly stark example, one of the studies in Pettigrew and Tropp's meta-analysis (by Van Dyk in 1990) investigated the effects of contact between White and Black South Africans during apartheid. These were circumstances that grievously violated Allport's optimal conditions (no equal status, no support of authority, minimal cooperation or common goals) but, even then, contact still worked! So, if for some reason your only option is competitive interracial paintball with your students, or perhaps a game of football pitting you and your same-race friends against your secret interracial lovers, it's certainly not ideal, but it's probably still better than nothing.

Education

It is a vicious and unhelpful stereotype to believe that racism is purely a characteristic of the unintelligent. It's a very simplistic belief. It ignores or implicitly denies the existence of very intelligent racist people: people who use their intelligence to excuse or justify their racist opinions, to invent convincing but ultimately pseudo-scientific racist arguments, or to do racist things while deceiving the people around them into perceiving them as egalitarian. As examples, I'd like to remind you of the racist people discussed in Chapter 6—the chapter on deception. Remember the woman who came up with an elaborate ruse about the White and Latino applicants needing to sign extra paperwork, just so she could send the equally qualified Black candidate away? Remember the man who pretended that he couldn't interview the Black candidate without first seeing references, but cheerfully interviewed the equally qualified White candidate on the spot for the same position? The people in these scenarios clearly carried out their racist acts with an awareness of who would be most likely to collaborate with their racism, considerations of the relative plausibility or deniability of the stories that they told to cover their racism, and the relative likelihood of facing any consequences for their racism. Their actions reveal a lack of morality, but *not* a lack of intelligence.

Perhaps more importantly, the notion that racist people are merely ignorant (or worse, merely uneducated) is a convenient narrative that can be used to distance oneself from racism. Along with her colleagues Andreouli and Howarth, Katy Greenland at the University of Cardiff does very interesting research on how people psychologically construct racism, and how they use these constructions to deny or downplay their own racism and the continued existence of racism in contemporary society. Specifically, one of their papers from 2016 found that people often pretend that racism is "located in other times, places and people." In other words, we discuss racism as if it were a characteristic limited to the older generation, or the unsophisticated country folk, or the ignorant and uneducated: the rednecks and the people from small towns. As well as being overtly ageist, classist, and ill-informed, this limited construction, this "othering" of racism, is used to protect us from perceiving ourselves as racist. It allows us to present ourselves and our societies as "post-racial," and, as the authors put it, "[to render] both racism and anti-racism irrelevant to contemporary societies, thus defusing and derailing a debate about racism." There is real danger to the oversimplified equating of racism and ignorance.

And yet.

In 2012, Hodson and Busseri analyzed two "large-scale, nationally representative United Kingdom data sets:" the 1958 National Child Development Study and the 1970 British Cohort Study. Combined, these data included 15,874 people—an enormous dataset from which statistical conclusions could be very reliably and confidently drawn.

Within these datasets were multiple measures of the participants' cognitive abilities. For example, at the ages of ten or eleven, the participants were assessed for, among other things, their verbal intelligence (recognizing similarities between words), nonverbal intelligence (recognizing similarities between shapes or symbols), matrix abilities (drawing missing aspects of shapes), and digit recall (accurately remembering a string of numbers). The datasets also contained measures of the participants' racism from later in their lives. For example, participants indicated their agreement with statements like "I wouldn't mind working with people from other races," or "I wouldn't mind if a family of a different race moved next door."

By combining these data, Hodson and Busseri could check to see whether there was a statistical relationship between an individual's cognitive ability in youth and their levels of racism later in life. And there was. Hodson and Busseri found a statistically significant "predictive effect of childhood cognitive ability on adult racism," specifically "lower *g* [lower general intelligence factor] in childhood predicts greater prejudice in adulthood." Put simply, less intelligent people grow up to be more racist.

Hodson and Busseri found similar results in a follow-up laboratory study using American participants. Furthermore, they weren't even the first people to posit or find a relationship between intelligence and prejudice. Far from it; as far back as fifty-eight years earlier, in 1954, Gordon Allport had also posited a negative relationship between intelligence and racism. Several other studies conducted over the intervening decades similarly found, as Hodson and Busseri put it, "negative correlations between scores on intelligence subscales and racism."

The explanations behind these relationships are rather complex, and can come across as politically skewed. I have tried as hard as possible to keep politics out of this book. It is, after all, a scientific book, not a political one. However, the research in this case is vast, reliable across several studies, and consistent in multiple populations, so here goes. According to a wealth of research, the connections between lower intelligence and racism often boil down to a lower capacity for abstract thinking, less cognitive flexibility, a resistance to change, and higher levels of social conservatism. In other words, less intelligent people have a harder time grappling with complex philosophical questions and just prefer to maintain the status quo (in this case, a very racist status quo) rather than to question it. They don't like thinking through the justifications for well-established customs and hierarchies, and they don't enjoy changes to the way society is run. As I said, this is repeatedly borne out in the data. Even Hodson and Busseri's 2012 data found that "of the total predictive effect of childhood cognitive ability on adult racism, between 92% and 100% was indirect, mediated via conservative ideology."

The good news, of course, is that we already know how to improve people's cognitive ability; it's called education. This is probably not the kind of claim for which you need much evidence. Nonetheless, I'll confirm there is indeed clear evidence that education, even from a very young age, boosts cognitive ability and tends to reduce personal and social problems later in life. For example, in 2001, Gorey conducted a meta-analysis of 35 experiments and quasi-experiments on education in preschool. Across this large and multi-faceted dataset, Gorey found that the effects of education on preschoolers were "statistically significant, positive, and large," and that these effects could be shown to endure for at least "5 to 10 years." A formal education is certainly not the only way to improve your intelligence, but it definitely has multiple short-term and long-term benefits for both your cognitive ability and social adjustment.

It is therefore unsurprising that it also has effects on racial attitudes and beliefs. In 2012, Wodtke surveyed 8,808 American adults (of varying racial identities) about their levels of education and their racial attitudes. He found that "whites, Hispanics, and blacks with higher levels of education are more likely to reject negative stereotypes," that "Education is ... related to more favorable attitudes toward race-targeted job training," and that "education has consistent positive effects on awareness of discrimination against minorities." None of these results were particularly surprising. Indeed, they fit quite well within the broader context of research on education and racism in White people. As Wodtke put it, "A large body of empirical evidence supports this view, showing that highly educated whites are more likely to reject negative racial stereotypes, agree with structural explanations for black–white inequality, and endorse principles of equal treatment."

Furthermore, while a general education is useful for all the reasons mentioned above, education specifically about race and racism is also important. For example, in 2001, Rudman, Ashmore, and Gary compared two groups of university students (47 in total). The first group of students (the control group) were enrolled in a research methods course taught by a White female professor. The second group (the experimental group) were enrolled in a prejudice and conflict seminar taught by an African American male professor. All the students completed the same measures: an explicit measure of their stereotypes about Black people (in which they responded to questions such as, "What proportion of Blacks are lazy?"), and an implicit measure of their stereotypes about Black people (i.e., an Implicit Association Test). These measures were taken twice: once at the beginning of the term and once at the end of the term, which would allow the researchers to see how both sets of students changed over time.

The results were remarkably clear. In the researchers' own words, "prejudice and conflict seminar students showed less anti-Black biases at the end of the semester, compared with the beginning. Moreover, they did so at both the implicit and explicit levels." In contrast, "control students did not show significant

252 THE SCIENCE OF RACISM

change in either implicit or explicit orientations." In a second study, reported in the same paper, Rudman and colleagues added a third condition—another course taught by the same African American professor that was unrelated to prejudice and conflict. Using this three-condition design, they were able to determine that it was the content of the course, not just the identity of the professor, that made the difference. In both prejudice-irrelevant courses, whether they were taught by a White or African American professor, the students' racism scores stayed the same. However, as in the first experiment, students in the prejudice and conflict course showed less implicit and explicit racism at the end.

Beyond this, a series of studies conducted by Phia Salter and her colleagues (see, for example, Bonam et al. 2018 and Nelson et al. 2013) have shown that denial and ignorance about past racism leads to a reduced ability to comprehend or recognize contemporary racism. Across a number of studies, they found that White people perform worse than Black people on measures of historical knowledge about racism; that White people are also less likely to perceive instances of contemporary racism; that White people's lower level of historical knowledge explains their lower likelihood of recognizing racism; and that interventions which teach White people about historical racism can improve their knowledge and their perceptions of contemporary racism.

All this makes a very convincing case for the power and importance of education, including education specifically about racism. It's part of the reason why I am unwilling to entirely denounce diversity training initiatives; some diversity training can be useful, provided it's done correctly. Research is very clear that educating ourselves, improving our cognitive flexibility, strengthening our abstract thinking and openness to change, and assimilating specific racism-related knowledge should reduce our implicit and explicit racial bias, and increase our ability to perceive instances of contemporary racism. I guess it's a good thing that you bought this book.

Media

Let's play a game. It's a game that I sometimes play with audiences when I give seminars on racism. It's best if you play the game in a group, so if you're reading this chapter with friends, colleagues, or students, this would be a great time to involve them. However, don't worry too much if you're reading alone. It still works reasonably well even if you play it by yourself.

Let's go.

Step 1 of the game: I'd like you to raise your hand if you either have children or remember being a child yourself. Yes, I know that this includes almost everyone, but it's just good game design that the first stage of every game should be very easy. It exists just to give you a sense of the mechanics of the game and an easy sense of accomplishment at getting through the first stage. So well done.

Step 2 of the game: I'd like you to think of ten children's books. These can either be books that you've read to your child (or children), or books that you used to read when you were a child. For example, thinking of my own children, I could list books such as *The Tiger Who Came to Tea*, *The Gruffalo*, *The Very Hungry Caterpillar*, *Thomas the Tank Engine*, and (when my boys got a bit older) *The Call of the Wild*. That's just five books, and that's a list from my life. I want you to offer a list from your life.

If you've completed the list of ten books, give yourself a hand.

For Step 3 of the game, I want you to count the number of books that contain actual human beings. That might seem like a weird request, but you may have noticed that many children's books don't contain human beings. Instead, animals and monsters feature prominently. Looking at my own list, for example, *The Gruffalo* has a mouse, a fox, an owl, a snake, and a Gruffalo, and that's it. No humans. *The Tiger Who Came to Tea* has humans, but also the eponymous tiger, who knocks on doors, speaks in very polite English, and, not to spoil the book for you, comes to tea. So, depending on the books you like to read, the number that contain actual humans might be a bit low. This number is important, however. (Looking at my own list, just three of the books contain humans: *The Tiger Who Came to Tea*, *Thomas the Tank Engine*, and *The Call of the Wild*.)

This is where things get interesting.

Step 4: Looking at your list of books that contain humans, I want you to write down the number of those books that contain any humans who aren't White.

Looking at my own list of five, for example, there are no non-White people in *The Tiger Who Came to Tea*. Sophie and her mummy (who welcome the tiger to tea) are White. Daddy (who is at work) is also White. There are also no non-White people in *Thomas the Tank Engine*. Sir Topham Hatt, all the other train staff, they're all White. Only *Call of the Wild* contains any non-White people. The main characters are all White, but there are also the Yeehats, a fictional tribe of bloodthirsty, savage Indians (i.e., Native Americans) who show up near the end and murder people. That's obviously not a great portrayal of an entire culture, but they're there, and it counts. So that's one: one book on my list that contains anyone who isn't White.

Step 5: Non-White is a very broad descriptor. Let's get more specific. Write down the number of books on your list that contain any Black people. Then write down the number of books that contain any East Asian people. Then do it for South Asian people, and then for Middle Eastern/North African people.

Step 6: Even Step 5 is a bit broad. We can be more specific. Write down the number of books on your list that contain a Black woman with a job, a Black man who takes care of children, a Middle Eastern person who isn't a refugee.

I could go on. But the point of the game should be clear by now. If you're like most people, for the last few steps in the game, you've probably been looking at a string of zeros. When I play this game with my audiences, it is both revealing and disheartening to see all the hands go down once the questions about ethnic minority characters begin. Indeed, even if you expand your list of children's books from your ten favorites to every single children's book you can remember, many people can't name a single children's book in which the main character is a human being who is not White.

This isn't entirely their fault. When it comes to children's books, non-White characters are hard to find. In 2022, the Center for Literacy in Primary Education published a report on ethnic representation within British children's literature between 2017 and 2021. Some of the findings were shocking. For example, among the 9,115 children's books published in the UK in 2017, just 1% of them featured a non-White person as a main character (compared to the 18% of the UK that isn't White). Indeed, almost all of the books (96%) depicted no non-White characters at all. Things improved somewhat between 2017 and 2021 and the proportion of non-White main characters rose from 1% to 9%, but that's still only half of what it should be if the books were representative of the UK population.

Things are even worse when we move away from all the published books and just focus on the most popular 100 books—the ones people actually tend to buy and read to their children. In 2018, using data from Nielsen BookScan, which provides data for the book publishing industry, the *Guardian* and the *Observer* analyzed the top 100 bestselling illustrated children's books of that year. Of these top 100, only five featured any non-White characters in leading roles. However, underrepresentation may not even have been the most serious concern. Rather, negative representation may have been the greater problem. Of these five books that contained any central non-White characters, three of them were from the *What the Ladybird Heard* series, a set of books that include the character Lanky Len, a non-White burglar. What a horrifyingly efficient way to teach young children that ethnic minorities are absent, or unimportant, or criminal.

There is some room for interpretation with these numbers. The Center for Literacy in Primary Education, for example, included books that were self-published and sometimes had to get ethnic diversity data indirectly. The *Guardian* analysis amalgamated data for the years in which books were published and the years in which books were sold, which may have also skewed their findings. Still, even if we assume some inaccuracy in these numbers, the scientific literature also shows severe underrepresentation and misrepresentation of racial minorities throughout a variety of seemingly innocuous media (not just children's books), and also that this negative representation has significant effects on levels of racism.

In a content analysis of all prime-time dramas and comedies from major American networks in 1999, Harwood and Anderson found in 2002 that White people were overrepresented while some ethnic minorities (for instance, Latinos) were underrepresented. In 2015, Facciani and colleagues performed an in-depth analysis of 28 randomly selected comic books from the most popular titles in the "Modern Age of Comics" (a particularly vibrant time in the history of American superhero comic books, between 1991 and 2005). This included 8,155 frames, 3,454 protagonists, 2,468 aggressors, and 23,243 characters in total. Unsurprisingly, Facciani and colleagues also found that White people were overrepresented and ethnic minorities were underrepresented. Indeed, they even found that "Aliens, demons, and other types of non-human lifeforms were more likely to be represented than all human racial minorities combined." That's right. If there are aliens out there in the universe reading human comics on the sly, it's entirely possible that they're getting better representation than Black people or Latinos.

But this isn't just limited to entertainment. Across a series of studies, Dixon and Linz investigated how people of different ethnicities are represented in the news, specifically across a variety of news stations in the Los Angeles area. In 2000, using a carefully selected representative sample of 116 different news programs from multiple stations, they too found the familiar pattern: White people were overrepresented while other people, such as Black people and Latinos, were underrepresented.

Except, that's not quite what they found. What they actually found was even worse. It wasn't just that the ethnic minorities were underrepresented. In a finding eerily reminiscent of the Lanky Len statistic, Dixon and Linz found that ethnic minorities were underrepresented in positive roles, but overrepresented in negative roles. For example, Black people were more likely to be portrayed as criminals than White people were—2.5 times as likely to be portrayed as felons, for example—but much less likely to be portrayed as guardians of the law, such as policemen or judges. Before you suggest that this is merely because the news was accurately reflecting real life, and that Black people really *are* more likely to be criminals and less likely to be judges: Dixon and Linz found that this was absolutely not the case. Black people made up almost twice the proportion of criminals in these news programs (37%) as they did in real life, according to the police's own numbers (21%). Other research finds similar things.

Turning back to Facciani and colleagues' 2015 analysis of comic books, they similarly found, for example, that "black characters were more likely to be represented as having lower socioeconomic status compared to white characters." Once again, if you're about to ask whether this was merely reflective of the reality—it wasn't. Facciani and colleagues found that 37% of Black comic-book characters were represented as low in socioeconomic status. That is a bit of a fuzzy and subjective term, so it's hard to find perfectly comparable numbers. However, according to statistics from the US Census Bureau, the percentage of Black people actually in poverty was only about 25% in 2015: significantly lower than the proportion represented in Facciani's study. This isn't accurate representation, just bad representation. So, whether it's a children's book, a comic book, or a news program—if you see ethnic minorities represented at all, they probably won't be represented favorably.

All this bad representation has consequences. In 2008, Dixon conducted a survey of White Americans' viewing habits and their attitudes toward Black people. Even after he statistically controlled for other factors such as gender, age, politics, education, and income, he still found that watching more network news (not extreme right-wing propaganda, just regular network news) predicted more anti-Black racism. Specifically, people who watched more network news thought that African Americans were poorer, more intimidating and more hostile.

Dixon's 2008 research relied on surveys and correlations, but genuine experiments also confirm these findings. In 2002, in a randomized controlled trial, Gilliam and colleagues exposed 390 White participants to real news stories minimally edited to make it seem as though they were about either White criminals or about Black criminals. Even after just twelve minutes of watching news stories about Black criminals—news stories of the kind that we know are overrepresented in the mainstream news media—Gilliam's participants expressed more negative, stereotypical ideas about Black people as a group, and endorsed more punitive policies to address crime. In 2017, in another randomized controlled trial, Dukes and Gaither found that after an unarmed civilian is shot by the police, even brief exposure to the kind of negative, stereotypical information often published about Black people is enough to make news consumers more likely to blame the victim for getting shot than the police officer for shooting him.

Fortunately, as was the case with education, this is a problem that suggests its own solution. As poor representations of ethnic minorities increase racism, so can positive representations decrease racism. In 1999, Fujioka surveyed 249 White and East Asian participants about their television consumption and their attitudes toward African Americans. Though there were some differences between the White and East Asian participants, the overall findings were very straightforward. Higher numbers of negative portrayals predicted more negative beliefs about African Americans, while higher numbers of positive portrayals predicted more positive beliefs about African Americans. Furthermore, Fujioka was also clear that the sheer number of African American representations was not the significant predictor of racist beliefs. Rather it was the positivity (or negativity) of the representations that mattered. This is important because we often discuss representation in terms of frequency while overlooking the nature of those representations. It's no good increasing the number of ethnic minorities in your media consumption if most of them are like Lanky Len.

Experimental findings confirm these results. For example, in 2001, Dasgupta and Greenwald recruited 73 participants for a study that was ostensibly about "general knowledge." After coming to the lab, the participants were split into three conditions and either shown (1) images of admired Black people and disliked White people (for example, Denzel Washington and Jeffrey Dahmer); (2) images of disliked Black people and admired White people (for example, Mike Tyson and Tom Hanks); or (3) pictures unrelated to race or people in any way, such as pictures of flowers. After looking at their assigned pictures, all the participants completed a White–Black Implicit Associations Test, the reaction-time test discussed in Chapter 5 that can detect racial bias even if you're unwilling or unable to admit to it. After just a few minutes looking at these pictures, the first condition (the Denzel Washington condition) showed significant reductions in their implicit anti-Black biases—reductions that did not occur for the other two conditions. When the experimenter checked on the participants a day later, the effects were still there, showing that this reduction in implicit racism didn't immediately fade away after the participants left the lab.

Finally, we must acknowledge that our control over the media available to us is sometimes limited. We don't always have the luxury of choosing books or television programs that represent everyone in a fair and balanced way. Sometimes it's just too much effort to wade through all the children's books published in a year to find the tiny proportion featuring positive examples of ethnic minorities as main characters. Fortunately, research has found ways of coping with that too. In 2007, Ramasubramanian recruited 158 White American participants. She showed all the participants five real news stories. However, depending on the conditions to which they were assigned, some of the participants saw negative news stories which reinforced stereotypes about ethnic minorities (that African Americans are violent and unemployed, or that Indians are hyper-traditional and very poor), while other participants saw either control news stories unrelated to race, or counter-stereotypical news stories.

However, before they were shown any news stories, participants were also randomly assigned to one of two other conditions. The first was a control condition, in which they were mostly told about memory; the second, a media literacy condition, which is the one we're really interested in. Media literacy is defined as "discriminating responsiveness to media," which is the habit of questioning what we see or read in the media, rather than passively taking it for granted as an accurate reflection of reality. If you're doing it well, it should, according to the authors, "foster critical thinking and discussion of media-related issues, including how media messages are created, marketed, and distributed as well as their potential influence." After getting their instructions (control or media literacy) and then watching their assigned media (negative stereotypes, counter-stereotypical, or control), all participants then completed implicit measures of their stereotypes of ethnic minorities.

This design might seem a bit confusing, but it's easier to follow when you realize that Ramasubramanian was trying to independently investigate the effects of the media we all watch (that is, whether you consume negative stereotypes about minorities) and your approach to watching that media (whether you consume it passively or critically). Can a more discriminating approach to media protect us, at least a bit, from the negative effects?

Well, to get the obvious results out of the way, Ramasubramanian found that positive, counter-stereotypical media led to less racial bias than the control or stereotypical media. That much is very similar to the findings of the other studies we've discussed so far. However, the more exciting finding was that media literacy appeared to have its own positive effects on racial bias. Furthermore, the strongest combination occurred when the participants viewed positive, counter-stereotypical media *and* approached media critically. The benefits were additive.

In Ramasubramanian's own words, "the current findings suggest that even the so-called subconscious, automatic process of stereotype activation can respond to motivational factors such as media literacy training and contextual factors such as exposure to counter-stereotypical information."

So, go pick up a copy of Malorie Blackman's *Marty Monster,* *Jabari Jumps* by Gaia Cornwall, *Where's That Cat?* by Manjula Padmanabhan, *The Adventures of Wrong Man and Power Girl!* by C. Alexander London and Frank Morrison, or *The Snowy Day* by Ezra Jack Keats (all children's books with strong, likeable, ethnic minority leads, two of which have a Black father taking care of his child). Read them to your children. Read them to yourself. Surround yourself with news programs, comic books, novels, and films that depict ethnic minorities often, and depict them positively. And if, for whatever reason, you can't do that, then at the very least learn to consume media with a pinch of skepticism. Acknowledge that the news stations don't just accurately report important events, but that they do so with a spin that reflects and perpetuates racial biases. Accept that even the most seemingly innocuous of media (like children's stories) can contain damaging, racist messages. Explain these facts to your children. That way, even if we can't always make the media around us better, we can still make ourselves better prepared for it.

Chapter 13

A Change Is Gonna Come
Remembering Systemic Racism

I've read a lot of articles about racism. I've been to a lot of talks and heard a lot of speeches about racism. Most of them end right there, where Chapter 12 ended. Now that the reader or listener has acquired a good understanding of what racism is, and now that they've learned a few proven strategies to help them *personally* lower their levels of racism, many people feel like it's time to draw things to a close.

I don't.

Indeed, in many ways, I feel as though the real conversation on how to address racism has hardly begun. To explain why, I will once again direct you to the quote from Stokely Carmichael that I referenced in Chapter 4. As he said, "If a White man wants to lynch me, that's his problem. If he's got the power to lynch me, that's my problem. Racism is not a question of attitude; it's a question of power."

To me, this quote highlights the clearest explanation of why so many approaches to tackling racism fail, why they were never set up to succeed in the first place, and why stopping at the end of Chapter 12 wouldn't be nearly enough. It's true that every strategy mentioned in that chapter (intergroup contact, education, and modifying our media) has been scientifically proven to reduce racism, but only in that they alter our *personal* racial attitudes, beliefs and behaviors. As Carmichael might have put it, they are only concerned with the issue of whether the White man *wants* to lynch me. They are only concerned with *his* (the White man's) problem. On the subject of *my* problem, on the issue of whether he has the *power* to lynch me, these solutions have very, very little to say.

Of course, both power and attitude matter. However, a bit of thought exposes which of the two should be more important. I personally would much rather live in a world in which every White man wanted to lynch me, but none of them had the power to do it, than a world in which no White men wanted to lynch me, but every single one of them had the power to do it. In the first instance, I may be disliked, but I am still perfectly safe. In the second, I am safe for the moment, but my life and security hang on the whims of people who could, at any time, and for any reason, withdraw that goodwill. No matter how effectively we do it, we will never solve racism by focusing exclusively on getting White people to like ethnic minorities more. Sooner or later, we must alter the nature of our society so that ethnic minorities can be less concerned about whether White people like them or not.

Brilliantly illustrative of this divergence is a study conducted by Saguy and colleagues in 2009, for which they recruited 210 undergraduate student participants and randomly assigned them to either a high-power condition, or a low-power condition. The participants in the high-power group were given control over the allocation of credits each person received for taking part in the study. They could decide to give themselves all the credits and give none to the low-power group. They could decide to give all the credits to the low-power group and keep none for themselves. They could decide to split them evenly. Either way, the choice was entirely theirs. Conversely, as was implied by the name, the participants in the low-power group had no say over how the credits were distributed. Whatever the high-power participants decided, they would have to live with it.

On top of this, Saguy and colleagues set up two other conditions to which participants could be randomly assigned. In all conditions, the participants were instructed to have a cross-group interaction. They were matched up in groups of six (that is, each group would contain three high-power participants and three low-power participants) and told to talk to each other for about six minutes. However, depending on the condition to which they were assigned, they were instructed to have either a conversation that focused on the similarities between the two groups (a condition meant to mimic positive intergroup contact), or a conversation that focused on the difference between the two groups—a condition that would highlight the injustice of the power differential between the groups.

Putting those two conditions together, a participant could end up in one of four circumstances: (1) high-power group + similarities-focused conversation; (2) high-power group + difference-focused conversation; (3) low-power group + similarities-focused conversation; or (4) low-power group + differences-focused conversation. After the conversations had ended, all the participants reported their attitudes toward the other group, the members of the low-power group indicated how many credits they expected to receive from the high-power group, and the high-power students got to decide how they would distribute the credits.

The specific purpose of this design was to reveal a potential weakness in strategies like those covered in Chapter 12. Saguy and colleagues were very much aware of the prior decades of intergroup contact research. They knew all too well that the similarities-focused conversation should produce more positive attitudes, and they expected that it would lead the low-power group to *expect* more favorable treatment from the high-power group. But would it actually lead to better treatment from the high-power group? On that point, they weren't so sure.

So, what were their results? As they hypothesized, Saguy and colleagues found "the expected main effect of contact type on out-group attitudes." Specifically, participants who took part in the similarities-focused discussions had more positive attitudes toward the members of the other group than did the participants in the differences-focused discussions. No surprises so far.

Also as hypothesized, Saguy and colleagues found that the "members of the disadvantaged groups tended to expect more out-group fairness following commonality-focused contact." Again, no surprises. After the friendlier interactions, the low-power people expected to receive better treatment (in the form of more credits) from the high-power people.

But did they?

No. They did not. As Saguy and colleagues put it, "In contrast to disadvantaged-group members' expectations, no effects of contact type (commonality- vs. difference-focused) emerged with respect to the number of credits advantaged-group members allocated to the out-group." Put more simply, even though the low-power participants expected to be treated better after their positive interactions with the high-power participants, these expectations did not match reality. Indeed, the researchers found that there were "no significant associations between out-group attitudes and credits allocated to the out-group." It didn't matter how much they liked you, they still weren't going to share any more of the credits. Whether the conversation was similarities-focused or differences-focused, the high-power students still assigned most of the credits to themselves. All that changed was whether or not the low-power students saw it coming.

Taking this back to Stokely Carmichael's quote, we can see

the real danger of interventions that focus solely on the attitudes of people in power: attitudes don't always translate into useful changes in behavior. Sometimes, the White man's feelings don't matter. Whether they're about lynching you, about discriminating against you in employment, or in healthcare, or in policing, or in the justice system, or immigration, or voting, or whatever! The feelings may not matter. What matters is the power. Had the low-power participants in Saguy's study acquired the power to decide on the distribution of the credits, you can be sure that this distribution would have been significantly more equitable, and to hell with the attitudes of the high-power participants.

This problem wasn't just limited to imaginary groups created for laboratory experiments. In 2010, Dixon and colleagues did a review of studies similar to Saguy's—studies that highlighted how boosting friendly cross-group attitudes might actually work *against* those in positions of less power. They found a devastating range of examples. One study (by Dixon, Durrheim, and Tredoux in 2007) found that "Black South Africans who reported having positive contact with Whites tended to be less supportive of such efforts [to overcome the country's legacy of racial inequality]." Another study (by Tausch, Saguy, and Singh in 2009), conducted in India, found that "Hindu friends improved Muslims' attitudes toward Hindus but also diminished their awareness of group inequalities and, in so doing, diminished their intentions to engage in actions to improve the situation of Muslims in India." Yet another study (by Saguy, Tausch, Dovidio, and Pratto in 2009) found that "cross-group friendship was positively associated with Israeli Arabs' perceptions of Israeli Jews as 'fair' and negatively associated . . . with support for social change to improve the situation of Arabs in Israel." And yet another study (by Wright and Lubensky in 2008) with African American and Latino students in the United States found that "contact with Whites diminished support for collective action to achieve racial equality."

These studies make it clear that we cannot afford to delude ourselves. Intergroup contact, education, and an improved media diet will almost certainly reduce racist attitudes, both implicit and explicit. They will almost certainly increase intergroup harmony. But, as Dixon and colleagues put it, we cannot "eat harmony." At some point, friendly conversations cease to be sufficient. We must fight for more power, and for better conditions. In this sense, the words of Frederick Douglass are as relevant today as they were when he delivered a speech on West Indian emancipation in New York in 1857:

> If there is no struggle there is no progress. Those who profess to favor freedom and yet deprecate agitation are men who want crops without plowing up the ground; they want rain without thunder and lightning. They want the ocean without the awful roar of its many waters.
>
> This struggle may be a moral one, or it may be a physical one, and it may be both moral and physical, but it must be a struggle. Power concedes nothing without a demand. It never did and it never will.

Back in Chapter 11, I discussed the research of professors Frank Dobbin and Alexandra Kalev, who reviewed the practices and diversity-related outcomes of over 700 large companies over multiple decades to determine which diversity initiatives were the most and least effective. I mentioned that diversity training initiatives, initiatives that lean heavily on education and changing attitudes, were among the least effective at increasing diversity in companies. But would you like to guess what the most effective strategies were?

Dixon and Saguy would probably be able to guess. The most effective strategies were not those that depended on personal attitudes, but those that relied on authority, transparency, and accountability. Dobbin and Kalev make this clear many times. For example, take it from Kalev and colleagues (2006): "Structures that embed accountability, authority, and expertise (affirmative action plans, diversity committees and taskforces, diversity managers and departments) are the most effective means of increasing the proportions of white women, black women, and black men in private sector management." Or perhaps take it from Dobbin and colleagues (2007): "Our analyses show that making a person or a committee responsible for diversity is very effective." Regardless of the personal feelings within the organizations, the best approaches are structural: approaches that make it clear who has the responsibility to increase diversity, and the powers they will have to effect those changes.

If the statistics on the prevalence of diversity training are at all accurate, you almost certainly belong to an organization that is trying to increase its diversity and inclusion in some way (or, at least, one that claims that it is). I invite you to seriously consider how that organization has approached this daunting task. Have they relied exclusively or almost exclusively on interventions that tackle personal feelings—intergroup contact, diversity education, media campaigns? Has it all been diversity training, awareness campaigns, encouraging posters, and blogs written by members of underrepresented groups? If so, then at best they are well-meaning, but limited. They may accomplish some genuine reductions in personal racism, but probably not much more.

By contrast, has your organization identified in clear, measurable terms what its diversity goals actually are, the specific person (or committee) with both the power and the responsibility to make sure those goals are met, and what the consequences will be if the goals are not met? Has your organization removed systemic barriers to involvement that keep ethnic minorities from full participation? Has it introduced systemic solutions like affirmative action policies?

And, speaking of affirmative action policies, we should note that what is true in the workplace also applies to broader society. Again, I acknowledge that personal attitudes can be important. I am not entirely disregarding the value of reducing individual racism or of making interracial interactions more positive. Still, rather than just obsessing over whether individual teachers like ethnic minority students, we should also investigate and restrict the policy failures that allow them to teach minority students poorly (recall Jacoby-Senghor and colleagues' findings from 2016), or to punish minority students unfairly for adopting the same behaviors as the White students (recall Gilliam and colleagues in 2016, as well as Shepherd in 2011). Rather than just worrying about how to make professors like ethnic minority doctoral candidates more, we should fix the flawed, unclear processes that allow these biased preferences to close doors for ethnic minority students in the first place (recall Milkman and colleagues 2015). Instead of just training police officers—and members of the public—to be more sympathetic toward ethnic minorities, we should address the serious systemic gaps that allow them to use disproportionate force against ethnic minorities (recall Bowling and Phillips 2007) or kill ethnic minorities with impunity (recall Correll and colleagues 2007). Instead of just worrying why doctors are more likely to offer White people thrombolytic therapy for myocardial infarction (recall Green and colleagues' research from 2007), we should have systems in place so that someone is held accountable when they do.

And, while we're at it, we should modify the British immigration system to undo the damage started in 1963. We should assign every American a free, easily sourced government ID, one that is acceptable for voting. We should reinstate university-level affirmative action programs. We should put our energy into dismantling every systemic obstacle, from sparse voting booths in ethnic minority neighborhoods, to the links between property taxes and funding for children's education, to openly discriminatory laws about dress, hairstyles, gun ownership and loitering. We should vote for people who will dismantle systemic racism and flatly refuse to consider voting for anyone who ignores it, perpetuates it or bolsters it. According to the research, these are the changes that will make the biggest difference. Or, as Stokely Carmichael might put it, these are the solutions that will address *my* problems, instead of just addressing *yours*.

Afterword

Spaceland
Other Dimensions of Bias

One of my favorite books of all time is *Flatland*, a novella by Edwin Abbott Abbott, published in 1884. It is the charming story of a square—a two-dimensional being who lives in a two-dimensional world called, no prizes for guessing, Flatland. In the story, the square meets a most confusing, shape-shifting, tele-porting creature. But this creature turns out to have no magical powers at all. It is merely a sphere, a being from the three-dimensional world of Spaceland, who can interact with the square's two-dimensional plane. When the sphere passes through the plane, he seems to appear out of nowhere, grow, shrink and disappear again. When the square locks a secret object away in his two-dimensional safe, the sphere (from his three-dimensional perspective) can still see it, and can even take the object out without ever opening the safe. In their adventures, the sphere takes the square under his wing, soaring "up" into the higher dimensions. Throughout, the story charmingly pretends to be the tale of how the sphere taught the square to understand a world of three dimensions, to elevate itself from Flatland into Spaceland. But, in truth, the gift of the story is the way it teaches us, as three-dimensional creatures, how to understand a world of four dimensions, how to elevate ourselves into something higher.

The Science of Racism is a one-dimensional book. It deals

with racism, and only racism. However, we do not live in a one-dimensional world. Racism is not the only widespread societal problem for which social psychology offers unique, science-based insights and solutions.

Let's go back to the study published by Eaton and colleagues (including myself) in 2020, which I last mentioned in Chapter 9. As you might remember, we sent out 251 CVs to large, public, research-active universities. The CVs were equivalent, but some of the CVs had White names on them and others had ethnic minority names. Despite being equally qualified, the White people were judged as more competent and hireable than the ethnic minorities.

Everything I just said about that study is true, but it's not the whole truth. Yes, some of the CVs had White names on them and some had ethnic minority names, but the CVs differed in another way as well. Some of them had men's names on them, and some had women's names.

What, then, was the effect of apparent gender on perceived competence and hireability? The full results are complex, because there were multiple types of ethnic minorities and what we found varied a little depending on the specific group. So, to demonstrate my next point as straightforwardly as possible, I'll narrow our focus to just the White and Black CVs. Looking at this limited subset, we have four types of CVs: (1) White men's CVs, (2) Black men's CVs, (3) White women's CVs, and (4) Black women's CVs. Remember, other than this change in apparent demographic identity, the CVs were all equivalent, so they should all have been seen as equally competent and equally hireable.

But of course, they weren't. You already know that the Black applicants were seen as less competent and hireable than the equally qualified White ones. What you should be able to guess is that the women were also seen as less competent and hireable than the equally qualified men. And what happened when these categories were combined? Well, the White man was seen as the most competent and hireable of the four. Behind him were the Black man and the White woman, who were seen as about equally competent and hireable. And then, significantly below these latter two, came the Black woman, who, despite having the same CV as everyone else, was seen as the least hireable and competent of all.

My point here is twofold. This book has taken pains to present the unassailable scientific knowledge that racism exists, and to explain the scientific methodology on which that knowledge is based. My first point is that the same scientific methodology also points us to the unassailable conclusion that sexism exists. It would have been entirely possible to write, instead of this book, a book called *The Science of Sexism*. It would have had its own chapters on methodology and meta-analysis, on implicit and explicit bias, on deception and psychological trickery, on diversity training and modifying media, on personal and structural biases. I do acknowledge that other books (for example, *The Authority Gap* by Mary Ann Sieghart, which I really enjoyed) have approached the topic of sexism and have used scientific findings to do so. For my part, and I fully acknowledge this as a matter of personal preference, I would like to see books that lean even more heavily into the science and rely less on the stories and anecdotes. The empirical research is there, waiting for someone to compile it and translate it for a broader audience. Perhaps someone should do that, although it won't be me.

My second point is that racism and sexism don't exist in separate worlds. There aren't two versions of Flatland, one in which racism affects outcomes and one in which sexism affects outcomes. There is only Spaceland, in which racism and sexism together affect outcomes all the time. Some Black people are women. Some women are Black people. And, as that last experiment showed, the experience of being a Black woman is not the same as either that of being a Black man or that of being a White woman.

But it gets more complicated.

That last experiment showed the simplest possible combination of the effects of racism and sexism. The two effects were in the same direction—that is, both Black people and women were perceived as less competent and hireable—and the combined effect was additive: the Black woman was perceived less favorably than either the Black man or the White woman. However, sometimes effects are more complex than that. Sometimes, they're interactive.

Recall the study I did in 2019 in which I asked about 3,500 White British people about their racialized dating preferences. In the earlier chapters of the book, I said that White people most strongly, and by a significant margin, preferred other White people and that next in line were Black people, then East Asian people, then South Asian people. All that was true, but it wasn't the whole truth. That pattern of preferences (White > Black > East Asian > South Asian) only applied to the sample as a whole. When I split the sample into people who were attracted to men versus people who were attracted to women, I got a different result.

Specifically, people who were attracted to men kept the same pattern I mentioned above: White > Black > East Asian > South Asian. However, for people who were attracted to women the pattern was subtly different: White > East Asian > Black > South Asian. In the paper, I explained that this pattern was a result of racialized sexual stereotypes: "Black people (both men and women) are stereotyped as being aggressive, hypersexual, and masculine . . . conversely, East Asians are stereotyped as being very submissive and feminine." It was therefore unsurprising that people who were attracted to men preferred (supposedly hypermasculine) Black partners to (supposedly hyperfeminine) East Asian partners, while people who were attracted to women preferred (supposedly hyperfeminine) East Asian partners to (supposedly hypermasculine) Black partners. In this case, it's not a simple matter of adding together the effects of racism and sexism. Instead, racism and sexism interact in complex ways to produce new patterns of discrimination. Is it easier to be a Black person or an East Asian person in a predominantly White dating scene? It depends on whether you're a man or a woman.

And that is just adding sexism to our list of potential dimensions. But there are still more dimensions. A wealth of research shows that sexual minorities are treated worse than heterosexual people, that religious minorities are treated worse than religious majorities, that disabled people are treated worse than able-bodied people, that working-class people are treated worse than middle-class and upper-class people, that immigrants are treated worse than non-immigrants, that transgender people are treated worse than cisgender people, that fat people are treated worse than thin people, and the list goes on and on and on. Each of these topics could be its own book. Each has its own studies, its own meta-analyses, its own caveats, its own false solutions, its own Trojan Horses. Furthermore, all these categories can occur in combination. Some working-class Black women are religious minorities. Some transgender people are disabled. Some Indian lesbians are immigrants. We do not live in Flatland. The world is terrifyingly more complex than that.

That said, complexity should not be your excuse for inaction. Personally, I abhor the kind of more-aware-than-thou one-upmanship that serves only to point out the flaws in other people's efforts and to ensure that no effort at all is ever truly made. I have sat in meetings in which people were tasked with designing initiatives to address racism, but ended up bickering with each other about whether the interventions also did enough to address this or that *other* social problem. And, in the end, because nobody could agree on anything, there was no antiracist intervention at all. Meanwhile, outside the meeting room, all the old racism, explicit and implicit, individual and systemic, continued unabated.

This is clearly counterproductive. It is unlikely that any intervention would even be capable of fully addressing racism, much less the dazzling array of prejudice that exists in contemporary society. We need not demand of ourselves such unrealistic perfection. So long as we are honest about what we're doing and what the limits of our efforts are, I firmly believe that it is better to do *something* (so long as that something is backed by science), than to be overwhelmed by complexity and do *nothing*.

Still, even with all that said, I think it's important to keep the complexity in mind. Move forward through Flatland as well as you can, reduce racism as well as you can, but never forget the wider Spaceland that surrounds it, and be ready to move into Spaceland when your knowledge and resources allow. Do your antiracism work, but don't lose sight of the fact that there are many types of prejudice in this world that have nothing to do with race, and others that interact with race to produce their own unique and horrible patterns of discrimination.

It would be a piss-poor form of antiracism that only benefited middle-class, able-bodied, heterosexual, cisgender, nonimmigrant men of color.

Acknowledgments

I am grateful to so many people for their contribution to this work. Thank you to my community in Jamaica who gave me a strong enough sense of who I am that I default to interpreting racism as a flaw in the other, rather than as a shortcoming in myself. Thank you to my old professors at Macalester who took an overconfident, sheltered young man and were the first to show him the complex, confusing workings of the world. This includes my White professors as well as the professors of color, and those in the French department as well as the psychology department. You opened my eyes. Thank you to the Rhodes Trust, Balliol College, the psychology department, and all my teachers and friends at Oxford University. You gave me time, freedom to explore, a rigorous, challenging, international, ambitious academic family, and the best scientific training anyone could hope for.

Thank you to my supportive colleagues at the University of Leeds, the University of Roehampton, and The University of London. As well as insight and guidance, many of you helped keep me sane as I struggled through the more opaque, unpleasant and unfair aspects of academic life. Thank you to all my colleagues at the Society for the Psychological Study of Social Issues. You have always been open, generous and supportive, and saw leadership potential in me before I even saw it in myself. Thank you to my research collaborators and research students. Without you, many of my own papers would never have been published or even conceived. I have become a better researcher through our partnerships. Thank you as well to my students who have taught me, through their feedback, how best to communicate complex academic ideas. Thank you to my friends and coworkers at Equality Group, with whom I honed my skills at communicating to the wider world outside of academia.

Thank you to two friends in particular—Caryn Franklyn and Natasha Devon—who have invested baffling amounts of time, energy and resources in my career. I can never repay you. Thank you to my friend and collaborator Katy Greenland for reading an earlier draft of this work and highlighting some of my omissions and oversights. The book is better because of you. Thank you to my agent, Jo Wander, who is just a brilliant agent and makes all the right connections for me. Thank you to my editors, Andrea Henry and Jamison Stoltz. Andrea, you were one of the first to believe in this book. And, without both of your knowledge, experience and patience, it wouldn't have been nearly as focused, interesting or approachable as it is. Thank you to my wife, Zoe Norridge, who talks about racism with me all the time, and picked up the pieces (practical and emotional) when I could no longer keep everything in place. And thank you to my sons, Thelonious West and Phoenix West, for reminding me every day that a better world is still worth fighting for.

References

Abrams, D., J. Broadwood, F. Lalot, K. D. Hayon, and A. Dixon
(2021). *Beyond Us and Them: Societal Cohesion in Britain through
Eighteen Months of COVID-19.* https://www.belongnetwork.co.uk
/wp-content/uploads/2021/11/Belong_SocietalCohesion_Report
_V5.pdf.

Allport, G. W. (1954). *The Nature of Prejudice.* New York: Perseus
Books.

Allport, G. W., and B. M. Kramer (1946). "Some Roots of Prejudice."
The Journal of Psychology, 22(1), 9–39. https://doi.org/10.1080
/00223980.1946.9917293.

Andreouli, E., K. Greenland, and C. Howarth (2016). "'I don't think
racism is that bad any more:' Exploring the 'end of racism'
Discourse among Students in English Schools." *European Journal
of Social Psychology*, 46, 171–84.

Apfelbaum, E. P., S. R. Sommers, and M. I. Norton (2008). "Seeing
Race and Seeming Racist? Evaluating Strategic Colorblindness in
Social Interaction." *Journal of Personality and Social Psychology*,
95(4), 918–32. https://doi.org/10.1037/a0011990.

Asbrock, F., L. Gutenbrunner, and U. Wagner (2013). "Unwilling, but
Not Unaffected: Imagined Contact Effects for Authoritarians and
Social Dominators." *European Journal of Social Psychology*, 43(5),
404–12.

Atewologun, D., T. Cornish, and F. Tresh (2018). *Unconscious Bias
Training: An Assessment of the Evidence for Effectiveness.*

https://www.equalityhumanrights.com/sites/default/files/research
-report-113-unconcious-bais-training-an-assessment-of-the
-evidence-for-effectiveness-pdf.pdf.

Awad, G. H., K. Cokley, and J. Ravitch (2005). "Attitudes toward
Affirmative Action: A Comparison of Color-Blind versus Modern
Racist Attitudes." *Journal of Applied Social Psychology*, 35(7),
1384–99. https://doi.org/10.1111/j.1559-1816.2005.tb02175.x.

Ayres, I., M. Banaji and C. Jolls (2015). "Race Effects on eBay." *The
RAND Journal of Economics*, 46(4), 891–917. https://doi.org/10
.1111/1756-2171.12115.

Banks, A. J., and H. M. Hicks (2016). "Fear and Implicit Racism:
Whites' Support for Voter ID Laws." *Political Psychology*, 37(5),
641–58. https://doi.org/10.1111/pops.12292.

Banton, O., K. West, and E. Kinney (2019). "The Surprising Politics
of Anti-Immigrant Prejudice: How Political Conservatism
Moderates the Effect of Immigrant Race and Religion on
Infrahumanization Judgments." *British Journal of Social Psychology*, 59(1), 157–70. https://doi.org/10.1111/bjso.12337.

Bavishi, A., J. M. Madera, and M. R. Hebl (2010). "The Effect of
Professor Ethnicity and Gender on Student Evaluations: Judged
before Met." *Journal of Diversity in Higher Education*, 3(4),
245–56. https://doi.org/10.1037/a0020763.

Bell, A. C., M. Burkley, and J. Bock (2019). "Examining the
Asymmetry in Judgments of Racism in Self and Others." *Journal
of Social Psychology*, 159(5), 611–27. https://doi.org/10.1080
/00224545.2018.1538930.

Bell, A. N., D. S. Smith, and J. Juvonen (2021). "Interpersonal
Attitudes toward Cross-Ethnic Peers in Diverse Middle Schools:
Implications for Intergroup Attitudes." *Group Processes and
Intergroup Relations*, 24(1), 88–107. https://doi.org/10.1177
/1368430219888020.

Bell, S. B., R. Farr, E. Ofosu, E. Hehman, and C. N. DeWall (2023).
"Implicit Bias Predicts Less Willingness and Less Frequent
Adoption of Black Children More Than Explicit Bias." *The Journal*

of Social Psychology, 163(4), 554–65. https://doi.org/10.1080/00224545.2021.1975619.

Berger, R., J. Benatov, H. Abu-Raiya, and C. T. Tadmor (2016). "Reducing Prejudice and Promoting Positive Intergroup Attitudes Among Elementary-school Children in the Context of the Israeli–Palestinian Conflict." *Journal of School Psychology*, 57, 53–72. http://dx.doi.org/10.1016/j.jsp.2016.04.003.

Bertrand, M., and S. Mullainathan (2004). "Are Emily and Greg More Employable than Lakisha and Jamal? A Field Experiment on Labor Market Discrimination." *American Economic Review*, 94, 991–1013.

Bonam, C. M., V. N. Das, B. R. Coleman, and P. Salter (2018). "Ignoring History, Denying Racism: Mounting Evidence for the Marley Hypothesis and Epistemologies of Ignorance." *Social Psychology and Personality Science*, 10(2), 257–65. https://doi.org/10.1177/1948550617751583.

Booth, A. L., A. Leigh, and E. Varganova (2012). "Does Ethnic Discrimination Vary across Minority Groups? Evidence from a Field Experiment." *Oxford Bulletin of Economics and Statistics*, 74(4), 547–73. https://doi.org/10.1111/j.1468-0084.2011.00664.x.

Bourabain, D., and P. P. Verhaeghe (2018). "Could You Help Me, Please? Intersectional Field Experiments on Everyday Discrimination in Clothing Stores." *Journal of Ethnic and Migration Studies*. https://doi.org/10.1080/1369183X.2018.1480360.

Bourget, D., and D. J. Chalmers (2014). "What Do Philosophers Believe?" *Philosophical Studies*, 170(3), 465–500. https://doi.org/10.1007/s11098-013-0259-7.

Bowling, B., and C. Phillips (2007). "Disproportionate and Discriminatory: Reviewing the Evidence on Police Stop and Search." *Modern Law Review*, 70(6), 936–61. https://doi.org/10.1111/j.1468-2230.2007.00671.x.

Burgess, S., and E. Greaves (2009). "Test Scores, Subjective Assessment and Stereotyping of Ethnic Minorities." *Journal of*

Labor Economics, 31(3), 535–76. https://www.bristol.ac.uk/media
-library/sites/cmpo/migrated/documents/wp221.pdf.

Butkowski, C., L. Humphreys, and U. Mall (2022). "Computing
Colorism: Skin Tone in Online Retail Imagery." *Visual
Communication*, 147035722210774. https://doi.org/
10.1177/14703572221077444.

Chisadza, C., N. Nicholls, and E. Yitbarek (2019). "Race and Gender
Biases in Student Evaluations of Teachers." *Economics Letters*, 179,
66–71. https://doi.org/10.1016/j.econlet.2019.03.022.

Choi, E., and K. L. Reddy-Best (2018). "Korean Fashion Media,
Beauty Ideals, and Colorism: Examining the Prominence of
Whiteness Between 2013 and 2017 in *Céci* Magazine."
International Textile and Apparel Association Proceedings, 1–2.

Correll, J., S. M. Hudson, S. Guillermo, and D. S. Ma (2014). "The
Police Officer's Dilemma: A Decade of Research on Racial Bias in
the Decision to Shoot." *Social and Personality Psychology
Compass*, 8(5), 201–13. https://doi.org/10.1111/spc3.12099.

Correll, J., B. Park, C. M. Judd, and B. Wittenbrink (2002). "The
Police Officer's Dilemma: Using Ethnicity to Disambiguate
Potentially Threatening Individuals." *Journal of Personality and
Social Psychology*, 83(6), 1314–29. https://doi.org
/10.1037/0022-3514.83.6.1314.

Correll, J., B. Park, C. M. Judd, and B. Wittenbrink (2007). "The
Influence of Stereotypes on Decisions to Shoot." *European
Journal of Social Psychology*, 37, 1102–17. https://doi.org
/10.1002/ejsp.450.

Correll, J., B. Park, and J. A. Smith (2008). "Colorblind and
Multicultural Prejudice Reduction Strategies in High-Conflict
Situations." *Group Processes and Intergroup Relations*, 11(4),
471–91. https://doi.org/10.1177/1368430208095401.

Crandall, C. S., A. Eshleman, and L. O'Brien (2002). "Social Norms
and the Expression and Suppression of Prejudice: The Struggle for
Internalization." *Journal of Personality and Social Psychology*,
82(3), 359–78. https://doi.org/10.1037/0022-3514.82.3.359.

Dasgupta, N., and A. G. Greenwald (2001). "On the Malleability of Automatic Attitudes: Combating Automatic Prejudice with Images of Admired and Disliked Individuals." *Journal of Personality and Social Psychology*, 81(5), 800–14. https://doi.org /10.1037/0022-3514.

Daumeyer, N. M., I. N. Onyeador, X. Brown, and J. A. Richeson (2019). "Consequences of Attributing Discrimination to Implicit vs. Explicit Bias." *Journal of Experimental Social Psychology*, 84, 103812. https://doi.org/10.1016/j.jesp.2019.04.010.

Decker, S. H., N. Ortiz, C. Spohn and E. Hedberg (2015). "Criminal Stigma, Race, and Ethnicity: The Consequences of Imprisonment for Employment." *Journal of Criminal Justice*, 43(2), 108–21. https://doi.org/10.1016/j.jcrimjus.2015.02.002.

Di Stasio, V., and A. Heath (2019). *Are Employers in Britain Discriminating against Ethnic Minorities? Summary Findings from the GEMM Project.* https://goo.gl/AdwyeX.

Dixon, J., L. R. Tropp, K. Durrheim, and C. Tredoux (2010). "'Let Them Eat Harmony:' Prejudice-Reduction Strategies and Attitudes of Historically Disadvantaged Groups." *Current Directions in Psychological Science*, 19(2), 76–80. https://doi.org /10.1177/0963721410363366.

Dixon, T. L. (2007). "Black Criminals and White Officers: The Effects of Racially Misrepresenting Law Breakers and Law Defenders on Television News." *Media Psychology*, 10(2), 270–91. https://doi.org/10.1080/15213260701375660.

Dixon, T. L. (2008a). "Network News and Racial Beliefs: Exploring the Connection between National Television News Exposure and Stereotypical Perceptions of African Americans." *Journal of Communication*, 58(2), 321–37. https://doi.org/10.1111/ j.1460-2466.2008.00387.x.

Dixon, T. L. (2008b). "Who Is the Victim Here? The Psychological Effects of Overrepresenting White Victims and Black Perpetrators on Television News." *Journalism*, 9(5), 582–605. https://doi.org /10.1177/1464884908094160.

Dixon, T. L. (2017). "Good Guys Are Still Always in White? Positive Change and Continued Misrepresentation of Race and Crime on Local Television News." *Communication Research*, 44(6), 775–92. https://doi.org/10.1177/0093650215579223.

Dixon, T. L., and D. Linz (2000). "Overrepresentation and Underrepresentation of African Americans and Latinos as Lawbreakers on Television Shows." *Journal of Communication*, 50(2), 131–54. https://doi.org/10.1111/j.1460-2466.2000 .tb02845.x.

Dobbin, F., and A. Kalev (2016). "Why Diversity Programs Fail." *Harvard Business Review*, 94(7), 14–20. https://hbr.org/2016/07 /why-diversity-programs-fail.

Dobbin, F., A. Kalev, and E. Kelly (2007). "Diversity Management in Corporate America." *Contexts*, 6(4), 21–7. https://doi.org/10.1525 /ctx.2007.6.4.21.

Dovidio, J. F., and S. L. Gaertner (2000). "Aversive Racism and Selection Decisions." *Psychological Science*, 11(4), 315–19. https:// doi.org/10.23959/sfjcr-1000005

Dukes, K. N., and S. E. Gaither (2017). "Black Racial Stereotypes and Victim Blaming: Implications for Media Coverage and Criminal Proceedings in Cases of Police Violence against Racial and Ethnic Minorities." *Journal of Social Issues*, 73(4), 789–807. https://doi.org /10.1111/josi.12248.

Eaton, A. A., J. F. Saunders, R. K. Jacobson, and K. West (2020). "How Gender and Race Stereotypes Impact the Advancement of Scholars in STEM: Professors' Biased Evaluations of Physics and Biology Post-Doctoral Candidates." *Sex Roles*, 82(3–4), 127–41. https://doi.org/https://doi.org/10.1007/s11199-019-01052-w.

Edwards, F., H. Lee, and M. Esposito (2019). "Risk of Being Killed by Police Use of Force in the United States by Age, Race–Ethnicity, and Sex." *Proceedings of the National Academy of Sciences of the United States of America*, 116(34), 16793–8. https://doi.org/10.1073 /pnas.1821204116.

Ervine, J. (2022). "Performing a Sense of Belonging: East Asian

Comedians in France." *Australian Journal of French Studies*, 59(4), 376–90. https://doi.org/10.3828/AJFS.2022.29.

Esen, E. (2005). *2005 Workplace Diversity Practices: Survey Report*. Society for Human Resource Management. https://books.google .com/books/about/2005_Workplace_Diversity_Practices_Surve .html?id=TSjyngEACAAJ.

Facciani, M., P. Warren, and J. M. C. Vendemia (2015). "A Content-Analysis of Race, Class, and Gender in American Comic Books." *Race, Gender and Class*, 22(3–4), 216–26. https://www.researchgate .net/publication/310328448.

Forrest-Bank, S., and J. M. Jenson (2015). "Differences in Experiences of Racial and Ethnic Microaggression among Asian, Latino/ Hispanic, Black, and White Young Adults." *Journal of Sociology and Social Welfare*, 42(1), 141–61. https://doi.org /10.15453/0191-5096.3885.

Franklyn, C., and K. West (2022). *Skewed: Decoding Media Bias* [audiobook]. Howes Publishing. https://www.audible.co.uk/pd /Skewed-Audiobook/B0B6GBC2W4.

Fujioka, Y. (1999). "Television Portrayals and African American Stereotypes: Examination of Television Effects when Direct Contact Is Lacking." *Journalism and Mass Communication Quarterly*, 76(1), 52–75.

Gallup (2021). "Race Relations." In *Gallup Historical Trends*. https://doi.org/10.1136/bmj.2.5971.618-a.

Gilliam, W. (2016). "Do Early Educators' Implicit Biases Regarding Sex and Race Relate to Behavior Expectations and Recommendations of Preschool Expulsions and Suspensions?" *Yale Child Study Center*, 1–18. papers3://publication/uuid/ DFEF674A-3825-41A7-8351-B8CFBA318B82.

Gilliam, F. D., N. A. Valentino, and M. N. Beckmann (2002). "Where You Live and What You Watch: The Impact of Racial Proximity and Local Television News on Attitudes About Race and Crime." *Political Research Quarterly*, 55(4), 755–80. https://doi .org/10.1177/106591290205500402.

Gilligan, T., P. S. Wang, R. Levin, P. W. Kantoff, and J. Avorn (2004). "Racial Differences in Screening for Prostate Cancer in the Elderly." *Archives of Internal Medicine*, 164(17), 1858–64. doi:10.1001/archinte.164.17.1858.

Gilmore, J. S., and A. Jordan (2012). "Burgers and Basketball: Race and Stereotypes in Food and Beverage Advertising Aimed at Children in the US." *Journal of Children and Media*, 6(3), 317–32. https://doi.org/10.1080/17482798.2012.673498.

Gorey, K. M. (2001). "Early Childhood Education: A Meta-Analytic Affirmation of the Short- and Long-Term Benefits of Educational Opportunity." *School Psychology Quarterly*, 16(1), 9–30. https://doi.org/10.1521/scpq.16.1.9.19163.

Gran-Ruaz, S., J. Feliciano, A. Bartlett, and M. T. Williams (2022). "Implicit Racial Bias across Ethnoracial Groups in Canada and the United States and Black Mental Health." *Canadian Psychology*, 63, 608–22. https://doi.org/10.1037/cap0000323.supp.

Green, A. R., D. R. Carney, D. J. Pallin, L. H. Ngo, K. L. Raymond, L. I. Iezzoni, and M. R. Banaji (2007). "Implicit Bias among Physicians and Its Prediction of Thrombolysis Decisions for Black and White Patients." *Journal of General Internal Medicine*, 22(9), 1231–8. https://doi.org/10.1007/s11606-007-0258-5.

Green, T. L., H. Vu, L. E. Swan, D. Luo, E. Hickman, M. Plaisime, and N. Hagiwara (2023). "Implicit and Explicit Racial Prejudice Among Medical Professionals: Updated Estimates from a Population-based Study." *The Lancet Regional Health–Americas*, 21. https://doi.org/10.1016/j.lana.2023.100489.

Greenland, K., E. Andreouli, M. Augoustinos, and R. Taulke-Johnson (2018). "What Constitutes 'Discrimination' in Everyday Talk? Argumentative Lines and the Social Representations of Discrimination." *Journal of Language and Social Psychology*, 37(5), 541–61.

Greenland, K., K. West, and C. van Laar (2022). "Definitional Boundaries of Discrimination: The Cultural Tools for Deciding

What Constitutes Discrimination (and What Doesn't)." *Journal of Applied Social Psychology*, 52(10), 945–64.

Greenwald, A. G., M. R. Banaji, L. A. Rudman, S. D. Farnham, B. A. Nosek, and D. S. Mellott (2002). "A Unified Theory of Implicit Attitudes, Stereotypes, Self-Esteem, and Self-Concept." *Psychological Review*, 109(1), 3–25. https://doi.org /10.1037/0033-295X.109.1.3.

Greenwald, A. G., D. E. McGhee, and J. L. K. Schwartz (1998). "Measuring Individual Differences in Implicit Cognition: The Implicit Association Test." *Journal of Personality and Social Psychology*, 74(6), 1464–80. https://doi.org/10.1037/0022-3514.74.6.1464.

Greenwald, A. G., C. T. Smith, N. Sriram, Y. Bar-Anan, and B. A. Nosek (2009). "Implicit Race Attitudes Predicted Vote in the 2008 US Presidential Election." *Analyzes of Social Issues and Public Policy*, 9(1), 241–53. https://doi.org /10.1111/j.1530-2415.2009.01195.x.

Gross, T. F. (2009). "Own-ethnicity Bias in the Recognition of Black, East Asian, Hispanic, and White Faces." *Basic and Applied Social Psychology*, 31(2), 128–35. https://doi.org /10.1080/01973530902880381.

Hachfeld, A., A. Hahn, S. Schroeder, Y. Anders, and M. Kunter (2015). "Should Teachers Be Colorblind? How Multicultural and Egalitarian Beliefs Differentially Relate to Aspects of Teachers' Professional Competence for Teaching in Diverse Classrooms." *Teaching and Teacher Education*, 48, 44–55. https://doi.org /10.1016/j.tate.2015.02.001.

Hagiwara, N., D. A. Kashy, and J. Cesario (2012). "The Independent Effects of Skin Tone and Facial Features on Whites' Affective Reactions to Blacks." *Journal of Experimental Social Psychology*, 48(4), 892–98. https://doi.org/10.1016/j.jesp.2012.02.001.

Haidt, J. (2017). "The Unwisest Idea on Campus: Commentary on Lilienfeld (2017)." *Perspectives on Psychological Science*, 12(1), 176–7. https://doi.org/10.1177/1745691616667050.

Hajnal, Z., N. Lajevardi, and L. Nielson (2017). "Voter Identification Laws and the Suppression of Minority Votes." *Journal of Politics*, 79(2), 363–79. https://doi.org/10.1086/688343.

Haney, C., C. Banks, and P. Zimbardo (1973). "A Study of Prisoners and Guards in a Simulated Prison." *Naval Research Review*, 9, 1–17.

Harper, K., and B. L. Choma (2019). "Internalised White Ideal, Skin Tone Surveillance, and Hair Surveillance Predict Skin and Hair Dissatisfaction and Skin Bleaching among African American and Indian Women." *Sex Roles*, 80(11–12), 735–44. https://doi.org /10.1007/s11199-018-0966-9.

Harwood, J., and K. Anderson (2002). "The Presence and Portrayal of Social Groups on Prime-Time Television." *International Journal of Phytoremediation*, 21(1), 81–97. https://doi.org /10.1080/08934210209367756.

Heath, A. F., and V. Di Stasio (2019). "Racial Discrimination in Britain, 1969–2017: A Meta-Analysis of Field Experiments on Racial Discrimination in the British Labor Market." *British Journal of Sociology*, 70(5), 1774–98. https://doi.org /10.1111/1468-4446.12676.

Hill, M. E. (2017). "Skin Color and the Perception of Attractiveness among African Americans: Does Gender Make a Difference?" *Social Psychology Quarterly*, 65(1), 77–91.

Hodson, G., and M. A. Busseri (2012). "Bright Minds and Dark Attitudes: Lower Cognitive Ability Predicts Greater Prejudice through Right-Wing Ideology and Low Intergroup Contact." *Psychological Science*, 23(2), 187–95. https://doi.org /10.1177/0956797611421206.

Hodson, G., H. Hooper, J. F. Dovidio, and S. L. Gaertner (2005). "Aversive Racism in Britain: The Use of Inadmissible Evidence in Legal Decisions." *European Journal of Social Psychology*, 35(4), 437–48. https://doi.org/10.1002/ejsp.261.

Howard, S. (2019). "Exonerees in Black and White: The Influence of Race on Perceptions of Those Who Falsely Confessed to a

Crime." *Psychology, Crime & Law*, 25(9), 911–24. https://doi.org
/10.1080/ 1068316X.2019.1597091.

Howell, J. L., S. E. Gaither, and K. A. Ratliff (2015). "Caught in the
Middle: Defensive Responses to IAT Feedback among Whites,
Blacks, and Biracial Black/Whites." *Social Psychological and
Personality Science*, 6(4), 373–81. https://doi.org
/10.1177/1948550614561127.

Jacoby-Senghor, D. S., S. Sinclair, and J. N. Shelton (2016). "A Lesson
in Bias: The Relationship Between Implicit Racial Bias and
Performance in Pedagogical Contexts." *Journal of Experimental
Social Psychology*, 63, 50–55. https://doi.org/10.1016/
j.jesp.2015.10.010.

Joseph-Salisbury, R., L. Connelly, and P. Wangari-Jones (2020).
"'The UK is Not Innocent:' Black Lives Matter, Policing and
Abolition in the UK." *Equality, Diversity and Inclusion*, 40(1),
21–28. https://doi.org/10.1108/EDI-06-2020-0170.

Kaiser, C. R., B. Major, I. Jurcevic, T. L. Dover, L. M. Brady, and J. R.
Shapiro (2013). "Presumed Fair: Ironic Effects of Organizational
Diversity Structures." *Journal of Personality and Social Psychology*,
104(3), 504–19. https://doi.org/10.1037/a0030838.

Kalev, A., F. Dobbin, and E. Kelly (2006). "Best Practices or Best
Guesses? Assessing the Efficacy of Corporate Affirmative Action
and Diversity Policies." *American Sociological Review*, 71,
589–617.

Kang, S. K., and K. A. Decelles (2016). "Whitened Résumés: Race and
Self-Presentation in the Labor Market." *Administrative Science
Quarterly*, 61(3), 469–502. https://doi.org
/10.1177/0001839216639577.

Kawakami, K., E. Dunn, F. Karmali, and J. F. Dovidio (2009).
"Mispredicting Affective and Behavioral Responses to Racism."
Science, 323(5911), 276–8. https://doi.org/10.1126/science
.1164951.

Kempf, A. (2020). "If We Are Going to Talk about Implicit Race Bias,
We Need to Talk about Structural Racism: Moving Beyond

Ubiquity and Inevitability in Teaching and Learning about Race." *Taboo: The Journal of Culture and Education*, 19(2), 115–30.

Kahn, K. B., P. A. Goff, J. K. Lee, and D. Motamed (2016). "Protecting Whiteness: White Phenotypic Racial Stereotypicality Reduces Police Use of Force." *Social Psychological and Personality Science*, 7(5), 403–411. https://doi.org/10.1177/1948550616633505.

King, E. B., S. A. Mendoza, J. M. Madera, M. R. Hebl, and J. L. Knight (2006). "What's in a Name? A Multiracial Investigation of the Role of Occupational Stereotypes in Selection Decisions." *Journal of Applied Social Psychology*, 36(5), 1145–59.

Kramer, R., and B. Remster (2018). "Stop, Frisk, and Assault? Racial Disparities in Police Use of Force During Investigatory Stops." *Law and Society Review*, 52(4), 960–93. https://doi.org/10.1111/lasr.12366.

Küpper, B., C. Wolf, and A. Zick (2010). "Social Status and Anti-Immigrant Attitudes in Europe: An Examination from the Perspective of Social Dominance Theory." *International Journal of Conflict and Violence*, 4(2), 205–19.

Leach, C. W., T. R. Peng, and J. Volckens (2000). "Is Racism Dead? Comparing (Expressive) Means and (Structural Equation) Models." *British Journal of Social Psychology*, 39(3), 449–65. https://doi.org/10.1348/014466600164507.

Leitner, M. (2021). *The Current Status of Equality, Diversity and Inclusion in the Further Education Sector in England*. https://feweek.co.uk/wp-content/uploads/2021/11/AoC-EDI-report.pdf.

Li, E. P. H., H. J. Min, and R. W. Belk (2008). "Skin Lightening and Beauty in Four Asian Cultures." *Advances in Consumer Research*, 35, 444–9.

Lilienfeld, S. O. (2017). "Microaggressions: Strong Claims, Inadequate Evidence." *Perspectives on Psychological Science*, 12(1), 138–69. https://doi.org/10.1177/1745691616659391.

Liu, R. Z., W. M. Liu, J. S. Wong, and R. Q. Shin (2023). "Anti-Black Racism and Asian American Local Educational Activism: A

Critical Race Discourse Analysis." *Educational Researcher.* https://doi.org/10.3102/0013189X231151939.

Liu, T., C. Liu, and Y. J. Chang (2022). "Asian American Mental Health amidst COVID-19 Anti-Asian Racism: Internalized Racism and Generational Status as Moderators." *Asian American Journal of Psychology*, 13(4), 328–38. https://doi.org/10.1037/aap0000284.

Lloret-Pineda, A., Y. He, J. M. Haro, and P. Cristóbal-Narváez (2022). "Types of Racism and Twitter Users' Responses Amid the COVID-19 Outbreak: Content Analysis." *JMIR Formative Research*, 6(5). https://doi.org/10.2196/29183.

Maddox, K. B., and S. A. Gray (2002). "Cognitive Representations of Black Americans : Reexploring the Role of Skin Tone." *Personality and Social Psychology Bulletin*, 28(2), 250–9.

Maghbouleh, N., A. Schachter, and R. D. Flores (2022). "Middle Eastern and North African Americans May Not Be Perceived, Nor Perceive Themselves, to Be White." *PNAS*, 119, e2117940119.

Mange, J., W. Y. Chun, K. Sharvit, and J. J. Belanger (2012). "Thinking about Arabs and Muslims Makes Americans Shoot Faster: Effects of Category Accessibility on Aggressive Responses in a Shooter Paradigm." *European Journal of Social Psychology*, 42(5), 552–6. https://doi.org/10.1002/ejsp.1883.

Marshall, J., A. Gollwitzer, K. Mermin-Bunnell, and T. Mandalaywala (2022). "The Role of Status in the Early Emergence of Pro-White Bias in Rural Uganda." *Developmental Science*, 25(4), e13240. https://doi.org/10.1111/desc.13240.

McConahay, J. B., B. B. Hardee, and V. Batts (1981). "Has Racism Declined in America?: It Depends on Who Is Asking and What Is Asked." *Journal of Conflict Resolution*, 25(4), 563–79. https://doi.org/10.1177/002200278102500401.

Mellor, J. "Police Cannot Explain 'Unfair' Use of Powers Against BAME People." The London Economic, 28 February 2021: https://www.thelondoneconomic.com/news/police-cannot-explain-unfair-use-of-powers-against-bame-people-222732/.

Mendelsohn, G. A., L. Shaw Taylor, A. T. Fiore, and C. Cheshire (2014). "Black/White Dating Online: Interracial Courtship in the 21st Century." *Psychology of Popular Media Culture*, 3(1), 2–18. https://doi.org/10.1037/a0035357.

Milkie, M. (1999). "Social Comparisons, Reflected Appraisals, and Mass Media: The Impact of Pervasive Beauty Images on Black and White Girls' Self-Concepts." *Social Psychology Quarterly*, 62(2), 190–210. https://doi.org/10.2307/2695857.

Milkman, K. L., M. Akinola, and D. Chugh (2015). "What Happens Before? A Field Experiment Exploring How Pay and Representation Differentially Shape Bias on the Pathway into Organizations." *Journal of Applied Psychology*, 100(6), 1678–1712. https://doi.org/10.1140/epjd/e2007-00070-4.

Miller, S. C., M. A. Olson, and R. H. Fazio (2004). "Perceived Reactions to Interracial Romantic Relationships: When Race Is Used as a Cue to Status." *Group Processes and Intergroup Relations*, 7(4), 354–69. https://doi.org/10.1177/1368430204046143.

Murstein, B. I., J. R. Merighi, and T. E. Malloy (1989). "Physical Attractiveness and Exchange Theory in Interracial Dating." *Journal of Social Psychology*, 129(3), 325–34. https://doi.org /10.1080/00224545.1989.9712049.

Nelson, J. C., G. Adams, and P. S. Salter (2013). "The Marley Hypothesis: Denial of Racism Reflects Ignorance of History." *Psychological Science*, 24(2), 213–18. https://doi.org /10.1177/0956797612451466.

Newheiser, A. K., and K. R. Olson (2012). "White and Black American Children's Implicit Intergroup Bias." *Journal of Experimental Social Psychology*, 48(1), 264–70. https://doi.org/10.1016/j. jesp.2011.08.011.

Nix, J., B. A. Campbell, E. H. Byers, and G. P. Alpert (2017). "A Bird's Eye View of Civilians Killed by Police in 2015: Further Evidence of Implicit Bias." *Criminology and Public Policy*, 16(1), 309–40. https://doi.org/10.1111/1745-9133.12269.

Noon, M. (2018). "Pointless Diversity Training: Unconscious Bias, New Racism and Agency." *Work, Employment and Society,* 32(1), 198–209. https://doi.org/10.1177/0950017017719841.

Norton, M. I., and S. R. Sommers (2011). "Whites See Racism as a Zero-Sum Game That They Are Now Losing." *Perspectives on Psychological Science,* 6(3), 215–18. https://doi.org/10.1177/1745691611406922.

Norton, M. I., S. R. Sommers, E. P. Apfelbaum, N. Pura, and D. Ariely (2006). "Color Blindness and Interracial Interaction." *Psychological Science,* 17(11), 949–53.

Nosek, B. A., M. R. Banaji, and A. G. Greenwald (2002). "Harvesting Implicit Group Attitudes and Beliefs from a Demonstration Web Site." *Group Dynamics, Theory, Research, and Practice,* 6(1), 101–15.

Nosek, B. A., A. G. Greenwald, and M. R. Banaji (2007). "The Implicit Association Test at Age 7: A Methodological and Conceptual Review," in J. A. Bargh (ed.), *Automatic Processes in Social Thinking and Behavior,* 265–92. New York: Psychology Press.https://doi.org/10.1016/j.mrfmmm.2009.01.007.

Nosek, B. A., F. L. Smyth, J. J. Hansen, T. Devos, N. M. Lindner, K. A. Ranganath, C. T. Smith, K. R. Olson, D. Chugh, A. G. Greenwald, and M. R. Banaji (2007). "Pervasiveness and Correlates of Implicit Attitudes and Stereotypes." *European Review of Social Psychology,* 18(1), 36–88. https://doi.org/10.1080/10463280701489053.

Offermann, L. R., T. E. Basford, R. Graebner, S. Jaffer, S. B. De Graaf, and S. E. Kaminsky (2014). "See No Evil: Color Blindness and Perceptions of Subtle Racial Discrimination in the Workplace." *Cultural Diversity and Ethnic Minority Psychology,* 20(4), 499–507. https://doi.org/10.1037/a0037237.

Pager, D. (2003). "The Mark of a Criminal Record." *American Sociological Review,* 108(5), 937–75. https://doi.org/10.1086/374403.

Pager, D., B. Western, and B. Bonokowski (2009). "Discrimination in a Low Wage Labor Market: A Field Experiment." *American Sociological Review*, 74(4469), 777–89.

Pager, D., B. Western, and N. Sugie (2009). "Sequencing Disadvantage: Barriers to Employment Facing Young Black and White Men with Criminal Records." *Annals of the American Academy of Political and Social Science*, 623(1), 195–213. https://doi.org /10.1177/0002716208330793.

Park, J., K. Felix, and G. Lee (2007). "Implicit Attitudes toward Arab-Muslims and the Moderating Effects of Social Information." *Basic and Applied Social Psychology*, 29(1), 35–45. https://doi.org /10.1080/01973530701330942.

Pauker, K., E. P. Apfelbaum, and B. Spitzer (2015). "When Societal Norms and Social Identity Collide: The Race Talk Dilemma for Racial Minority Children." *Social Psychological and Personality Science*, 6(8), 887–95. https://doi.org/10.1177/1948550615598379.

Pearson, A. R., J. F. Dovidio, and S. L. Gaertner (2009). "The Nature of Contemporary Prejudice: Insights from Aversive Racism." *Social and Personality Psychology Compass*, 3, 1–25. https://doi.org /10.1111/j.1751-9004.2009.00183.x.

Perszyk, D. R., R. F. Lei, G. V. Bodenhausen, J. A. Richeson, and S. R. Waxman (2019). "Bias at the Intersection of Race and Gender: Evidence from Preschool-aged Children." *Developmental Science*, 22(3), e12788. https://doi.org/10.1111/desc.12788.

Pettigrew, T. F., and L. R. Tropp (2006). "A Meta-Analytic Test of Intergroup Contact Theory." *Journal of Personality and Social Psychology*, 90(5), 751–83. https://doi.org /10.1037/0022-3514.90.5.751.

Pierson, E., C. Simoiu, J. Overgoor, S. Corbett-Davies, D. Jenson, A. Shoemaker, V. Ramachandran, P. Barghouty, C. Phillips, R. Shroff, and S. Goel (2020). "A Large-Scale Analysis of Racial Disparities in Police Stops across the United States." *Nature Human Behavior*, 4(7), 736–45. https://doi.org/10.1038/ s41562-020-0858-1.

Quillian, L., D. Pager, O. Hexel, and A. H. Midtbøen (2017). "Meta-Analysis of Field Experiments Shows No Change in Racial Discrimination in Hiring over Time." *Proceedings of the National Academy of Sciences of the United States of America,* 114(41), 10870–5. https://doi.org/10.1073/pnas.1706255114.

Ramasubramanian, S. (2007). "Media-Based Strategies to Reduce Racial Stereotypes Activated by News Stories." *Journalism and Mass Communication Quarterly,* 2, 249–64.

Reece, R. L. (2016). "What Are You Mixed With: The Effect of Multiracial Identification on Perceived Attractiveness." *Review of Black Political Economy,* 43(2), 139–47. https://doi.org/10.1007/s12114-015-9218-1.

Richeson, J. A., and R. J. Nussbaum (2004). "The Impact of Multiculturalism Versus Color-Blindness on Racial Bias." *Journal of Experimental Social Psychology,* 40(3), 417–23. https://doi.org/10.1016/j.jesp.2003.09.002.

Rooth, D. O. (2010). "Automatic Associations and Discrimination in Hiring: Real World Evidence." *Labor Economics,* 17(3), 523–34. https://doi.org/10.1016/j.labeco.2009.04.005.

Rosado Marzán, C. F. (2021). "Wage Theft As Crime: An Institutional View." *SSRN Electronic Journal.* http://ssrn.com/abstract=3558726.

Rosen, M. (2014). "'Microaggression' is Hypersensitive Nitpicking." *Denver Post,* 20 May, pp. 1–5. https://www.denverpost.com/2014/05/20/rosen-microaggression-is-hypersensitive-nitpicking/.

Rudlin, J. (2021). *Life and Power in a Hostile Environment: An Exploration of Civil Resistance to Immigration Policy in the UK.* https://www.ucl.ac.uk/bartlett/development/sites/bartlett/files/wp206.pdf.

Rudman, L. A., and R. D. Ashmore (2007). "Discrimination and the Implicit Association Test." *Group Processes & Intergroup Relations,* 10(3), 359–72. https://doi.org/10.1177/1368430207078696.

Rudman, L. A., R. D. Ashmore, and M. L. Gary (2001). "'Unlearning' Automatic Biases: The Malleability of Implicit Prejudice and

Stereotypes." *Journal of Personality and Social Psychology*, 81(5), 856–68. https://doi.org/10.1037/0022-3514.81.5.856.

Rutland, A., L. Cameron, L. Bennett, and J. Ferrell (2005). "Interracial Contact and Racial Constancy: A Multi-Site Study of Racial Intergroup Bias in 3–5-year-old Anglo-British Children." *Applied Developmental Psychology*, 26, 699–713. https://doi.org/10.1016/j. appdev.2005.08.005.

Sadler, M. S., J. Correll, B. Park, and C. M. Judd (2012). "The World is Not Black and White: Racial Bias in the Decision to Shoot in a Multiethnic Context." *Journal of Social Issues*, 68(2), 286–313. https://doi.org/10.1111/j.1540-4560.2012.01749.x.

Saguy, T., N. Tausch, J. F. Dovidio, and F. Pratto (2009). "The Irony of Harmony: Intergroup Contact Can Produce False Expectations for Equality." *Psychological Science*, 20(1), 114–22. https://doi.org /10.1111/j.1467-9280.2008.02261.x.

Sanchez, D. T., K. E. Chaney, S. K. Manuel, and J. D. Remedios (2018). "Theory of Prejudice and American Identity Threat Transfer for Latino and Asian Americans." *Personality and Social Psychology Bulletin*, 44(7), 972–83. https://doi.org/ 10.1177/0146167218759288.

Sayler, R. I. (1969). "An Exploration of Race Prejudice in College Students and Interracial Contact." PhD dissertation, University of Washington.

Schreer, G. E., S. Smith, and K. Thomas (2009). "'Shopping while Black:' Examining Racial Discrimination in a Retail Setting." *Journal of Applied Social Psychology*, 39(6), 1432–44.

Schwartz, G. L., and J. L. Jahn (2020). "Mapping Fatal Police Violence across U.S. Metropolitan Areas: Overall Rates and Racial/Ethnic Inequities, 2013–2017." *PLoS ONE*, 15(6), e0229686. https://doi.org /10.1371/journal.pone.0229686.

Shepherd, M. A. (2011). "Effects of Ethnicity and Gender on Teachers' Evaluation of Students' Spoken Responses." *Urban Education*, 46(5), 1011–28. https://doi.org/10.1177/0042085911400325.

Shook, N. J., and R. H. Fazio (2008). "Interracial Roommate Relationships: An Experimental Field Test of the Contact Hypothesis." *Psychological Science*, 19(7), 717–23. https://doi.org /10.1111/j.1467-9280.2008.02147.x.

Skinner, B. F. (1948). "'Superstition' in the Pigeon." *Journal of Experimental Psychology*, 38(2), 168–72. https://doi.org/http:// dx.doi.org/10.1037/h0055873.

Smedley, A., and B. D. Smedley (2005). "Race as Biology is Fiction, Racism as a Social Problem is Real: Anthropological and Historical Perspectives in the Social Construction of Race." *American Psychologist*, 60(1), 16–26. https://doi.org /10.1037/0003-066X.60.1.16.

Soble, J. R., L. B. Spanierman, and H. Y. Liao (2011). "Effects of a Brief Video Intervention on White University Students' Racial Attitudes." *Journal of Counseling Psychology*, 58(1), 151–7. https:// doi.org/10.1037/a0021158.

Statista. (2021). *Number of People Shot to Death by the Police in the United States from 2017 to 2020, by Race.* https://www. statista.com /statistics/585152/people-shot-to-death-by-us- police-by-race/.

Sturdivant, T. D., and I. Alanis (2021). "'I'm Gonna Cook My Baby in a Pot:' Young Black Girls' Racial Preferences and Play Behavior." *Early Childhood Education Journal*, 49(3), 473–82. https://doi.org /10.1007/s10643-020-01095-9.

Sullivan, J., L. Wilton, and E. P. Apfelbaum (2020). "Adults Delay Conversations about Race Because They Underestimate Children's Processing of Race." *Journal of Experimental Psychology: General.* https://doi.org/10.31234/osf.io/5xpsa.

Tate, S. A., and D. Page (2018). "Whiteliness and Institutional Racism: Hiding Behind (Un)Conscious Bias." *Ethics and Education*, 13(1), 141–55. https://doi.org/10.1080/17449642.2018.1428718.

Tatum, B. D. (1999). *"Why Are All the Black Kids Sitting Together in the Cafeteria?" and Other Conversations about Race.* New York: Basic Books.

Tawa, J., R. Ma, and S. Katsumoto (2016). "'All Lives Matter:' The Cost of Colorblind Racial Attitudes in Diverse Social Networks." *Race and Social Problems*, 2(8), 196–208. https://doi.org/10.1007/s12552-016-9171-z.

Thijssen, L., F. van Tubergen, M. Coenders, R. Hellpap, and S. Jak (2022). "Discrimination of Black and Muslim Minority Groups in Western Societies: Evidence From a Meta-Analysis of Field Experiments." *International Migration Review*, 56(3), 843–80. https://doi.org/10.1177/01979183211045044.

Turner, R. N., and K. West (2011). "Behavioral Consequences of Imagining Intergroup Contact with Stigmatized Outgroups." *Group Processes and Intergroup Relations*, 1–10. https://doi.org/10.1177/1368430211418699.

Van Boven, L. (2000). "Pluralistic Ignorance and Political Correctness: The Case of Affirmative Action." *Political Psychology*, 21(2), 267–76. https://doi.org/10.1111/0162-895X.00187.

Vittrup, B. (2018). "Color Blind or Color Conscious? White American Mothers' Approaches to Racial Socialization." *Journal of Family Issues*, 39(3), 668–92. https://doi.org/10.1177/0192513X16676858.

Wallrich, L., K. West, and A. Rutland (2020). "Painting All Foreigners with One Brush? How the Salience of Muslims and Refugees Shapes Judgments." *Journal of Social and Political Psychology*, 8(1), 246–65. https://doi.org/10.5964/jspp.v8i1.1283.

Watson, J. B., and R. Rayner (1920). "Conditioned Emotional Responses." *Journal of Experimental Psychology*, 3, 1–14.

West, K. (2019a). "Interethnic Bias in Willingness to Engage in Casual Sex versus Committed Relationships." *Journal of Sex Research*, 57(4), 409–20. https://doi.org/10.1080/00224499.2018.1546372.

West, K. (2019b). "Testing Hypersensitive Responses: Ethnic Minorities Are Not More Sensitive to Microaggressions, They Just Experience Them More Frequently." *Personality and Social Psychology Bulletin*, 45(11), 1619–32. https://doi.org/10.1177/0146167219838790.

West, K., and A. A. Eaton (2019). "Prejudiced and Unaware of It: Evidence for the Dunning–Kruger Model in the Domains of Racism and Sexism." *Personality and Individual Differences*, 146(3), 111–19. https://doi.org/10.1016/j.paid.2019.03.047.

West, K., and K. Greenland (2016). "Beware of 'Reducing Prejudice:' Imagined Contact May Backfire if Applied with a Prevention Focus." *Journal of Applied Social Psychology*, 46(10), 583–92. https://doi.org/10.1111/jasp.12387.

West, K., K. Greenland, and C. van Laar (2021). "Implicit Racism, Color Blindness, and Narrow Definitions of Discrimination: Why Some White People Prefer "All Lives Matter" to "Black Lives Matter"." *British Journal of Social Psychology*, 60, 1136–53. https://doi.org/10.1111/bjso.12458.

West, K., K. Greenland, C. van Laar, and D. Barnoth (2022). "It's Only Discrimination when They Do It to Us: When White Men Use Ingroup-Serving Double Standards in Definitional Boundaries of Discrimination." *European Journal of Social Psychology*, 52(4), 735–47. https://doi.org/10.1002/ejsp.2849.

West, K., and M. Hewstone (2012a). "Culture and Contact in the Promotion and Reduction of Anti-Gay Prejudice: Evidence from Jamaica and Britain." *Journal of Homosexuality*, 59(1), 44–66. https://doi.org/10.1080/00918369.2011.614907.

West, K., and M. Hewstone (2012b). "Relatively Socially Acceptable Prejudice Within and Between Societies." *Journal of Community and Applied Social Psychology*, 22(3), 269–82. https://doi.org/10.1002/casp.1112.

West, K., V. Hotchin, and C. Wood (2017). "Imagined Contact Can Be More Effective for Participants with Stronger Initial Prejudices." *Journal of Applied Social Psychology*, 47(5), 282–92.

West, K., and J. Lloyd (2017). "The Role of Labeling and Bias in the Portrayals of Acts of 'Terrorism:' Media Representations of Muslims vs. Non-Muslims." *Journal of Muslim Minority Affairs*, 37(2), 211–22. https://doi.org/10.1080/13602004.2017.1345103.

West, K., R. Lowe, and V. Marsden (2017). "'It don't matter if you're Black or White'?: Aversive Racism and Perceptions of Interethnic Romantic Relationships." *Social Psychology Review*, 19(1), 11–19.

Wilson, D. C., and P. R. Brewer (2013). "The Foundations of Public Opinion on Voter ID Laws: Political Predispositions, Racial Resentment, and Information Effects." *Public Opinion Quarterly*, 77(4), 962–84. https://doi.org/10.1093/poq/nft026.

Wisniewski, J. M., and B. Walker (2020). "Association of Simulated Patient Race/Ethnicity with Scheduling of Primary Care Appointments." *JAMA Network Open*, 3(1), e1920010-e1920010. doi:10.1001/jamanetworkopen.2019.20010.

Wodtke, G. T. (2012). "The Impact of Education on Intergroup Attitudes: A Multiracial Analysis." *Social Psychology Quarterly*, 75(1), 80–106. https://doi.org/10.1177/0190272511430234.

Zou, L. X., and C. L. Dickter (2013). "Perceptions of Racial Confrontation: The Role of Color Blindness and Comment Ambiguity." *Cultural Diversity and Ethnic Minority Psychology*, 19(1), 92–6. https://doi.org/10.1037/a0031115.

Notes and Sources

Introduction

p. x   **Dinesh D'souza's *The End of Racism***: Dinesh D'souza, *The End of Racism: Principles for a Multiracial Society* (New York: Free Press, 1995), p. 736.

p. x   **Larry Elder's *Stupid Black Men: How to Play the Race Card—and Lose***: Larry Elder, *Stupid Black Men: How to Play the Race Card—and Lose* (New York: Macmillan, 2008).

p. x   **Ijeoma Oluo's *Mediocre: The Dangerous Legacy of White Male America***: Ijeoma Oluo, *Mediocre: The Dangerous Legacy of White Male America* (New York: Seal Press, 2020).

p. x   **Layla Saad's *Me and White Supremacy***: Layla Saad, *Me and White Supremacy: How to Recognize Your Privilege, Combat Racism and Change the World* (New York: Hachette, 2020).

Chapter 1

p. 4   **2018 *Guardian* poll of British adults**: Aamna Mohdin, "Up to 40% of Britons think BAME People do Not Face More Discrimination," *Guardian*, 20 December 2018: https://www.theguardian.com/world/2018/dec/20/up-to-40-of-britons-think-bame-people-do-not-face-more-discrimination.

p. 4   **A 2021 Gallup Poll . . . while the other half do not**: "Race Relations," *Gallup*: htttps://news.gallup.com/poll/1687/Race-Relations.aspx#5.

p. 5   **Trump's Executive Order 13950**: The full text of Executive Order 13950 can be found here: https://www.federal register.gov /documents/2020/09/28/2020-21534/combating- race-and-sex -stereotyping.

p. 5   **"Let this front page serve as a reminder of how white supremacy is aided by—and often relies upon—the cowardice of mainstream institutions:"** https://x.com/aoc/status/1158557383767052293.

p. 5   **"Your weakness will help build a monument to white supremacy:"** https://x.com/AOC/status/955112863726743553.

p. 6   **According to US Senator Ted Cruz . . . the color of their skin**: "Ted Cruz Says Critical Race Theory is 'Every Bit as Racist as Klansmen in White Sheets'," *Newsweek*, 18 June 2021: https://www.newsweek.com /ted-cruz-says-critical-race-theory-every-bit-racist-klansmen -white-sheets-1602105.

p. 6   **"What I Discovered about Critical Race Theory in Public Schools and Why It Shouldn't Be Taught:"** Christopher F. Rufo, "What I Discovered about Critical Race Theory in Public Schools and Why It Shouldn't Be Taught," *USA Today*, 6 July 2021: https://eu.usatoday.com/story/opinion/voices/2021 /07/06/critical-race-theory-schools-racism-origins-classroom /7635551002/.

p. 6   **"Today the struggle against institutional racism continues. From Stephen Lawrence to George Floyd, Black Lives Matter:"** https://x.com/jeremycorbyn/status/1385223671757877249?lang =en.

p. 7   **Kemi Badenoch . . . attempts to "politicize" her skin color**: Fraser Nelson, "Kemi Badenoch: The Problem With Critical Race Theory," *Spectator*, 24 October 2020: https://www.specta tor.co.uk/article/kemi-badenoch-the-problem-with-critical -race-theory/.

p. 7   **Further still, Badenoch has stated that British teachers would be breaking the law**: Jessica Murray, "Teaching White Privilege as Uncontested Fact is Illegal, Minister Says," *Guardian*, 20 Octo-

ber 2020: https://www.theguardian.com/world/2020/oct/20
/teaching-white-privilege-is-a-fact-breaks-the-law-minister-says.

p. 7   **In 2021, the British government . . . "no evidence of systemic
or institutional racism" in the UK**: *Commission on Race and
Ethnic Disparities: The Report* : https://assets.publishing.service
.gov.uk/government/uploads/system/uploads/attachment_data
/file/974507/20210331_-_CRED_Report_-_FINAL_-_Web
_Accessible.pdf.

Chapter 2

p. 14   **the unemployment rate for Black people in the United States
is much higher than the unemployment rate for White people**:
"Gap in U.S. Black and White Unemployment Rates is Widest in
5 Years," *Thompson Reuters Foundation News*, 2 July 2020:
https://news.trust.org/item/20200702150904-zd222.

p. 14   **unemployment rates among Black British people being
twice as high as those among White British people**:
"Unemployment—Ethnicity Facts and Figures," *GOV.UK*: https://
www.ethnicity-facts-figures.service.gov.uk/work-pay-and
-benefits/unemployment-and-economic-inactivity/unemploy
ment/ latest.

Chapter 3

p. 33   **At 6.09 p.m., within mere hours of Archie's birth, BBC Radio
host Danny Baker . . . the caption "Royal baby leaves hospital:"**
Amy Walker, "Danny Baker Fired by BBC over 'Offensive' Royal
Baby Ape Tweet," *Guardian*, 9 May 2019: https://www.theguardian.
com/media/2019/may/09/danny-baker- apologizes-for-chimp
-tweet-about-royal-baby.

p. 33   **While they were there, an eighteen-year-old man jumped on
the baby while saying "Go back to your country" and "You
don't even speak English:"** Charlie Gates, "Newborn Baby Taken

to Hospital after Suspected Hate Crime at Christchurch Park,"
Radio New Zealand News, 18 December 2022: https://www.rnz
.co.nz/news/national/481004/newborn-baby-taken-to-hospital
-after-suspected-hate-crime-at-christchurch-park.

p. 34   **The bullet had already pierced Aiyana's neck. Aiyana was already dead**: Rose Hackman, "'She was only a baby:' Last Charge Dropped in Police Raid that Killed Sleeping Detroit Child," *Guardian*, 31 January 2015: https://www.theguardian.com/us -news/2015/jan/31/detroit-aiyana-stanley-jones-police-officer -cleared.

p. 34   **Amrita's mother alerted the hospital five times about her daughter's breathing difficulties**: Kamin Gock and Sian Johnson, "Review Reveals Failings in Lead-Up to Amrita Lanka's Death at Monash Children's Hospital," *ABC News*, 6 October 2022: https:// www.abc.net.au/news/2022-10-07/amrita-lanka-death-review -uncovers-failings-in-care/101507652.

p. 34   **Chikayzea Flanders was twelve years old . . . the school's uniform and appearance policy**: "School Discriminated against Rastafarian Boy by Telling Him to Cut His Dreadlocks," Equality and Human Rights Commission, 12 September 2018: https://www.equalityhumanrights.com/en/our-work/news /school- discriminated-against-rastafarian-boy-telling-him-cut -his-dreadlocks#:~:text=On%20his%20first%20day%20at,and %20must%20be%20cut%20off.

p. 35   **Loehmann shot Tamir almost immediately upon arrival. The car hadn't even stopped**: Elliott C. McLaughlin, "Cleveland: 12-Year-Old's Police Shooting Death His Own Fault," *CNN*, 2 March 2015: https://edition.cnn.com/2015/03/01/us/cleveland -responds-lawsuit-police-shooting-tamir-rice/index.html.

p. 35   **Oprah Winfrey . . . "she couldn't afford it:"** Tanya Ballard Brown, "Why Didn't the Store Just Let Oprah Buy the $38,000 Handbag?," *NPR*, 10 August 2013: https://www.npr.org/ sections /codeswitch/2013/08/10/210574193/why-didnt-the-store- just-let -oprah-buy-the-38-000-handbag.

p. 35 **Millard Scott's family reported that he was still limping, still in pain**: Vikram Dodd, "Family of Man Tasered in His Home Consider Suing Met Police," *Guardian*, 15 July 2020: https://www.theguardian.com/uk-news/2020/jul/16/family-of-man-tasered-in-his-home-consider-suing-met-police.

p. 36 **Gendron had come to the Tops armed with a Bushmaster AR-15 style rifle and concerns about White people being "replaced:"** Peter Nickeas, Casey Tolan and Virginia Langmaid, "How the 18-Year-Old Suspect Legally Obtained Guns before the Buffalo Mass Shooting," *CNN*, 18 May 2022: https://edition.cnn.com/2022/05/17/us/buffalo-mass-shooting-guns-suspect/index.html.

p. 37 **some have argued that the focal explanation should be Gendron's mental health problems, not his racism**: Ashley Southall, Chelsia Rose Marcius and Andy Newman, "Before the Massacre, Erratic Behavior and a Chilling Threat," *New York Times*, 15 May 2022: https://www.nytimes.com/2022/05/15/nyregion/gunman-buffalo-shooting-suspect.html.

Chapter 4

p. 55 **'its restrictive effect is intended to and would, in fact, operate on colored people almost exclusively**: Grace Brown, "The Origins of the Windrush Scandal Lie in 30 Years of Racist Immigration Legislation," *Runnymede Trust*, 22 June 2022: https://www.runnymedetrust.org/blog/the-origins-of-the-windrush-scandal-lie-in-30-years-of-racist-immigration-legislation.

p. 60 **only thirteen cases of alleged personation fraud were recorded by police forces in 2022, and only seven of those cases involved allegations in polling stations**: "2022 Electoral Fraud Data," Electoral Commission: https://www.electoralcommission.org.uk/who-we-are-and-what-we-do/our-views-and-research/our-research/electoral-fraud-data/2022-electoral-fraud-data.

p. 60   **millions of Americans (about 7%) do not have a form of government-issued identification that would be acceptable for voting**: "Fact Sheet on ID Voter Laws," American Civil Liberties Union (August 2021): https://www.aclu.org/wp-content/uploads/document/aclu_voter_id_fact_sheet_-_final__1_.pdf.

p. 61   **According to a 2015 report by Project Vote**: https://www.projectvote.org/wp-content/uploads/2015/06/AMERICANS-WITH-PHOTO-ID-Research-Memo-February-2015.pdf.

p. 62   **Perhaps you, like author and journalist Douglas Murray, see voter ID laws as something that can "unite the American Left and Right:"** Douglas Murray, "Voter ID Laws Are Not Racist," *UnHerd*, 23 July 2021: https://unherd.com/2021/07/voter-id-laws- are-not-racist/.

p. 62   **Maybe, like the British government, you believe that voter ID laws will "prevent voter fraud and protect democracy:"** Graeme Demianyk, "Electoral Commission: Voters Were Turned Away Thanks to New Photo ID Laws," *HuffPost*, 4 May 2023: https:// www. huffingtonpost.co.uk/entry/voters-turned-away-due-to-new-photo-id-requirement-electoral-commission-says_uk_645 42b76e4b00eb7e63a72b2#:~:text=The%20new%20compulsory%20ID%20rules,voter%20fraud%20and%20protect%20democracy.

Chapter 5

p. 71   **For example, in the 2022 documentary series *Harry & Meghan* . . . other members of his family**: *Harry & Meghan*, Netflix, 2022.

p. 71   ***The Leader's Guide to Unconscious Bias* by Pamela Fuller**: Pamela Fuller, *The Leader's Guide to Unconscious Bias* (New York: Simon and Schuster, 2020).

p. 71   ***Sway: Unraveling Unconscious Bias* by Pragya Agarwal**: Pragya Agarwal, *Sway: Unraveling Unconscious Bias* (London: Bloomsbury, 2021).

p. 71 ***Unconscious Bias: Everything You Need to Know about Our Hidden Prejudices* by Annie Burdick**: Annie Burdick, *Unconscious Bias: Everything You Need to Know about Our Hidden Prejudices* (London: Octopus Publishing Group, 2021).

p. 71 ***UNBIAS: Addressing Unconscious Bias at Work* by Stacey A. Gordon**: Stacey A. Gordon, *UNBIAS: Addressing Unconscious Bias at Work* (New York: Wiley, 2021).

p. 72 ***The Authority Gap* by Mary Ann Sieghart**: Mary Ann Sieghart, *The Authority Gap* (London: Transworld, 2022).

p. 72 **The Project Implicit website**: https://implicit.harvard.edu /implicit/takeatest.html.

p. 77 **In 2019, three years after Jacoby-Senghor's research . . . Richard Adams, the education editor of the *Guardian*, published an article on the "degree gap:"** Richard Adams, "Universities Urged to Close 'Degree Gap' Between Black and White Students," *Guardian*, 2 May 2019: https://www.theguardian.com/educa tion/2019/may/02/universities-urged-to-close-degree-gap-betwe en-black-and-white-students.

Chapter 6

p. 89 **Matt Rowan . . . when he called a group of high-school girls "fucking niggers." He just thought that his microphone was off**: Deon Osborne, "Racial Slur: Announcer Calls Kneeling High School Basketball Girls N-Word," *Black Wall Street Times*, 12 March 2019: https://theblackwallsttimes.com/2021 /03/12/announcer-calls-high-school-basketball-girls-nggers-for -kneeling/.

p. 90 **Jo Marney . . . she would never have sex with a "negro" because they are "ugly:"** Glen Owen, "'Meghan's Seed Will Taint Our Royal Family:' UKIP Chief's Glamor Model Lover, 25, is Suspended from the Party over Racist Texts about Prince Harry's Wife-to-Be," *Daily Mail*, 13 January 2018: https://www.dailymail. co.uk/news/article-5266657/Ukip-leaders-girlfriends-racist -Meghan-Markle-messages.html.

p. 90   **In 2002, employees at Target ... "routinely destroying the job applications of Black individuals who attended job fairs held at several Milwaukee universities:"** EEOC *v.* Target Corporation, case no. 02-C-146, 16 May 2007: https://casetext.com/case/equal-employment-opportunity-comm-v-target-corp. As cited in D. Pager, "The Use of Field Experiments for Studies of Employment Discrimination: Contributions, Critiques, and Directions for the Future," *Annals of the American Academy of Political and Social Science*, 609:1 (2007), 104–33.

p. 90   **In 2002, the then Mayor of London ... "flag-waving piccaninnies" with "watermelon smiles:"** Boris Johnson, "If Blair's So Good at Running the Congo, Let Him Stay There," *Daily Telegraph*, 10 January 2002: https://www.telegraph.co.uk/politics/0/blairs-good-running-congo-let-stay/.

p. 90   **In 2017, Conservative candidate Derek Bullock ... Manchester Arena bombing**: John Stevens, "EXCLUSIVE: Tory Council Candidate Kicked Out over Racist 'Shoot The P***s' Facebook Post," *Daily Mirror*, 5 April 2023: https://www.mirror.co.uk/news/politics/tory-council-candidate-kicked-out-29639810.

p. 90   **In 2018, Buford (Georgia) City Schools superintendent Geye Hamby ... "Don't send us a deadbeat nigger from a temp site:"** Michael Harriot, "Audio Recording Catches Georgia School Superintendent Using N-Word Like It's 1799," *The Root*, 23 August 2018: https://www.theroot.com/audio-recording-catches-georgia-school-superintendent-u-1828556692.

p. 90   **In 2022, Grégoire de Fournas wasn't trying not to be racist when he shouted "Go back to Africa" at Carlos Martens Bilongo, a Black, French lawmaker**: Kim Willsher, "'Go back to Africa:' French MP Banned after Racist Outburst in Parliament," *Guardian*, 4 November 2022: https://www.theguardian.com/world/2022/nov/04/back-to-africa-outrage-at-mps-racist-outburst-in-french-parliament#:~:text=De%20Fournas%20apologized%20to%20Bilongo,should%20go%20back%20to%20Africa%E2%80%9D.

p. 90   **In 2023, Conservative councillor Alexis McEvoy wasn't trying not to be racist when she called Ian Wright a "typical black hypocrite:"** Miriam Burrell, "Tory Councillor Quits after Calling Ian Wright a 'Typical Black Hypocrite'," *Evening Standard*, 21 March 2023: https://www.standard.co.uk/news/uk/alexis-mcevoy-ian- wright-tory-resign-new-forest-twitter-b1068935.html.

Chapter 7

p. 95   **In 1999, in an article titled "When Discrimination Makes Sense," social commentator Dinesh D'souza . . . reasonable responses to real-world data**: Dinesh D'souza, "When Discrimination Makes Sense," *Hoover Institution*, 30 October 1999: https://www.hoover.org/research/when-discrimination-makes-sense.

p. 96   **In 2000, in an article in the *Guardian*, Boris Johnson . . . in the park at night**: Boris Johnson, "Am I Guilty of Racial Prejudice? We All Are," *Guardian*, 21 February 2000: https://www.theguardian.com/uk/2000/feb/21/lawrence.ukcrime3.

p. 96   **A 2016 article by Philip Bump in the *Washington Post* . . . so that—not the police—should be the real focus of our attention**: Philip Bump, "Maybe the Iraq War and George W. Bush Aren't the Albatrosses We Think," *Washington Post*, 14 August 2015: https://www.washingtonpost.com/news/the-fix/wp/2015/08/14/is-jeb-bush-signaling-that-his-brothers-iraq-legacy-isnt-the-albatross-one-might-think/.

p. 97   **In 2016, Simon Denyer of the *Washington Post* reported . . . "accompanied by another person when traveling:"** Simon Denyer, "Air China's Shocking Advice for London Visitors: 'Precautions are needed' in Indian, Pakistani, Black Neighborhoods," *Washington Post*, 7 September 2016: https://www.washingtonpost.com/news/worldviews/wp/2016/09/07/stay- away-from-indian-pakistani-black-neighborhoods-air-chinas-shocking-advice-for-london-visitors/.

p. 98   **The most recent statistics on the UK prison population . . . in prison in the UK in 2023**: Georgina Sturge, "UK Prison Population Statistics," House of Commons Library: https://researchbriefings.files .parliament.uk/documents/SN04334/SN04334.pdf, 8 September 2023.

p. 99   **The US Bureau of Justice Statistics regularly publishes the results of a National Crime Victimization Survey**: Alexandra Thompson and Susannah N. Tapp, "Violent Victimization by Race or Hispanic Origin, 2008–2021," Bureau of Justice Statistics, July 2023: https://bjs.ojp.gov/violent-victimization-race-or -hispanic-origin-2008-2021.

p. 100   **the Office of National Statistics estimated that in 2022, the total population of England and Wales was 60,236,400**: "Population and Migration Statistics Transformation, England And Wales Case Study: 2023," Office for National Statistics, 27 June 2023: https://www.ons.gov.uk/peoplepopulationandcom munity/populationandmigration/populationestimates/articles /populationandmigrationstatisticstransformationenglandan dwalescasestudy/2023.

p. 101   **the shooting of Justine Damond**: "Mohamed Noor: Ex-Officer Who Killed Unarmed Woman Freed on Parole," *Guardian*, 27 June 2022: https://www.theguardian.com/us-news/2022/jun/27 /mohamed-noor-freed-parole-justine-damond-minneapolis.

p. 104   **in 2021, the Public Policy Institute of California released a report based on almost 4 million stops of motorists and pedestrians by police in 2019**: Magnus Lofstrom, Joseph Hayes, Brandon Martin, and Deepak Premkumar, and Alexandria Gumbs, "Racial Disparities in Law Enforcement Stops," Public Policy Institute of California, October 2021: https://www.ppic. org/?show-pdf=true&docraptor=true&url=https%3A%2F%2F www.ppic.org%2Fpublication%2Fracial-disparities -in-law-enforcement-stops%2F.

p. 106   **the internally conflicted Dr. Jekyll**: Robert Louis Stevenson, *The Strange Case of Dr. Jekyll and Mr. Hyde* (London: New English Library, 1974).

p. 116 **the BBC television program *The Capture***: BBC One, *The Capture*, written and directed by Ben Chanan, first aired 3 September 2019: https://www.bbc.co.uk/programs/m00085sx.

p. 118 **On 6 July 2013, Asiana Airlines Flight 214 from Incheon International Airport near Seoul, Korea, crashed on its approach to San Francisco International Airport**: Alan Taylor, "The Crash of Asiana Airlines Flight 214," *Atlantic*, 11 July 2013: https://www.theatlantic.com/photo/2013/07/the-crash-of-asiana-airlines-flight-214/100551/.

p. 118 **news anchor Tori Campbell read the names of the pilots who were supposedly in charge of Flight 214**: Chelsea J. Carter and Susan Candiotti, "KTVU Anchor Apologizes for Bogus Crew Names in Crash Story," *CNN Travel*, 13 July 2013: https://edition.cnn.com/2013/07/12/travel/asiana-offensive-names/index.html.

p. 118 **an article about the incident published online in the *Journal*, several people took to their keyboards to explain that it was, in fact, not racist**: "US TV Station Caught Out by Racist Joke about Plane Crash Pilots' Names," *Journal*, 17 November 2023: https://www.thejournal.ie/us-tv-fake-racist-names-asiana-pilots-991410-Jul2013/.

p. 119 **certain scenes in the 1994 film *Pulp Fiction***: Quentin Tarantino, dir., *Pulp Fiction*. Miramax, 1994.

p. 120 **Aaron Sibarium raised similar concerns on 6 February 2023, via Twitter. His specific tweet read: "ChatGPT says it is never morally permissible to utter a racial slur:"** Aaron Sibarium, "ChatGPT says it is never morally permissible to utter a racial slur," Twitter, 6 Feb 2023: https://twitter.com/aaronsibarium/status/1622425697812627457.

p. 121 **The 2003 musical *Avenue Q* offers a similar line of reasoning**: Jeff Whitty's *Avenue Q*, directed by Jason Moore, opened on Broadway at the Golden Theater on 31 July 2003.

p. 130 **As one Reddit user put it: "There's nothing wrong with having racial preferences in dating . . . because it's their ideal type, then so be it:"** AingealPenance, "CMV: There's nothing wrong

with having a racial preference in dating," Reddit: https://www
.reddit.com/r/changemyview/comments/tcs4rn/cmv_theres
_nothing_wrong_with_having_a_racial/.

Chapter 8

p. 142   **Her full quote was, "We've gone from the rich diversity of the
Abbey to a terribly white balcony. I was very struck by that:"**
Craig Simpson, "Coronation Balcony Scene Was 'Terribly
White,' says *Bridgerton* Star Adjoa Andoh," *Daily Telegraph*, 7
May 2023: https://www.telegraph.co.uk/royal-family/2023/05
/07/bridgerton-adjoa-andoh-coronation-balcony-terribly
-white/.

p. 142   **London paper the *Metro's* . . . "terribly white:"** "Bridgerton:
Adjoa Andoh Dubs Buckingham Palace Balcony 'Terribly
White'," *Metro*, 7 May 2023: https://metro.co.uk/2023/05/07
/bridgerton-adjoa-andoh-dubs-buckingham-palace-balcony
-terribly-white-18742946/.

p. 142   **The *Daily Mail* ran with . . . "terribly white:"** Chloe Louise,
"Bridgerton Star Adjoa Andoh Stuns ITV by Calling the Buckingham Palace Balcony 'Terribly White' during Live Coronation
Coverage," *Daily Mail*, 6 May 2023: https://www.dailymail.co.uk
/usshowbiz/article-12055129/Bridgerton-star-Adjoa-Andoh
-stuns-ITV-calling-Buckingham-Palace-balcony-terribly-white
.html.

p. 142   **The *Telegraph* said . . . "the Hypocrisy of the Woke Left:"**
Michael Deacon, "The Row over the 'Terribly White' Royal
Balcony Exposes the Hypocrisy of the Woke Left," *Daily Telegraph*,
13 May 2023: https://www.telegraph.co.uk/columnists/2023/05
/13/terribly-white-royal-balcony-adjoa-andoh/.

p. 142   **From the *Metro*: "Bridgerton Star Adjoa Andoh's 'Terribly
White' Coronation Comments Attract over 4,000 Ofcom
Complaints:"** Tori Brazier, "Bridgerton Star Adjoa Andoh's
'Terribly White' Coronation Comments Attract over 4,000
Ofcom Complaints," *Metro*, 10 May 2023: https://metro.co.uk

/2023/05/ 10/adjoa-andohs-coronation-comments-attract-4000 -ofcom-complaints-18759510/.

p. 142 **From the *Daily Mail* barely a week later . . . "Coronation Balcony Row:"** Tom Pyman, "Now ITV is Hit with Record 8,252 Ofcom Complaints over 'Terribly White' Coronation Balcony Row," *Daily Mail*, 17 May 2023.

p. 142 **One Talk TV presenter, Kevin O'sullivan . . . "You are allowed to be a White family, surely?:"** "'Am I Too White?' Kevin O'sullivan Seethes as Royal Family Described as 'Terribly White'," YouTube, 11 May 2023: https://www.youtube.com /watch?v=EDXuXA7gIDc.

p. 142 **Julia Hartley-Brewer . . . "something that people find very frustrating:"** "'If That Isn't Racist, I Don't Know What Is!' Julia Hartley-Brewer on 'Terribly White' Comments," YouTube, 11 May 2023: https://www.youtube.com/watch?v=LEgrEu51_aM.

p. 143 **In 2015 in Canada, an Indigenous woman, Tamara Crowchief . . . "not satisfied beyond a reasonable doubt that this offense was, even in part, motivated by racial bias:"** Peter Holley, "Yelling 'I Hate White People' and Punching One Isn't a Hate Crime, Canadian Judge Rules," *Washington Post*, 7 July 2016: https://www.washingtonpost.com/news/worldviews /wp/2016/07/07/canadian-judge-punching-a-caucasian-and-yel ling-i-hate-white-people-isnt-a-hate-crime/.

p. 143 **Jeong had (in 2013 and 2014) tweeted derogatory things about White people . . . the tweets had been taken out of context**: "Sarah Jeong: *NY Times* Stands by 'Racist Tweets' Reporter," *BBC News*, 2 August 2018: https://www.bbc.co.uk/news/world- us -canada-45052534.

p. 143 **this did little to appease public figures like Governor Mike Huckabee**: Mike Huckabee, "If @nytimes keeps Sarah Jeong as writer given her vulgar, racist, anti-police, sexist rants, then the paper has no shame, no standards," Twitter, 3 August 2018: https://twitter.com/govmikehuckabee/status/102545868920 8139776.

p. 143   **the then Fox News host Tucker Carlson**: Ian Schwartz, "Tucker Carlson on Sarah Jeong: Left Thinks Racism Against White People 'Impossible'," *Real Clear Politics*, 3 August 2018: https:// www.realclearpolitics.com/video/2018/08/03/tucker_carlson_ on _sarah_jeong_left_thinks_racism_against_white_people _impossible.html.

p. 143   **In 2018, the French rapper Nick Conrad . . . kidnapped, tortured, shot and hanged from a tree**: "'Pendez les Blancs:' la polémique créée par le clip du rappeur Nick Conrad résumée en quatre actes," *FranceInfo Culture*, 27 September 2018: https:// www.francetvinfo.fr/culture/musique/pendez-les-blancs -la-polemique-creee- par-le-clip-du-rappeur-nick-conrad-resumee -en-quatre-actes_ 2959449.html.

p. 143   **Conrad denied being a racist . . . comment on contemporary racism**: "Hang White People: Rapper Nick Conrad Fined over YouTube Song," *BBC News*, 19 March 2019: https://www.bbc .co.uk/news/world-europe-47633459.

p. 144   **On Netflix, you can still watch *White Chicks* . . . spend most of the movie in "whiteface:"** Keenen Ivory Wayans, dir., *White Chicks*. Columbia, 2004.

p. 144   **In 2015, Heron Creek, a middle school in Florida . . . were not welcome to participate in the program:** Andrea Hubbell, "School Accused of 'Reverse-Racism'," *NBC News*, 12 November 2015: https://www.nbcnews.com/video/school- accused-of -reverse-racism-565408835748.

p. 144   **in 2023, Rasmussen Reports conducted a national survey of 1,000 American adults . . . 21% were not sure how they felt**: Rachel Hartman, "How Do Black Americans Really Feel about the Phrase 'It's OK to be White'?," Cloud Research: https://www .cloudresearch.com/resources/blog/its-ok-to-be- white-rasmussen -poll/.

p. 144   **These findings caused Scott Adams . . . "that's a hate group:"** Janell Ross, "The Death of Dilbert and False Claims of White

Victimhood," *Time*, 1 March 2023: https://time.com/6259311
/dilbert-racism-scott-adams/.

p. 145 **since 1958, a series of yearly Gallup polls . . . marriages
between White people and non-White people**: Joseph Carroll,
"Most Americans Approve of Interracial Marriages, Blacks
More Likely than Whites to Approve of Black–White Unions,"
Gallup, 16 August 2007: https://news.gallup.com/poll/28417/
most-americans-approve-interracial-marriages.aspx#:~:text=
Gallup's%20long%2Dterm%20trend%20on,marriages%20
between%20whites%20and%20blacks.

p. 150 **in 2021, the Community Security Trust . . . including 173 vio-
lent assaults**: *Antisemitic Incidents Report 2021*, Community
Security Trust: https://cst.org.uk/data/file/f/f/Incidents%20
Report%202021.1644318940.pdf.

p. 150 **In 2017, a group of White supremacists . . . "Jews will not replace
us:"** Yair Rosenberg, "'Jews will not replace us:' Why White Supremacists Go after Jews," *Washington Post*, 14 August 2017: https://www.
washingtonpost.com/news/acts-of-faith/wp/2017/08/14/jews
-will-not-replace-us-why-white-supremacists-go-after-jews/.

p. 151 **As Trinidadian-born American civil rights activist Stokely
Carmichael once said . . . "it's a question of power:"** From
Shirley Anne Tate, *Post-Intersectionality to Black Decolonial
Feminism: Black Skin Affections* (New York: Routledge, 2022).

p. 154 **British government's own figures . . . 92% of the House of
Lords is White**: Elise Uberoi and Helena Carthew, "Ethnic
Diversity in Politics and Public Life," House of Commons
Library, 2 October 2023: https://commonslibrary.parliament
.uk/research-briefings/sn01156/.

p. 154 **The number of business CEOs in the UK . . . Black chairpersons, CEOs or CFOs in any FTSE 100 company at the time?
Zero**: James Cook, "Why Are There No Black CEOs in the UK?,"
Business Leader, 27 October 2022: https://www.businessleader
.co.uk/why-are-there-no-black-ceos-in-the-uk/.

p. 154   **According to the United States Census Bureau, non-Hispanic White people account for about 58.9% of the US population**: United States Census Bureau, Quick Facts United States— Population Estimates, 1 July 2022: https://www.census.gov /quickfacts/fact/table/US/EDU685221.

p. 154   **However, they also account for 76% of American millionaires**: "Breakdown of U.S. Millionaires by Race/Ethnicity," as of 2013, Statista:https://www.statista.com/statistics/300528/us-millionaires- race-ethnicity/#:~:text=As%20of%202013%2C   %20about%20 76,U.S.%20millionaires%20were%20White%2FCaucasian .&text=The%20issue%20of%20racial%20inequality,history%20 of%20the%20United%20States.

p. 154   **77% of Congress**: Katherine Schaeffer, "Racial, Ethnic Diversity Increases Yet Again with the 117th Congress," Pew Research Center, 28 January 2021: https://www.pewresearch.org/short -reads/2021/01/28/racial-ethnic-diversity-increases-yet-again -with-the-117th-congress/.

p. 154   **88.8% of CEOs, CFOs and COOs in the United States**: Bryan Strickland, "Diversity among CEOs, CFOs Continues to Rise," *Journal of Accountancy*, 23 August 2022: https://www.journalo- faccountancy.com/news/2022/aug/diversity-among-ceos -cfos-continue-rise.html#:~:text=Overall%2C%2088.8%25%20 of%20CEOs%2C,numbers%20over%20the%20last%20decade.

p. 154   **Taking a particularly chilling example of the dangerous use of that power . . . primarily by White people**: "Lynchings: By State and Race, 1882–1968," University of Missouri-Kansas City School of Law, Archives at Tuskegee Institute, 26 July 2010: https://web.archive.org/web/20100629081241/http://www.law .umkc.edu/faculty/projects/ftrials/shipp/lynchingsstate.html.

p. 154   **the Equal Justice Initiative estimates that about 6,500 Black Americans were lynched . . . every week for eighty-five unin- terrupted years**: "Reconstruction in America, Racial Violence after the Civil War," Equal Justice Initiative: https://eji.org /reports/reconstruction-in-america-overview.

p. 155   **The Equal Justice Initiative has also assembled a record of the reasons for these lynchings, some of which are as petty and absurd as they are tragic:** "The Legacy Museum offers a powerful, immersive journey through America's history of racial injustice:" https://legacysites.eji.org/about/museum/?gad_source =1&gclid=Cj0KCQiApOyqBhDlARIsAGfnyMqolrzzCjcEV0nY 3dYHh_oyh9C5fxZJ9-SNvR_gbfu_pKkVR4upq_8aAsK NEALw_wcB.

p. 155   **Frank Dodd was lynched in DeWitt, Arkansas, in 1916 for annoying a White woman by "talk[ing] insultingly" to her:** "Frank Dodd (Lynching of)," *Encyclopedia of Arkansas*, 16 June 2023: https://encyclopediaofarkansas.net/entries/frank -dodd- 13428/.

p. 155   **Henry Patterson was lynched in Labele, Florida, in 1926 for asking a White woman for a drink of water:** "White Mob in Florida Lynches Black Man for Requesting Drink of Water," Equal Justice Institute: https://calendar.eji.org/racial-injustice /may/11#:~:text=On%20May%2011%2C%201926%2C%20 a,for%20a%20drink%20of%20water.

p. 155   **Ernest Green and Charlie Lang (both fourteen years old) were lynched in Shubuta, Mississippi, in 1942, because a White girl said they attempted to attack her:** "2 NEGRO BOYS LYNCHED; Victims, 14, Accused of Attacking Girl, Hanged in Mississippi," *New York Times*, 13 October 1942: https://www.nytimes. com/1942/10/13/archives/2-negro-boys-lynched-victims-14 -accused-of-attacking-girl-hanged-in.html.

p. 155   **And things didn't end in 1968. The last official lynching to take place in the United States was that of nineteen-year-old Michael Donald, a Black teenager from Mobile, Alabama:** Breeanna Hare, "Inside the Case that Bankrupted the Klan," *CNN*, 11 April 2021: https://edition.cnn.com/2021/04/10/us /michael-donald-case-timeline/index.html.

p. 155   **The unofficial list includes people like Robert Fuller . . . the Black community was deeply unconvinced:** Tim Arango and

Maria Abi-Habib, "In California, Hanging Deaths of Two Black Men Summon a Dark History and F.B.I. Scrutiny," *New York Times*, 19 June 2020: https://www.nytimes.com/2020/06/19/us /hanging-deaths-california.html.

p. 157   **When Cloud Research replicated Rasmussen's survey ... to figure out why Black people might disagree that "It's OK to be White:"** Rachel Hartman, "How Do Black Americans Really Feel about the Phrase 'It's OK to be White'?," Cloud Research: https://www.cloudresearch.com/resources/blog/its-ok-to-be -white-rasmussen-poll/.

p. 159   **As Rahman put it: "If after hundreds and hundreds and hundreds of years ... that would be reverse racism:"** "Aamer Rahman (Fear of a Brown Planet)—Reverse Racism," FEAR OF A BROWN PLANET, YouTube, 28 November 2013: https:// www.youtube.com/watch?v=dw_mRaIHb-M.

Chapter 9

p. 163   **In this chapter, I will take the advice often attributed to Einstein and "make everything as simple as possible, but not simpler:"** Andrew Robinson, "Did Einstein Really Say That?," *Nature*, 30 April 2018: https://www.nature.com/articles/d41586- 018-05004-4#:~:text=%E2%80%9CEverything%20should%20 be%20made%20as,possible%20without%20having%20to%20 surrender.

p. 174   *How to Argue with a Racist* **by British geneticist Adam Rutherford**: Adam Rutherford, *How to Argue With a Racist: History, Science, Race and Reality* (London: Hachette, 2020).

p. 175   **Neda Maghbouleh ... has written a book about just this issue, titled** *The Limits of Whiteness: Iranian Americans and the Everyday Politics of Race*: Neda Maghbouleh, *The Limits of Whiteness: Iranian Americans and the Everyday Politics of Race* (Redwood City: Stanford University Press, 2017).

p. 176 **"Are Jews White?" by Atiya Husain**: Atiya Husain, "Are Jews White? A Recent Judicial Ruling Defining Jewish as a Protected Race Follows a Long and Often Ugly History," *Slate*, 14 August 2018: https://slate.com/news-and-politics/2018/08/are-jews-white-a -judge-tries-to-answer-the-question-in-a-messy-lawsuit.html.

p. 176 **"Are Jews White? Yes. And No" by Dave Schechter**: Dave Schechter, "Are Jews White? Yes. And No," *Atlanta Jewish Times*, 28 January 2021: https://www.atlantajewishtimes.com/are-jews -white-yes-and-no/.

p. 177 **"Are Jews White? Or, The History of the Nose Job" by Sander L. Gilman**: Sander L. Gilman, "Are Jews White? Or, The History of the Nose Job," in Les Back and John Solomos (eds), *Theories of Race and Racism* (New York: Routledge, 2020), pp. 294–302.

p. 177 **"Are Jews White? It's a Mistake Even to Ask" by Gershom Gorenberg**: Gershom Gorenberg, "Are Jews White? It's a Mistake Even to Ask," *American Prospect*, 29 August 2017: https://prospect.org/civil-rights/jews-white-mistake-even-ask.

p. 177 **In 2020, in an interview with *Dalit Camera* reproduced on *Monthly Review Online* . . . "Indian racism toward Black people is almost worse than White peoples' racism:"** " 'Indian racism toward Black people is almost worse than white peoples' racism:' An Interview with Arundhati Roy," *MR. Online*, 13 July 2020: https://mronline.org/2020/06/13/indian-racism-toward -black-people-is-almost-worse-than-white-peoples-racism-an -interview-with-arundhati-roy/.

p. 178 **In 2021, in a letter addressed to the Department of Justice in the US . . . "political favoritism or privilege:"** Yukong Zhao, "AACE Urges the U.S. Department of Justice to Take A Nonpartisan, Holistic Approach," 6 April 2021: https://asianamerican foreducation.org/wp-content/uploads/2021/04/AACE-Letter-to -US-Attorney-General-202104.pdf.

p. 179 **In a 2021 article in the *Guardian*, Pulitzer-winning author Viet Thanh Nguyen . . . being mocked with a "ching-chong"**

accent: Viet Thanh Nguyen, "From Colonialism to Covid: Viet Thanh Nguyen on the Rise of Anti-Asian Violence," *Guardian*, 3 April 2021: https://www.theguardian.com/books/2021/apr/03/from-colonialism-to-covid-viet-thanh-nguyen-on-the-rise-of-anti-asian-violence.

p. 179   **In 2022, an East Asian TikTok user in the US ... "go do some nails or some feet or something, bitch:"** Ryan General, "Woman Unleashes Racist Tirade at Asian Woman; Throws Rocks at Asian Journalist after Being Confronted," 25 November 2022: https://news.yahoo.com/woman-unleashes-racist-tirade-asian- 225242901.html?guccounter=1&guce_referrer=aHR0cHM6Ly93d3cuZ29v Z2xlLmNvbS8&guce_referrer_sig=AQAAAKEBevWnNwykAeJ1d gkVdin1w1zZkjhcwYucyDr29oCyQCk- kzv_11X8IVcn2QJDXsMs GwkJIhxd_EHegTP_b9RMzitppuatLSRe5DrT5QTe9G-2RioFewJ 0ebPi2XCtdFUPcFiO3J9sXUEAynJzFVXmJCHOVD6NI rfy-plDMdjI.

p. 180   **Professor Jennifer Ho ... racism in majority White countries still serves the "ideology of White supremacy:"** Jennifer Ho, "Anti-Asian Racism, Black Lives Matter, and COVID-19," *Japan Forum*, 2020: https://doi.org/10.1080/09555803.2020.1821749.

p. 181   **South Asian identification with and explicit support for the Black Lives Matter movement, including the groups South Asians for Black Lives**: southasians4blacklives, Instagram: https://www.instagram.com/southasians4blacklives/.

p. 181   **the Alliance of South Asians Taking Action**: AACRE: https://aacre.org/south-asian-solidarity-blacklivesmatter/, 1 December 2015.

p. 181   **Sadiq Khan, the Muslim Mayor of London ... accused the Labor Party of being "far too slow" to tackle antisemitism**: Matt Honeycombe-Foster, "Sadiq Khan Joins Jewish Labor Movement as He Says Party Has Been "Far Too Slow" to Tackle Antisemitism," *Politics Home*, 15 April 2019: https://www.politicshome.com/news/article/sadiq-khan-joins-jewish-labor

-movement-as-he-says-party-has-been-far-too-slow- to-tackle
-antisemitism.

p. 181   **Khan has also been outspoken about "the anti-Black racism,
injustice and other systemic inequalities:"** Sadiq Khan, "We
can't wait any longer. We must address the anti-black racism,
injustice and other systemic inequalities in our society, and do it
now," Twitter, 5 June 2020: https://twitter.com/MayorofLondon
/status/1268966470400315394.

p. 185   **I've written a whole book about bias in the media**: Caryn
Franklyn and Keon West, *Skewed: Decoding Media Bias*
(Rearsby: Howes Publishing, 2022): https://adbl.co/3ozD4cQ.

Chapter 10

p. 195   **In 2005, in an interview on the American television show *60
Minutes* . . . "How are we going to get rid of racism?:"** Interview by Mike Wallace with Morgan Freeman, *60 Minutes* (New
York, NY: Columbia Broadcasting System, 2005): https://search
.alexanderstreet.com/preview/work/bibliographic_ entity%7C
video_work%7C2860766.

p. 196   **Coleman Hughes is an African American author, writer and
commentator . . . he argued that color blindness was the best
perspective**: Coleman Hughes, "Actually, Color-Blindness Isn't
Racist," *Free Press*, 20 December 2022: https://www.thefp.com
/p/actually-color-blindness-isnt-racist.

p. 196   **Dr Carson also supports color blindness . . . "the very idea
that we should be divided based on race at all:"** Ben Carson,
"Reflecting on Dr. King's Vision—How Are We Faring in Pur-
suit of the Just Society?" *Fox News Opinion*, 16 January 2022:
https://www.foxnews.com/opinion/martin-luther-king-vision-j
ust-society-dr-ben-carson.

p. 196   **Like Dr. Carson, many other politicians and authority figures have used that very line from Dr. King's "I Have a
Dream" speech . . . This list includes, among others, US**

Representative Charles Eugene "Chip" Roy: Hajar Yazdiha, "How the Distortion of Martin Luther King Jr's Words Enables More, Not Less, Racial Division within American Society," *The Conversation*, 14 January 2023: https://theconversation.com/how-the-distortion-of-martin-luther-king-jr-s-words-enables-more-not-less-racial-division-within-american-society-195177.

p. 197   **Conservative MP Maxime Bernier**: Maxime Bernier, "I thought the ultimate goal of fighting discrimination was to create a color-blind society where everyone is treated the same. Not to set some Canadians apart as being 'racialized'," Twitter, 2 March 2018: https://twitter.com/MaximeBernier/status/969583307817209857.

p. 197   **Dennis Prager**: Dennis Prager, "Should we be Colorblind?," Prageru.com, 1 November 2021: https://www.prageru.com/video/should-we-be-colorblind.

p. 197   **American politician Peter Navarro (who is White) . . . "we have got real problems in this country:"** Maia Niguel Hoskin, "Dear White People, Cut It Out with the 'Colorblindness.' It Perpetuates White Supremacy," *Forbes*, 13 July 2020: https://www.forbes.com/sites/maiahoskin/2020/07/13/dear-white-people-cut-it-out-with-the-colorblindness-it-perpetuates-white-supremacy/.

p. 197   **In a 2023 interview . . . Elba explained why he stopped describing himself as "a Black actor:"** Alex Bilmes, "Becoming Idris Elba," *Esquire*, 8 February 2023: https://www.esquire.com/uk/culture/a42621203/idris-elba-interview-luther/.

p. 197   **Boris Becker . . . "I'm color blind. I didn't see she was darker than me and I just fell in love with the woman:"** Sudipto Pati, "'I'm Colorblind'—In an Emphatic Confession, Tennis Legend Boris Becker Defends a Sensitive Marriage Move," *Essentially Sports*, 4 August 2023: https://www.essentiallysports.com/atp-tennis-news-im-colorblind-in-an-emphatic-confession-tennis-legend-boris-becker-defends-a-sensitive-marriage-move/.

p. 198   **Even Nigel Farage . . . a party built on the explicit dislike of immigrants and foreigners**: Nigel Farage, "We, As a Party, Are Color-Blind," *BBC News*, 12 March 2015: https://www.bbc .co.uk/news/av/uk-31847535.

p. 198   **the party of councillor Rozanne Duncan who was filmed saying she had a "problem with people with negroid features:"** "Ex-UKIP Councillor Rozanne Duncan: 'No Regrets' over Comments," *BBC News*, 22 February 2015: https://www.bbc .co.uk/news/uk-politics-31565770.

p. 198   **the party of councillor Dave Small . . . "all around me I could hear the sound of jabbering in an alien voice . . . we also have the Pakistani's [*sic*] and the Somali's [*sic*]:"** "New Ukip Councillor Suspended over Claims of Racism by the Newsroom," *Yorkshire Post*, 29 May 2014: https://www.yorkshirepost.co.uk/ news/politics/new- ukip-councillor-suspended-over-claims-of -racism-1841149.

p. 198   **the party of candidate Joseph Quirk, who has said, "Well, I reckon dogs are more intelligent, better company and certainly better behaved than most Muslims:"** Ruby Stockham, "Is UKIP a Racist Party? These 15 Comments Would Suggest So," *Left Foot Forward*, 23 February 2015: https://leftfootforward .org/2015/02/is-ukip-a-racist-party-these-15-comments-would -suggest-so/.

p. 199   **the original Facebook post about Jax and Reddy had been shared over 27,000 times and liked more than 88,000 times**: Love What Matters, "This morning Jax and I were discussing his wild hair," Facebook, 27 February 2017: https://www.facebook .com/lovewhatreallymatters/photos/a.710462625642805/14250 65474182513/?type=3.

p. 199   **The news aggregation website** Newsner . . . **"we have a lot to learn by watching the youngest generation:"** "5-Year-Old BFFs Get Same Haircut So They'll No Longer Have Any Differences," *Newsner*, 4 March 2017: https://en.newsner.com/family/5-year -olds-bffs/.

p. 199   **Madeline Holcombe of CNN called it a "message of love in this boy's haircut:"** Madeline Holcombe, "Black and White Friends Try to Trick Teacher with Matching Haircuts," *CNN*, 3 March 2017: https://edition.cnn.com/2017/03/03/us/black-and -white-friends-haircut-trnd/index.html.

p. 199   **The boys' parents echoed similar sentiments . . . "There's an innocence children have that sometimes we lose:"** Holcombe, "Black and White Friends Try to Trick Teacher."

p. 199   **Jax's mother . . . "If this isn't proof that hate and prejudice is something that is taught, I don't know what is:"** "5-Year-Old BFFs Get Same Haircut," *Newsner*.

p. 201   **In 2014, MTV partnered with David Binder Research . . . found overwhelming support for color-blind ideas**: DBR MTV Bias Survey Summary, April 2014: https://d1fqdnmgwphrky .cloudfront.net/studies/000/000/001/DBR_MTV_Bias_Survey _Executive_Summary.pdf?1398858309.

p. 207   **As Coleman Hughes has argued . . . striving to treat people equally, without considerations of race, in both our public policy and private lives**: Coleman Hughes, "Actually, Color-Blindness Isn't Racist," *Free Press*, 20 December 2022: https://www.thefp.com/p/actually-color-blindness-isnt-racist.

p. 211   **In 2023, the US Supreme Court called an end to affirmative action policies in university selection . . . "a step toward a more colorblind society:"** Anthony Zurcher, "Affirmative Action: Supreme Court Justices Clash Over 'Colorblind' America," *BBC News*, 29 June 2023: https://www.bbc.co.uk/news /world-us-canada-66058664.

p. 212   **Coleman Hughes, for example, has argued at length . . . color blindness has its roots in the Enlightenment, or that it was developed during the fight against slavery**: Hughes, "Actually, Color-Blindness Isn't Racist."

p. 213   **the philosopher Charles Mills: "Ignorance is usually thought of as the passive obverse to knowledge . . . imagine an ignorance**

that resists:" Katherine Wall, "Overcoming the Desire Not to Know: Addressing White Ignorance to Create Reparative Futures," CIRE Bristol, 12 January 2021: https://cire-bristol.com /2021/01/12/overcoming-the-desire-not-to-know-addressing -white-ignorance-to-create-reparative-futures/.

Chapter 11

p. 215   **Sir Keir Starmer . . . "I would have no truck with that . . . my support for the police is very, very strong:"** "Black Lives Matter: Sir Keir Starmer 'Regrets' Calling Movement a 'Moment'," *BBC News*, 2 July 2020: https://www.bbc.co.uk/news/uk-politics -53267989.

p. 215   **Earlier that year, on 25 May 2020, George Floyd . . . suffocated and died:** Olive Enokido-Lineham, "George Floyd Killing: Last Minneapolis Police Officer Sentenced to Nearly Five Years," *Sky News*, 8 August 2023: https://news.sky.com/story/george -floyd-killing-last-minneapolis-police-officer-sentenced-to -nearly-five-years-12935796.

p. 215   **Those on the right . . . were openly critical of the movement:** Jessica Murray, "Teaching White Privilege as Uncontested Fact is Illegal, Minister Says," *Guardian*, 20 October 2020: https:// www.theguardian.com/world/2020/oct/20/teaching- white-priv ilege-is-a-fact-breaks-the-law-minister-says.

p. 216   **Members of Black Lives Matter were not impressed . . . suggested that we should not "allow former prosecutors to tell us what our demands are:"** Maximillian Jeffery, "Slapped Down: Black Lives Matter say 'cop in expensive suit' Keir Starmer has 'no right to tell us' Not to Demand Police Are Abolished," *Sun*, 29 June 2020: https://www.thesun.co.uk/news/11986324/black -lives-matter-cop-in-expensive-suit-keir-starmer/, 29 June 2020.

p. 216   **Perhaps worst of all, Nigel Farage . . . heartily agreed with Keir Starmer's stance:** Nigel Farage, "Heartily agree with @ Keir_Starmer's condemnation of the Black Lives Matter organization," Twitter, 29 June 2020: https://twitter.com/Nigel _Farage/status/1277635418746425352.

p. 216 **Labor MP Florence Eshalomi explained . . . that he regretted that people thought he had meant something else**: "Black Lives Matter: Sir Keir Starmer 'Regrets' Calling Movement a 'Moment'," *BBC News.*

p. 217 **the day of George Floyd's funeral in Texas . . . he tweeted the photograph of himself taking the knee**: Keir Starmer, "We kneel with all those opposing anti-Black racism. #BlackLives-Matter," Twitter, 9 June 2020: https://twitter.com/Keir_Starmer /status/1270374388488167428, 9 June 2020.

p. 217 **Sir Keir did manage to do one thing that was a bit surprising . . . "I think everybody should have unconscious bias training:"** Damien Gayle, "Keir Starmer to Sign Up for Unconscious Bias Training amid Criticism," *Guardian*, 6 July 2020: https://www.the guardian.com/politics/2020/jul/06/keir-starmer-to-sign-up-for -unconscious-bias-training-amid-criticism.

p. 219 **Betsy McCaughey . . . unconscious bias "ideology" is intended to "humiliate" White people and frame them as "oppressors:"** Betsy McCaughey, "Biden's Race Training for Federal Workers is Designed to Humiliate Whites," *New York Post*, 29 June 2020: https://nypost.com/2021/06/29/bidens-race-training-for -federal-workers-is-designed-to-humiliate-whites/.

p. 219 **Ben Bradley . . . "Orwellian re-education courses . . . that tell ordinary people they are racists:"** Ben Bradley, "MP Ben Brad-ley: Why I Refuse to Take Part in the Orwellian 'Re-education' Courses on 'Unconscious Bias' That Tell Ordinary People They Are Racists," *Daily Mail*, 19 September 2020: https://www.daily mail.co.uk/debate/article-8750961/BEN-BRADLEY-refuse-edu cation-tells-ordinary-people-racists.html.

p. 219 **Trump's 2020 "Executive Order on Combating Race and Sex Stereotyping . . ." largely a complaint designed to stop any-body from talking about racism (or sexism)**: "Executive Order on Combating Race and Sex Stereotyping," 22 September 2020:

https://trumpwhitehouse.archives.gov/presidential-actions
/executive-order-combating-race-sex-stereotyping/.

p. 220 **According to an article by Pamela Newkirk . . . "companies were spending an estimated $8 billion a year on diversity efforts:"** Pamela Newkirk, "Diversity Has Become a Booming Business. So Where Are the Results?," *Time*, 10 October 2019: https://time.com/5696943/diversity-business/.

p. 220 **In 2014, Google alone reportedly spent $114 million on its diversity program:** Newkirk, "Diversity Has Become a Booming Business."

p. 220 **In 2018, Indeed, a popular job website, reported that positions for diversity and inclusion professionals had increased by 35% over the previous two years:** Newkirk, "Diversity Has Become a Booming Business."

p. 221 **Later, a 2021 article by Nazia Parveen in the *Guardian* indicated that 81% of companies have conducted some kind of unconscious bias training:** Nazia Parveen, "'Unconscious bias training alone will not stop discrimination,' Say Critics," *Guardian*, 2 March 2021: https://www.theguardian.com/money/2021/mar/02/unconscious-bias-training-alone-will-not-stop-discrimination-say-critics.

p. 221 **According to a report by Leitner . . . much of this training focuses on unconscious bias:** M. Leitner, *The Current Status of Equality, Diversity and Inclusion in the Further Education Sector in England* (2021): https://feweek.co.uk/wp-content/uploads/2021/11/AoC-EDI-report.pdf.

Chapter 12

p. 236 **As an investigation by the *Guardian* revealed . . . "it was not, in fact, the practice to appoint colored immigrants or foreigners" to clerical roles in the royal household:** David Pegg and Rob Evans, "Buckingham Palace Banned Ethnic Minorities from Office Roles, Papers Reveal," *Guardian*, 2 June 2021:

https://www.theguardian.com/uk-news/2021/jun/02/
buckingham-palace-banned-ethnic-minorities-from-office
-roles-papers-reveal#:~:text=They%20reveal%20how%20in%20
1968,unclear%20when%20the%20practice%20ended.

p. 236   **one of his arguments in favor of segregation was his staunch belief in the inferiority of Black people . . . disproportionately criminal and disproportionately diseased**: Dan T. Carter, *The Politics of Rage: George Wallace, the Origins of the New Conservatism, and the Transformation of American Politics* (New York: Simon & Schuster, 1995), pp. 237–8.

p. 237   **the speech delivered by Enoch Powell . . . now widely known as the "Rivers of Blood" speech, continues to echo in the British consciousness to this day**: Andy Richards, "Enoch Powell: What Was the 'Rivers of Blood' Speech? Full Text Here," *Birmingham Mail*, 30 March 2015: https://www.birminghammail .co.uk/news/midlands-news/enoch-powell-what-rivers-blood -8945556.

p. 237   **in a 2018 article for the *Atlantic*, Samuel Earle described what he called the "unsettling shadow of Powell . . ." an event more commonly referred to as "Brexit:"** Samuel Earle, "'Rivers of Blood:' The Legacy of a Speech That Divided Britain," *Atlantic*, 20 April 2018: https://www.theatlantic.com/international / archive/2018/04/enoch-powell-rivers-of-blood/558344/.

p. 238   **both White people and Black people preferred "their own pattern of society, their own churches and their own schools— which history and experience have proven are best for both races:"** George Wallace to Ms. Martin, 14 April 1964, Gilder Lehrman Institute of American History (GLC00295): https:// www.gilderlehrman.org/sites/default/files/inline-pdfs/00295 _FPS_0.pdf.

p. 239   **Jerry Falwell, a White American pastor and conservative activist, criticized the US Supreme Court's 1954 anti-segregation ruling**: Max Blumenthal, "Agent of Intolerance," *Nation*, 28

May 2007: https://www.thenation.com/article/archive/ agent -intolerance/.

p. 245 **We learned the choreography to "Bumbro," a song made famous by its part in the 2000 Indian Hindi-language Bolly- wood action thriller** *Mission Kashmir*: Vidhu Vinod Chopra, dir., *Mission Kashmir.* Shankar–Ehsaan–Loy, 2000.

p. 255 **among the 9,115 children's books published in the UK in 2017, just 1% of them featured a non-White person as a main char- acter**: *Reflecting Realities: Survey of Ethnic Representation within UK Children's Literature 2017*, Center for Literacy in Primary Education: https://clpe.org.uk/system/files/CLPE%20Reflecting %20Realities%20Report%20July%202018.pdf.

p. 255 **In 2018, using data from Nielsen BookScan, which provides data for the book publishing industry, the** *Guardian* **and the** *Observer* **analyzed**: Donna Ferguson, "'Highly concerning:' Picture Books Bias Worsens as Female Characters Stay Silent," *Guardian*, 13 June 2019: https://www.theguardian.com/ books /2019/jun/13/highly-concerning-picture-books-bias-worsens-a s-female-characters-stay-silent.

p. 258 **according to statistics from the US Census Bureau, the per- centage of Black people actually in poverty was only about 25% in 2015**: John Creamer, "Poverty Rates for Blacks and His- panics Reached Historic Lows in 2019," United States Census Bureau, 15 September 2020: https://www.census.gov/library/ stories/2020/09/poverty-rates-for-blacks-and-hispanics -reached-historic-lows-in-2019.html#:~:text=In%202019%2C %20the%20share%20of,share%20in%20the%20general%20 population.

Chapter 13

p. 263 **the quote from Stokely Carmichael . . . "Racism is not a ques- tion of attitude; it's a question of power:"** From Shirley Anne

Tate, *Post-Intersectionality to Black Decolonial Feminism: Black Skin Affections* (New York: Routledge, 2022).

p. 268   **the words of Frederick Douglass are as relevant today as they were when he delivered a speech on West Indian emancipation in New York in 1857**: "(1857) Frederick Douglass, 'If there is no struggle, there is no progress'," *Blackpast*, 25 January 2007: https://www.blackpast.org/african-american-history/1857-fred erick-douglass-if-there-no-struggle-there-no-progress/.

Afterword

p. 272   **One of my favorite books of all time is *Flatland*, a novella by Edwin Abbott Abbott, published in 1884**: Abbott, Edwin Abbott, *Flatland: A Romance of Many Dimensions* (London: Seeley, Service & Co, 1884).

Index

Professor Keon West is a social psychologist at University College London. He earned his doctorate from Oxford University in 2010 as a Rhodes Scholar and has since published more than seventy quantitative papers on prejudice and discrimination in many of the best peer-reviewed social-psychology journals, including *Personality and Social Psychology Bulletin*, *The Journal of Experimental Social Psychology* and *Perspectives on Psychological Science*. Professor West has written for national and international newspapers and been the host of numerous radio and television shows on the topics of prejudice and discrimination. He is a citizen of three countries and has, over his life, been a resident of four. He is a husband, a father of two boys, a hobby photographer and a huge fan of *Star Trek*. He has always been Black. *The Science of Racism* is his second book.